# MOTHER'S BEST

# MOTHER'S BEST

COMFORT FOOD THAT
TAKES YOU HOME AGAIN

150 Favorites from
MOTHER'S BISTRO & BAR

Lisa Schroeder
with Danielle Centoni

photographs by Ellen Silverman

The Taunton Press

To those who have loved and supported me through thick and thin: my sister Sherry and brother-in-law Steve; my daughter Stephanie; my true love Rob; and Isabella and Taylor, who taught me the true beauty of motherhood—grandmotherhood.

Text © 2009 by Lisa Schroeder
Photographs © 2009 by Ellen Silverman

The Taunton Press, Inc., 63 South Main Street, PO Box 5506, Newtown, CT 06470-5506
e-mail: tp@taunton.com

Editor: Carolyn Mandarano
Copy editor: Valerie Cimino
Indexer: Heidi Blough
Jacket/Cover design: Sowins Design
Interior design: Sowins Design
Layout: Sowins Design, Sandy Mahlstedt, Lynne Phillips
Photographer: Ellen Silverman
Food stylist: Heidi Johannsen
Prop stylist: Heather Chontos

Library of Congress Cataloging-in-Publication Data

Schroeder, Lisa, 1957-
  Mother's best : comfort food that takes you home again / Lisa Schroeder with Danielle Centoni.
      p. cm.
  Includes index.
  ISBN 978-1-60085-017-2
  1.  Cookery, International.  2.  Mother's Bistro & Bar.  3.  Mama Mia Trattoria.  I. Centoni, Danielle.  II. Title.
  TX725.A1S4223 2009
  641.59--dc22

                         2009026452

Printed in the United States of America
10 9 8 7 6 5 4 3 2

The following names/manufacturers appearing in *Mother's Best* are trademarks:
Academy Awards®, Baker's®, Barilla®, Callebaut®, Chao Koh®, Chef'sChoice®, Chicken of the Sea®, Cholula®, De Cecco®, Disaronno®, Droste®, Frangelico®, Ghirardelli®, Godiva®, Grand Marnier®, Jell-O®, Jif®, Kahlúa®, Lindt®, Mae Ploy®, Malibu®, Microplane®, Nabisco® Famous Chocolate Wafers, Ritz®, Rogue Creamery® Oregon Blue cheese, Scharffen Berger®, Starbucks℠, Tabasco®, Tapatío®, Thai Kitchen®, X-Acto®

# ACKNOWLEDGMENTS

The idea for *Mother's Best* was years in the making and almost as many in the writing. I couldn't have done it without the support of all my amazing restaurant staff, both front-of-house and back, past and present, particularly those who upheld my exacting standards even when I banished myself to my computer to write—my faithful assistant, Amanda Harp; managers Eddie Phillips, Bryon Deisher, Stephanie Cohen, Stephanie Pasquini, Howard Tang, Jessica Whalen, and Sierra Buryn; chefs Joseph Bialek, Kim Cress, Rebecca McGrath, and Debra Putnam; sous chefs Adam Harpe and Jennifer Orozco. This book would not have been possible if not for my entire dedicated crew, who spread the love through everything they do—whether seating a guest, making a cocktail, taking an order, cooking a dish, serving a guest, clearing plates, or washing a pot. I couldn't do it and would be nowhere without them.

I am so thankful for my wonderful life partner, Rob Sample, who believed in me and has put up with me during the most stressful times—I couldn't have done it without you, your compassion, and your love.

I am extremely grateful to my co-writer, Danielle Centoni, who answered my prayers for a co-writer who understood my "voice" and could translate it to the written word, giving up precious time with her young children to make these pages happen.

Thank you to my agent, Stacey Glick; editor at Taunton Press, Carolyn Mandarano; and Lisa Donoghue from LAD Communications, who helped get all this off the ground.

Special thanks to my colleagues Diane Morgan and Joan Cirillo, who answered my many questions about how the world of publishing works, and my culinary mentors chefs Gray Kunz, Sottha Khunn, Sylvain Portay, and all the chefs at The Culinary Institute of America who taught me the importance of quality and meticulousness in everything I do.

I would be nowhere without the support of my amazing friends and family: Elizabeth Ludwig Bailey, Ellen Walsh, Barbara Moore, Sherry, Steve, Michael, Colette, Marc, Lisa, Paul, Melissa, Judy, Merrill, Loretta, and Irv, who helped me believe in myself and my dreams, encouraging me every step of the way.

A special thanks goes out to all our recipe testers who made sure everything would work in a home kitchen: Caroline Brezing, Dave and Yvette Centoni, Kathleen Chetlain, Alexandra Clark, Josh Cohn, Tonka Formigle, Cathy Francioch, Sandi Francioch, Elly Fryer, Holly Hancey, Nathan Hostler, Corinna Kell, Candice Kimberling-Tarr, Anthony Ledbetter, Kate Leeper, Ariel Maclean, Cindy Pickens, Shannon Pickens, Joanna Rodriguez, Katherine Ross and Art Krug, Mary Roth, Carrie Thompson, Jaime Waugh, and Abbie Witscher.

Thank you to my mother, Belle, from whom I inherited the burning desire to cook, even though she chased me out of her kitchen.

And finally, thanks to all our former Mothers of the Month and mothers everywhere who show their love through food and who have proven that the way to any family's heart is through their stomachs!

# CONTENTS

# THE BIRTH OF MOTHER'S

It's 5:45 P.M. on a Thursday night in 1992. I'm still at work, trying to figure out what I'm going to do for dinner for the family. I'm exhausted and don't feel like cooking, but we've already done take-out twice this week. I wrack my brain, trying to think of a place where we could get the kind of wholesome, comforting food I would make—if I had the time. Nothing came to mind.

That was the moment my restaurant, Mother's Bistro & Bar, was born. I realized there weren't any restaurants serving real home cooking—not the flavorless, out-of-a box stuff of diners and chain restaurants, but flavorful, familiar, and nutritious dishes that mothers around the world have been cooking for their families for generations.

This epiphany changed my life, inspiring me to switch careers at the age of 35 and enroll at The Culinary Institute of America in Hyde Park, New York. There I learned not only how to cook professionally but also how to develop a menu, price the food, and determine how much of it to make. I lived and breathed food, going to classes for eight hours a day and then participating in every extracurricular activity. On weekends I traveled to Manhattan to see my daughter, Stephanie, and work as a server to make some money to live.

After cooking school I knew I still needed real-world experience before I could launch my own place, so I got a job as a cook at Le Cirque, a four-star restaurant in Manhattan, where I was paid $350 for a 60-hour work week. This was hardly enough to support myself and my daughter, so I got a second job waiting tables. For an entire year I worked 90 hours a week, six days a week, learning everything I could and trying to keep my head above water.

When Stephanie left for college a year later and Le Cirque closed to move to a new location, I decided it was time to head to Europe and find out what it was like to work in real French kitchens and eat the foods of France, Italy, Spain, and Morocco at their source. These travels changed my perceptions about food forever, but the most eye-opening experience happened in Morocco. After I searched high and low and found very few restaurants, it occurred to me—Moroccan matriarchs *live* to cook for their families, so why would Moroccans go out for Moroccan food? That's when I realized that the soul of a country's cuisine is not found in its restaurants but rather in the foods cooked at home—what I call "Mother Food"—meals made with love and shared by families.

While restaurants in Morocco were few and far between, they certainly weren't in short supply in this country. Americans were, and still are, cooking less and eating out more. And yet, our country's Mother Food was rarely offered in restaurants. I was sure that busy people like me had to be craving these foods, and I definitely didn't want to see a generation of kids growing up and not knowing what brisket was or that chicken noodle soup didn't always come from a can. My concept of Mother's Bistro became even clearer: Along with my dream of opening a restaurant, I had a mission to help preserve Mother Food for posterity.

It took a few more years and a move across the country to join my life and business partner, Rob Sample, in Portland, Oregon, before my dream and mission became reality. We turned a dark and dank Irish pub into a bright and airy ode to all things motherly, with pictures of moms and children on the wall, flowing curtains, cushy chairs, and a corner of books and toys for kids. On our first day of business we turned our sign from "closed" to "open" and 90 people walked in the door. It's been nine years and we've never once looked back.

The birth of Mother's wasn't easy (more like a caesarian section with no anesthetic), and I worked harder than I had ever worked in my life (yes, harder than my 90-hour work weeks in New York). But it was all worth it—so much so that I couldn't resist opening a second restaurant, called Mama

Mia Trattoria, right next door. There are days when I look out into my dining rooms and see the happy faces of the guests and my eyes well up with tears of joy. My dream has come true.

But now I want to take my dream one step further. Instead of just providing my guests with the home-style food their mother, grandmothers, and great-grandmothers might have made, I want to teach people how to make these dishes themselves. Many of us have become alienated from our kitchens, but even in these heady, hectic times—or maybe because of them—many of us are looking to find our way back. We want the pride and satisfaction that comes from making our own meals and gathering our families around the table to enjoy them. We want to take charge of what's in our food and know exactly what we're putting in our mouths. We want to spend less money and more time together. And we want the familiar, nourishing dishes that we grew up on—or wish we did.

And that's how *Mother's Best* was born. I have gathered many of the best recipes from my two restaurants into this book and seasoned them generously with advice gleaned from all my years behind the stove. Like the restaurants from which it evolved, this book pays homage to mothers and their cuisine from around the world. It introduces some of the mothers we have featured at Mother's Bistro over the years, women from Hungary, Ireland, Greece, France, and Italy (to name a few), as well as mothers from different regions of the United States. At Mother's Bistro we feature a "Mother of the Month," or "M.O.M.," who collaborates with me to create a special menu with some of her best dishes, and we cook them together so I can learn how to make her dishes firsthand. Now you can learn, too.

But the recipes in this book aren't just simple rehashings of old standards. I've used my training in classic French cooking to take things to a higher level. Whereas a typical mother uses water in her braised beef brisket, I use veal or beef stock. While one of our Mothers of the Month calls for margarine in her pastry, I use butter. A mother may regularly use canned cream of mushroom soup as an ingredient, but I make my own mushroom sauce. So it's mother's food, only better.

These subtle but significant changes are what I like to call the "love." It's that one secret ingredient that makes any dish taste better and keeps families coming back for more. It's taking time to heat a pan, sauté an onion, reduce a sauce, taste a dish, and adjust the seasonings.

You don't have to be a mom, or even a parent, to get something out of this book. It's for anyone who wants to learn how to create comforting, delicious, family-friendly food worthy of a restaurant. It offers ways to help you work cooking into your busy life. And it takes the fear out of the equation by demystifying each step of the process and offering "Love Notes" to guide you through. Although this book is aimed at inexperienced cooks, even experts will likely learn something new. You'll get ideas on how to coax more flavor out of your ingredients and how to "plate" food so that it's a feast for the eyes.

But most of all, you'll learn how to cook with love and how to find love through cooking (let's face it, the way to your family's heart *is* through their stomachs). With love as the mantra, let *Mother's Best* inspire a return of the heart to the hearth of your home.

# starters

When you're planning a party or a special dinner, it's tempting to either skip the starters or let the grocery store do the cooking. Tubs of dip and trays of precut vegetables are just so easy. But the first course sets the tone for the meal, getting your guests' palates geared up for the main event. Do you really want their first bites to taste canned, bland, and loaded with preservatives?

Of course not. But that doesn't mean you have to spend all day making fussy filled canapés, either. In this chapter you'll find easy yet flavorful beginnings for any occasion.

When deciding what to serve before the meal, first consider the event. Vegetables with dips like Hummus (page 11) are quick to make and perfect for casual get-togethers like potlucks and football parties. Special occasions call for a little more formality. Try setting out one or two little things, such as roasted nuts and crostini topped with Belle's Chopped Liver (page 14), so that guests have something to nibble on while waiting for everyone else to arrive. Make it more sophisticated, yet still simple, by serving the topping on the bread with a garnish (like a basil leaf) rather than in a bowl alongside. Then as a first course, serve a plated appetizer such as the Three Cheese and Spinach Stuffed Portabella Mushrooms (page 17) or a salad like the Poached Pear, Rogue River Blue Cheese, and Hazelnut Salad (page 32).

Since the first course is the prologue to the main meal, be sure it complements what's to come. Serving Mama's Italian Chopped Salad (page 43) before a tropical plate of Macadamia Nut–Crusted Red Snapper with Mango Salsa & Coconut Rice (page 161) would be quite a surprise for your guests. However, it might be nice before Pan-Seared Cod Puttanesca (page 164), even though the two are from very different cuisines. Start by considering what region or climate the dishes come from. Foods from Mediterranean countries, for example, will likely be more compatible with each other than with a combination of dishes from every corner of the world.

That being said, compatible doesn't mean matching—too much of one thing is tiresome. So mix it up, offer a variety of textures as well as flavors, and balance rich foods with lighter ones, hot dishes with cold ones.

### CREATING SENSATIONAL SALADS

Salads, like other starters, can be simple or fancy, and these days the choices for greens include not only the old reliables, like iceberg, romaine, and green leaf, but also an increasing selection of toothsome and slightly bitter greens, like radicchio, escarole, Belgian endive, and frisée. Watercress and arugula also have a slightly spicy bite, though with a tender texture. While iceberg, romaine, and leaf lettuces provide a mild backdrop that allows the ingredients to shine, the bitter greens provide a welcome contrast to the sweet, sour, and savory notes you find in most salads, helping you notice those delicious flavors even more. A good compromise is mesclun mix, an assortment of tender young leaves that range from the mild to the assertive ends of the spectrum.

Since any delicious salad starts with the greens, it's important to prepare them correctly. Some salad green leaves, such as Belgian endive and arugula, are better left whole because they're already small enough to eat without cutting. But most other lettuces should be cut or torn into bite-size pieces. Some cooks argue that lettuce edges are less likely to turn brown if they are torn. While that's true, you don't have to worry about browning unless you're prepping the lettuce in advance. Otherwise, just cut it and make life easy.

To efficiently cut lettuce, tear the leaves away from the core, stack a few, and cut into bite-size pieces. In the case of romaine and red and green leaf lettuces, leave the head intact, cut it lengthwise in thirds, and then cut crosswise to yield perfect pieces with just a few strokes of your chef's knife.

### CLEANING THE GREENS

Washing lettuce is a crucial step. No one wants to bite into a mouthful of dirt, sand, or worse—bugs! Instead of painstakingly washing each leaf individually, cut or tear them first, then swish the pieces around in a bowl of fresh, cold water. If you have a salad spinner (which I highly recommend), you can use its bowl for swishing, then lift the lettuce out of the water and right into the spinner's basket (don't pour the lettuce into the basket or you'll dump the dirt and debris right back onto the clean lettuce leaves). Change the water and repeat this process until no more grit falls to the bottom of the bowl.

Salad dressings will slide right off lettuce that's wet, so use a salad spinner to get the lettuce really dry, making sure to occasionally stop and drain the water that accumulates in the bowl. And don't pack the lettuce or it won't get properly dried. If you don't have a salad spinner, lay the lettuce in a single layer between two clean kitchen towels or paper towels and gently roll it up. If working ahead, you can keep washed lettuce crisp by wrapping it loosely in dry paper towels or a clean kitchen towel and refrigerating in an airtight bag or container.

## MAKING DRESSINGS

A vinaigrette can be as simple as tossing some greens with a good olive oil and wine vinegar, but I prefer to spend a little extra time to make an emulsified vinaigrette, which does a better job of coating the lettuce.

An emulsion is a mixture of two insoluble liquids like oil and vinegar. When shaken or stirred together, these liquids will separate quickly, but it is possible to delay the separation by adding an emulsifier like egg yolk (used in Caesar dressing and mayonnaise) or Dijon mustard or by adding the oil in a very slow, thin stream to the vinegar while vigorously beating with a whisk. Introducing the oil too quickly—or not incorporating it quickly enough—will prevent the two liquids from staying together. But once the dressing has begun to thicken, the remaining oil can be added a bit more rapidly, with any additional seasonings whisked in after all the oil has been incorporated.

My gadget of choice for mixing larger quantities of dressings is the immersion blender, also known as a "stick blender." Not only is it really easy to use but cleanup is also a snap. To use, lower it into the middle of the ingredients, turn it on, and slowly move it up and down while adding the oil in a slow, thin stream. Continue blending until the dressing is nice and thick. A tall cylindrical container works best with this tool.

If you don't have an immersion blender, a regular blender, electric mixer fitted with the whisk attachment, or a food processor fitted with the metal blade will also work. In each of those cases, you want to have the machines running when you begin adding the oil in a slow, thin stream. When you see the mixture becoming creamy and emulsified, you can add the rest of the oil a little faster.

### ASSEMBLING AND SERVING SALADS

It's far better to dress your salad lightly than to overdress it. (Put another way, it's easier to add more dressing than it is to come up with more salad ingredients!) You can prevent overdressing by placing the greens in a large bowl with ample space for tossing. Begin with less dressing, gradually adding more in small amounts after the greens have been tossed and tasted. You want the leaves to glisten, not drip. I prefer to mix salad with my hands, so that I can mix it thoroughly without bruising the leaves. You can also use tongs, but be gentle.

Don't dress salads until just before serving or the greens will end up limp. If you want to get ahead, assemble the salad and place it in the refrigerator. Then toss it with the dressing just before serving.

A deep bowl makes tossing the salad easier, but it's not the best choice to bring to the table because you can't really see the ingredients. Instead, transfer the salad to a wide, shallow bowl to better show off your creation. If you plan to serve the salad individually, mound the leaves in the center of each plate to give them height. Strategically place additional ingredients like nuts or cheese on top for maximum eye appeal.

# Hummus

ALTHOUGH HUMMUS IS TRADITIONALLY EATEN WITH WARM PITA BREAD, IT IS JUST AS delicious with raw vegetables or slathered on sandwiches. It takes just a few minutes to whip up and costs a fraction of the price of store-bought; plus you can make it just how you like it—chunky or smooth, heavy on garlic or lemon. You can also add other flavors or spices, like sun-dried tomatoes, olives, fresh herbs, curry powder, or hot sauce. The sambal oelek chile paste adds a touch of spice that keeps things interesting.

2 (15-ounce) cans garbanzo beans (chickpeas), drained and rinsed (Love Note 1)

1 cup plus 1 tablespoon cold water

5 large cloves garlic, finely chopped (about 2 tablespoons)

⅔ cup lemon juice (about 4 medium lemons)

2½ teaspoons kosher salt

1⅓ cups tahini (sesame paste), stirred well (Love Note 1, Grilled Salmon with Sesame Noodles, page 159)

2 teaspoons ground cumin

1 tablespoon sambal oelek (spicy chile paste; Love Note 2; optional)

4 Kalamata or other black olives (optional)

Warmed pita bread or pita chips (Love Note 3), or cut raw vegetables

1.  Place the garbanzo beans, water, garlic, lemon juice, salt, tahini, and cumin in the bowl of a food processor fitted with a metal blade or in a blender. Process until smooth, at least 3 minutes. You may have to stop to scrape down the sides of the bowl. Alternatively, you can purée the ingredients with an immersion blender. Taste and add additional salt or lemon juice if desired.

2.  To serve, spoon the hummus onto individual plates or onto a medium dinner plate, spreading it in an even layer to the rim. Spoon the chile paste in the center and top with the olives, if using. Arrange pita wedges or vegetables around the plate. Hummus can be refrigerated in an airtight container for several days. For best flavor, allow it to come to room temperature before serving. *continued*

# LOVE NOTES

**1** I draw the line at **cooking dry garbanzo beans,** even though I'm the kind of cook who loves to do everything from scratch. You could start with dry garbanzos, soak them overnight, and then cook them for 3 to 4 hours, but it just doesn't seem worth it for this dish. It's so much easier when you start with the canned beans, and no one (even you) will notice the difference. I do like to rinse the beans, though, to reduce the sodium and get rid of that "tinny" taste.

**2** There are all sorts of **spicy condiments** on the market, but my favorite for hummus is the bright red chili sauce called sambal oelek. The chunky condiment comes from Indonesia, but it's used all over Southeast Asia. It gets its spicy-sour taste from ground chiles, vinegar, and garlic. Sambal oelek has many uses, and once you have it in your kitchen, you'll find yourself adding it to noodle soups, stir-fries, vegetable dishes—even mayonnaise.

**3** **Cold pita bread** isn't appetizing, but a quick stint in the oven warms it up, softens the texture, and releases its toasty flavors. To do this, heat the oven to 350°F and wrap the pita in foil to keep them from drying out. Place on the middle rack of the oven for about 5 minutes, or until warmed through. (If you're going to keep an eye on the pita, don't bother to wrap them in foil. Check after 3 minutes, and if they are almost too hot to handle, they are warm enough.) Remove from the oven, cut into 8 wedges (a pizza cutter works well for this), and arrange around the hummus on the plate.

We've tested all kinds of pita and found that the best one for dips is the Greek kind. Unless you need a pocket to stuff for sandwiches, this fluffy, tasty pita is a perfect accompaniment to hummus and other dips. If you want to turn pita bread into delicate, fresh-baked chips, buy the pocket kind and cut into wedges, splitting the two layers so the chips will be thin. Toss them on a baking sheet with a little olive oil, salt, and pepper (or other herbs and spices such as garlic salt, paprika, oregano . . . whatever you like). Spread the triangles out and bake at 350°F for 3 to 5 minutes, or until golden brown and crisp.

# Belle's Chopped Liver

BEFORE I OPENED MOTHER'S AND WHILE I WAS STILL WORKING OUT THE MENU,
I stopped by the only Jewish deli in Portland at the time to check out my chicken
soup competition. One look at the stacks of canned broth behind the counter and
I knew it would be no contest. I also noticed they sold chopped liver, so I ordered
some and took it with me to a coffee shop across the street. As I waited for my drink,
I unwrapped the liver and gave it a try and then promptly wrapped it right back up
and threw it away, washing out the taste as fast as I could with a cup of strong coffee.
Right then and there I decided that the chopped-liver lovers of Portland deserved better and vowed to put my version on the menu.

I called my recipe chopped-liver pâté, hoping to entice those who hadn't tried
chopped liver before. But one diner didn't approve of my tactic, saying that it was
not pâté at all, and thus the name was misleading. That was a valuable lesson for me.
I immediately changed the name to reflect what it truly is—chopped liver—and let
its delicious taste speak for itself.

1 pound chicken livers, defrosted if
previously frozen

3 tablespoons chicken fat (divided;
Love Note 1)

1 large onion, thinly sliced

1 teaspoon kosher salt

½ teaspoon freshly ground black
pepper

5 hard-cooked eggs, 1 yolk
removed and discarded or reserved
for another use (Love Note 2)

1.  Place the livers in a colander set in the sink to drain any excess liquid.

2.  Heat a large (12- to 14-inch) sauté pan over medium-high heat for about 2 minutes,
    or until very hot. Add 2 tablespoons of the chicken fat. Once it has almost melted,
    add the onions and sauté until they start to color and soften. Lower the heat to
    medium and continue to sauté until the onions are lightly caramelized, but not
    dark brown, 15 to 20 minutes. Remove the onions from the pan (try to leave as
    much fat in the pan as possible) and set aside.

3. Place the empty pan over high heat until it is very hot, about 2 minutes. Add the remaining 1 tablespoon of chicken fat. When it's hot, add the chicken livers. (It's important that the fat and the pan be searing hot so that the livers sauté rather than steam.) Season with the salt and pepper. Sauté for 4 to 5 minutes, or until the livers are cooked through. They should be brown on the outside and pink in the center. Do not overcook or the chopped liver will be dry.

4. Transfer the livers to a bowl and allow to cool slightly. Using a food processor, meat grinder, or the grinder attachment of an electric mixer, process or grind half the livers with half the hard-cooked eggs and half the sautéed onions. If using a food processor, pulse the mixture, stopping to scrape the sides of the bowl, until it is a coarse purée. (It should be smooth but not the consistency of baby food.) Scrape the puréed liver mixture into a bowl.

5. Repeat with the remaining livers, sautéed onions, and hard-cooked eggs. Add to the mixing bowl with the first batch and taste for seasoning. Adjust with additional salt and pepper if desired.

6. Spoon the chopped liver into a serving bowl or individual ramekins or press it into a greased mold (Love Note 3). Cover tightly with plastic wrap or a lid (so the surface doesn't get dried out), and refrigerate for up to 2 days. Or freeze in small portions and thaw overnight in the refrigerator. Serve with crackers, thin slices of toasted challah, or brioche bread (Love Note 4).

*continued*

# LOVE NOTES

**1 Sautéing the livers and onions** with chicken fat is traditional, authentic, and definitely a way to add another layer of flavor. I tried to make this dish with canola oil but chopped liver aficionados complained, so I switched to the more traditional chicken fat and have heard nothing but compliments ever since. Ask your local butcher for chicken fat, or look for it in the kosher frozen foods section of your supermarket.

An even cheaper option? Save the fat you skim off when making chicken stock or chicken soup. Freeze it in small plastic deli containers, and you can take spoonfuls out as needed. Liver is already high in cholesterol, so if you're watching your intake you can substitute vegetable oil for the chicken fat. But don't be tempted to use olive oil, which will smoke when sautéing the livers at high heat.

**2 Hard-cooking** (not boiling!) an egg is an important technique to learn. To hard-cook eggs: Place the eggs in a saucepan just large enough to accommodate them in a single layer. Cover them by 1 inch with hot water. Place the pan over high heat. Bring to a boil, cover, turn off the heat, and let sit for 12 minutes. Remove the cover, pour out most of the hot water, place the pot in the sink, and run cold water over the eggs to cool them quickly. To peel, knock the eggs on a hard surface a few times to break apart the shell. Peel and rinse under cold water.

**3 To unmold the liver,** fill a sink or bowl with hot water, dip the bottom of the mold into the water until the water comes up to an inch from the top, and hold it there for about 30 seconds. Place the mold on the counter and run a knife along the inside edge. Place a plate on top of the mold and carefully flip the mold over onto it. Give it a shake or two until you feel it release. If it doesn't happen on the first try, dip the mold in the hot water again.

**4 Serve this** with something mild like matzoh, water crackers, or crostini (page 172). A strongly flavored cracker will muddle the taste of the chopped liver.

# Three Cheese and Spinach–Stuffed Portabella Mushrooms

WARM, SAVORY STUFFED MUSHROOMS ARE ONE OF THOSE THINGS PEOPLE CAN'T get enough of. And a large portabella makes a perfectly sized appetizer for one. But this filling is also great stuffed into button mushrooms for a platter of bite-size hors d'oeuvre. This recipe was created by Kimberley Cress, my former chef de cuisine at Mama Mia Trattoria, and is one of my most favorite starters.

6 large (6-inch-diameter) portabella mushrooms, stems and gills removed (Love Note 1)

2 tablespoons extra-virgin olive oil, divided

¼ teaspoon kosher salt (divided)

¼ teaspoon freshly ground black pepper (divided)

1 large shallot, finely chopped (about 2 tablespoons)

1 clove garlic, finely chopped (about 1 teaspoon)

1 pound fresh spinach, stemmed and cleaned (Love Note 2)

1½ tablespoons dried breadcrumbs (Love Note 3)

2 cups shredded mozzarella cheese

½ cup grated Parmesan cheese (Love Note 4)

⅓ cup grated pecorino romano cheese

6 tablespoons Roasted Red Pepper Coulis (page 21)

1. Heat the oven to 350°F. Place the cleaned mushrooms on a baking sheet, gill side up. Brush with 1 tablespoon of the olive oil, sprinkle with ⅛ teaspoon salt and ⅛ teaspoon pepper, and bake for 6 minutes. Remove from the oven and set aside to cool on the baking sheet for at least 15 to 20 minutes.

2. Heat a large (12- to 14-inch) sauté pan over medium-high heat. Add the remaining tablespoon of olive oil. Add the shallots and the garlic and sauté, stirring, for a minute or so. Add a few handfuls of spinach, carefully turning with tongs or a spatula, and cook until wilted; add more spinach as room becomes available. Season with the remaining ⅛ teaspoon salt and ⅛ teaspoon pepper.

*continued*

3. Drain the spinach in a fine-mesh strainer set in the sink, pressing on the spinach with your hands or a rubber spatula to ensure that all the liquid drains off. Set aside until cool enough to handle, and then finely chop.

4. In a medium mixing bowl, combine the chopped spinach, breadcrumbs, mozzarella, Parmesan, and pecorino romano. Taste and adjust the seasoning as necessary by adding more salt and pepper.

5. Divide the filling evenly among the baked and cooled mushrooms (about $\frac{1}{4}$ cup filling per mushroom; Love Note 5). Bake for about 10 minutes, or until the filling is hot and bubbly.

6. To serve, place 1 mushroom on each plate and drizzle 1 tablespoon Roasted Red Pepper Coulis around each mushroom.

*continued*

**1** **To remove the gills,** pull the stem out, hold the cap in the palm of your hand, gill side up, and use a spoon to gently scrape them out and discard. If using button mushrooms, just pull off the stems and fill them.

This recipe will perfectly stuff six 6-inch mushrooms. If you can only find small, 4-inch portabellas, then use eight mushrooms instead of six.

**2** **To clean fresh spinach,** first cut through the stems close to the leaves. Then fill a large bowl with cold water and swish the leaves around in it, scooping the spinach from the water with your hands. Set the spinach in a colander, discard the water, and repeat until the spinach is completely clean and there is no dirt in the bowl.

To save time buy "cello" spinach—bags of fresh, trimmed, cleaned spinach leaves. If serving raw, wash it before using.

**3** **Use stale bread** to create breadcrumbs. If the bread is hard, break it into chunks and process in a food processor until the texture of sand, or use the grater attachment. For fully dry crumbs, which can be stored longer, spread them out on a large baking sheet and leave them out overnight or place in a 300°F oven for 10 minutes, stirring occasionally, until they feel dry and rough.

If the bread is soft, dry it in the oven first, then break it up before processing it, grating it, or sealing it in a plastic bag and crushing with a rolling pin until fine. Freeze breadcrumbs in a zip-top freezer bag for several months.

**4** **Hard cheeses, like Parmesan,** should be finely grated shortly before use to best release their flavor and aroma and help them melt quickly and evenly. A rasp-style grater with small holes (I like the Microplane® brand) is the most effective, plus it can double as a zester. If using hard cheeses as a garnish, shaving thin slices with a vegetable peeler is a nice alternative.

Cheese labeled *Parmesan* or *Grana Padano* is affordable and perfectly acceptable for most recipes. For dishes where Parmesan plays a key flavor role, such as fettuccine Alfredo, use Parmigiano-Reggiano because it has the most intense and complex flavor.

**5** **Unbaked mushrooms** can be stuffed and refrigerated in an airtight container for up to 2 days. Allow an extra 10 minutes of baking time.

## ROASTED RED PEPPER COULIS

*COULIS* (COO-LEE) IS A FRENCH TERM THAT ORIGINALLY WAS USED TO DESCRIBE the juices from cooked meat, but these days it usually refers to a smooth sauce made from puréed vegetables or fruits. While the most common coulis is made from tomatoes, this one is made from roasted red peppers blended with sautéed garlic, shallots, and a touch of cream for a rich, smoky sweetness.

This recipe makes more than you'll need for the stuffed portabellas, but it's extremely versatile. Try it as a sauce for salmon, grilled steak, and crab cakes. You can freeze the leftovers in 1-cup portions to use later. It might look a little broken when defrosted, but just whisk it well while reheating to re-emulsify it.

2 tablespoons olive oil

2 shallots, finely chopped (Love Note 1)

2 cloves garlic, minced

4 roasted red bell peppers, peeled, cored, seeded, and sliced (Love Note 2)

1½ cups Vegetable Stock (page 84) or Chicken Stock (page 87)

½ teaspoon granulated sugar

¼ cup heavy cream

½ teaspoon kosher salt

¼ teaspoon freshly ground black pepper

1.  Heat the olive oil in a medium (8- to 10-inch) sauté pan over medium-high heat. Add the shallots, lower the heat to medium, and sauté until soft and translucent, about 5 minutes. Add the garlic and sauté until fragrant, about 1 minute more.

2.  Add the red peppers and continue to sauté until heated through and the shallots are very soft, about 3 minutes more.

3.  Add the broth and sugar and cook, stirring, until nearly all of the liquid has evaporated and the mixture is almost dry.

*continued*

4. Spoon the mixture into the bowl of a food processor fitted with the metal blade. Purée the mixture, then slowly add the cream through the feed tube while the motor is running. Check to make sure it's smooth, season with the salt and pepper, and pulse once or twice more to combine.

5. Serve immediately, or refrigerate the coulis for up to 2 days in a tightly covered container. The coulis is best served warm. Reheat in a saucepan over low heat just before serving.

## LOVE NOTES

**1** **Shallots** are members of the onion family, but they look more like small, reddish brown heads of garlic. They have a milder yet more complex flavor than regular onions. There's usually at least 2 "cloves" covered in papery skin per "head," so it can be confusing to know what is meant when a recipe specifies 1 shallot. Honestly, it's a matter of taste, but when I say 1 shallot, I'm referring to 1 clove. The cloves are much bigger than garlic cloves, usually about 2 inches tall and wide. If you have gigantic shallots, you might only need half a clove to equal 1 normal-size shallot.

**2** **Roast peppers** on the grill, under the broiler, or on the flame of a gas stove. Regardless of the method you choose, blacken all sides then place in a bowl and cover with plastic wrap; the steam will loosen the skins. Rub the skin off with your fingers, then rinse the peppers under cold water to get off the last bits of blackened skin. Remove the seeds by cutting off the top of the pepper, slicing it lengthwise, and using your fingers or a paring knife to pull out the membranes and scrape away the seeds.

# Spicy Shrimp Rémoulade

ALTHOUGH RÉMOULADE SOUNDS FUSSY AND FRENCH, IT'S TRADITIONALLY JUST homemade mayonnaise doctored up with capers and diced gherkins (tiny pickles). In this version, created by Alberta Williams, a M.O.M. and second mother to our friend and regular guest Glen Zoller, hot sauce and cayenne pepper give it plenty of Cajun-style kick. The sauce is tossed with boiled or grilled shrimp and served on a bed of shredded lettuce, but you can also serve it with crab or fish. You might even want to save some, mix it with an equal amount of mayonnaise, and use it as a sandwich spread with chicken or turkey. Try to make the rémoulade sauce a day ahead, which gives the flavors a chance to meld and develop.

**FOR THE RÉMOULADE SAUCE**

1 clove garlic, minced

1 medium rib celery, finely chopped

2 tablespoons chopped fresh Italian (flat-leaf) parsley

¼ cup thinly sliced scallions (white and green parts, about 2 scallions)

2 tablespoons white-wine vinegar

1 tablespoon paprika

⅛ teaspoon kosher salt

1½ teaspoons prepared horseradish

¼ cup Creole or stone-ground mustard

1 tablespoon ketchup

1½ teaspoons Tabasco® sauce

½ cup olive oil

**FOR THE SHRIMP**

1 large carrot, peeled and sliced

1 medium onion, sliced

1 rib celery, sliced

1 bay leaf

2 tablespoons kosher salt

1 tablespoon black peppercorns

2 tablespoons lemon juice (about 1 lemon)

5 cups cold water

1 pound extra-large shrimp, unpeeled (Love Note 1)

**FOR THE GARNISH**

1 cup shredded iceberg lettuce

1 bunch scallions, thinly sliced diagonally (white and green parts, ends trimmed)

*continued*

**TO MAKE THE RÉMOULADE SAUCE**

1.  Place the garlic, celery, parsley, scallions, vinegar, paprika, salt, horseradish, mustard, ketchup, and hot sauce in a blender or the bowl of a small food processor fitted with the metal blade. Blend until combined.

2.  With the machine running, add the oil in a slow, steady stream. Continue processing until the oil is incorporated and emulsified, giving the sauce a thick, creamy consistency. Taste and add more salt, if necessary.

3.  Using a rubber spatula, scrape the sauce into an airtight container and chill for at least 30 minutes before serving, preferably a few hours or overnight. (This helps meld the flavors and mellow out the scallions.) The sauce can be made up to 3 days ahead and stored, tightly covered, in the refrigerator.

**TO MAKE THE SHRIMP**

1.  Place the carrots, onions, celery, bay leaf, salt, peppercorns, lemon juice, and water in a large saucepan. Bring to a boil over high heat, reduce the heat, and simmer, uncovered, for 15 minutes. Meanwhile, prepare an ice bath with 4 cups of ice cubes and 4 cups of cold water in a large bowl.

2.  Turn off the heat, add the shrimp, cover the pot, and let sit for 5 to 6 minutes (stirring the shrimp once or twice to make sure they all get submerged in the water), or until they are white all the way through (peel one to check).

3.  Strain the shrimp through a sieve set over a bowl and place in the ice bath to cool for about 1 minute before peeling. Reserve the cooking liquid to make shrimp stock, if desired (Love Note 2).

4.  Peel the shrimp and devein them (Love Note 3), keeping the tails intact (they look more appetizing that way).

*continued*

5. Place the shrimp in a large bowl. Add about ⅓ cup of the rémoulade and gently toss to generously coat the shrimp. Allow the shrimp to marinate in the sauce for 20 minutes.

**TO SERVE**

Place a thin layer of lettuce on each plate. Arrange the shrimp on top of the lettuce, allowing 4 or 5 per serving. Top with the scallions and serve.

## LOVE NOTES

**1** **Shrimp are sized** according to how many you get in a pound. The size categories are: colossal (10 or fewer per pound), jumbo (11 to 15 per pound), extra-large (16 to 20), large (21 to 30), medium (31 to 35), small (36 to 45), and miniature (roughly 70 to 90). In general, the different sizes of shrimp, except the miniatures, can be substituted for each other.

**2** **I boil the shrimp** with aromatic vegetables such as onion and celery to give the shrimp added flavor. Even better, the shrimp add their own essence to the broth, which you can strain and reuse as shrimp stock.

**3** **To peel shrimp,** turn one over so the legs are facing you and use your thumbs to pull them away from each other, tearing the shell down the middle of its thin underside. Next, peel back the shell until you reach the tail, then tear the shell away.

To devein the shrimp, run a paring knife along the top of the shrimp to expose the vein. Remove the vein with your finger, the tip of your knife, or under a stream of cold water.

# Alberta Williams
{ SPICY SHRIMP RÉMOULADE }

Glen Zoller, a good friend and regular guest of Mother's Bistro & Bar, suggested we honor a woman who is a great cook and a major part of his life. Here's how he tells her story.

Alberta Williams was born on June 28, 1937, in Waterproof, Louisiana, about 40 miles from Natchez, Mississippi. She had three sisters and two brothers and learned to cook from her grandmother. Alberta says, "Growing up in the country you had to cook . . . we made soul food; things like hominy and scrambled eggs, corn pone, monkey bread, and greens." In 1955 she moved to New Orleans with her kids and her "ole man," who took a job at the riverfront. Aged 18, Alberta went to Hayes Chicken Shack to get a job. Though told by the owner that she was just a "country girl," she convinced him to let her work for free for the week. A successfully catered party where all the food got gobbled up earned her big thanks, a new job, and even a bonus. She moved on to various restaurants over the years, getting experience with lots of different foods, especially seafood.

In 1969, Alberta answered an ad placed by Linda Zoller, my mother. Linda needed a nanny to help out with her fourth child, Diana. "Berta" (as the family called her) got the job and began to clean the house and cook out of boredom while the baby slept. One day she made a pot roast, and from that day on, Berta was recruited to make all the family meals (especially since my mother was unable to make toast without a recipe)—red beans and rice, seafood gumbo, jambalaya, hot sausage sandwiches, crawfish étouffée . . . you name it! When our parents had dinner parties, their friends would come into the kitchen and eat right out of the pot. Berta says she got used to the party moving from the dining room into the kitchen. We Zoller kids grew up on Cajun and Creole food, literally eating for dinner nightly what people travel to New Orleans to enjoy in the finest restaurants. "Ya'll taught other kids how to eat," says Alberta.

In 1978, Berta "ran away" to Las Vegas and got a job at the Aladdin Hotel as a cook. She remembers meeting Redd Foxx and Rodney Dangerfield and laments not having started a little place of her own right downtown "not on the 'strip,' but downtown." She missed her eight kids and the Zollers, so she moved back to New Orleans.

Berta continues working and has remained an integral part of the Zoller family for nearly 33 years. She is the matriarch of her own large family, a wonderful cook, and as much a mother to the Zoller children as was their own mother.

# Mama Mia Trattoria's House Salad

I REALLY DELIBERATED OVER THE SIGNATURE SALAD FOR MAMA MIA TRATTORIA, my Italian restaurant. I wanted it to feature mesclun greens and to be different from other salads already on the menu. Since I love the color and flavor that red onion brings to a salad, that was a given. I thought blue cheese or Gorgonzola would offer something salty and savory, but my chef, Benny, suggested ricotta salata, a crumbly sheep's milk cheese.

Benny also suggested we use pecans, which go perfectly with this salad. Candying the nuts not only makes them sweeter but also simultaneously roasts and crisps them. This salad offers a symphony of flavors and textures in every bite.

6 cups mesclun greens, washed and dried

2½ tablespoons Balsamic Vinaigrette (page 30)

½ small red onion, thinly sliced (Love Note 1)

⅓ cup Candied Pecans, coarsely chopped (facing page)

⅓ cup crumbled ricotta salata cheese (Love Note 2)

1. Place the greens in a medium bowl and add the vinaigrette; toss to coat.

2. Place the dressed greens in a serving bowl or on individual plates.

3. Top the greens with the onion rings, Candied Pecans, and ricotta salata; serve immediately.

## CANDIED PECANS

MAKE A BIG BATCH OF THESE AND KEEP THEM IN AN AIRTIGHT CONTAINER FOR salads. They're great to have on hand for guests to snack on or as part of a cheese plate.

4 cups raw pecan halves

1 cup confectioners' sugar

4 cups vegetable oil (for frying)

1. Bring a large pot of water to a boil over high heat. Add the pecans and blanch for 2 minutes. Drain and rinse under cold water until cool.

2. Shake off some of the excess water. Place the pecans in a large bowl. Sprinkle with the confectioners' sugar and toss to coat (a little water clinging to the nuts will help "melt" the sugar so it can coat the nuts). Spread the nuts on a parchment-lined baking sheet for 10 minutes to allow the coating to dry.

*continued*

## LOVE NOTES

**1** **Use a mandoline** on the thinnest setting to slice the onions. To make the peeled onion easier to handle when slicing, cut it in half lengthwise, and then turn it on its side to run it along the mandoline blade. (Don't cut off the hairy root end; use that for the "handle.")

**2** **Ricotta salata** is made from sheep's milk curds that have been salted, pressed, dried, and aged for about 3 months. It's white, with a firm, dry texture, so you can grate it or crumble it. The flavor goes well with grilled vegetables and meats.

3. Place a medium saucepan over medium-high heat and add the oil. Heat the oil until it registers 350°F on a deep-fry thermometer. Working in batches, fry 1 cup of pecans at a time until the sugar has caramelized and the pecans are toasted, 4 to 5 minutes (watch carefully because they burn easily). Use a spider (Love Note 1, page 223, Spaetzle) to scoop the nuts out; transfer to a paper towel–lined baking sheet to cool. Store candied nuts in an airtight container for about 1 month.

## BALSAMIC VINAIGRETTE

MAKES ABOUT 2 CUPS

I LEARNED HOW *ACETO BALSAMICO TRADIZIONALE* (TRUE BALSAMIC VINEGAR) IS MADE during my "last hurrah" trip to Europe. After Le Cirque closed in June of 1996, my friend Claire and I traveled for three months, working in Spain, Italy, France, and Morocco.

During a stop in Modena, Italy, we toured an organic farm. In the farmhouse attic were row upon row of small barrels made of different types of wood, all containing vinegar. Each barrel had a small linen napkin covering a square opening. I was told that it allowed for evaporation over the 25-year aging period. After a determined amount of time in a particular wood barrel, the vinegar would be moved to another barrel made of a different wood, which would impart its own unique flavor. Understanding this painstaking process made it perfectly clear to me why true balsamic vinegar is so expensive (and why it shouldn't be used in a vinaigrette)!

½ cup balsamic vinegar (Love Note 1)

½ tablespoon Dijon mustard

¾ cup extra-virgin olive oil

¾ cup canola or other vegetable oil

1 teaspoon kosher salt

½ teaspoon freshly ground black pepper

1.  Whisk the balsamic vinegar and mustard together in a small bowl. Very slowly drizzle the oils into the vinegar mixture while whisking vigorously (Love Note 2). Continue whisking until all the oil has been incorporated and the dressing is thickened. Alternatively, you can do this with an immersion blender (see Making Dressings, page 9).

2.  Add the salt and pepper and whisk again to incorporate. The dressing will keep covered and refrigerated for up to 2 weeks.

## LOVE NOTES

**1  There are many kinds** of balsamic vinegar on the market, but when it comes to salad dressings, almost any inexpensive balsamic from Modena, Italy, will do. True balsamic vinegar has a wonderful, sweet, nuanced flavor, but it would be hard to appreciate it in a salad dressing. Plus, it's very expensive. If you can afford the real stuff, use it as the Italians do—drizzled over strawberries or a special pasta or sipped as a liqueur.

**2  Emulsifying salad dressings** by hand is a technique everyone should know how to do. It will come in handy when you're away from home and don't have your immersion blender. The trick is to add the oil extremely slowly while whisking as fast as you can. It definitely helps if your bowl stays firmly in place while you do this, so if your bowl doesn't have a rubber grip on the bottom, you can keep it in place by wrapping a damp kitchen towel around the bottom of it. Be patient, as it will take several minutes of constant whisking and incremental drizzling to create a thick emulsion.

# Poached Pear, Rogue River Blue Cheese, and Hazelnut Salad

I LOVE THE INTERPLAY BETWEEN SWEET AND SAVORY THAT FRUIT CAN ADD TO salads. Here, fresh pears are poached in red wine to give them a gorgeous color and deeper flavor that's delicious with the assertive blue cheese and toasty hazelnuts. This is definitely a company-worthy dish, although if you make the components ahead you can enjoy it even on a busy weeknight. Store any leftover vinaigrette in an airtight container in the fridge and use within a couple of weeks.

¼ cup red-wine vinegar

1 teaspoon Dijon mustard

⅓ cup hazelnut oil (optional; Love Note 1)

⅓ cup canola oil (or ⅔ cup if not using hazelnut oil)

½ teaspoon kosher salt

¼ teaspoon freshly ground black pepper

6 cups mesclun greens, washed and dried

2 Red Wine–Poached Pears (page 35)

2½ ounces Rogue Creamery® Oregon Blue or other blue cheese, crumbled (about 1 cup)

½ cup hazelnuts, lightly toasted, skins removed, and chopped (Love Notes 2 and 3)

1. In a small bowl, whisk together the vinegar and mustard. Add the oils in a slow, steady stream while whisking vigorously. Continue whisking until all of the oil is incorporated and the dressing is thickened. Add the salt and pepper. (Alternatively, you can use an immersion blender; see Making Dressings, page 9).

2. In a large bowl, toss the mesclun with 2½ tablespoons of the dressing and taste. Add more dressing, if needed. Divide the greens among four plates.

3. Halve and core the poached pears. Cut lengthwise into ¼-inch slices and evenly distribute on the greens. They also look nice sliced but held together by the upper part of the pear (called "fanning"). Sprinkle with cheese and hazelnuts, drizzle with reduced syrup if desired (Love Note 2, page 36) and serve.

*continued*

# LOVE NOTES

**1. Nut oils** are a wonderful way to add depth to salads and tie the dressing into the rest of the ingredients. Hazelnut oil is available in the gourmet section of most grocery stores and through online gourmet retailers.

Nut oils go rancid rather quickly, so buy them in small quantities and store in the refrigerator. The oil will solidify when chilled, so set the bottle out 10 minutes before using so it has a chance to liquefy again. Sniff your oil before using to ensure it hasn't gone bad. If it smells soapy or acrid, or like linseed oil, throw it out.

**2. To toast or roast hazelnuts,** heat the oven to 275°F. Spread the shelled hazelnuts in a single layer on a baking sheet. Toast for 20 to 30 minutes, or until the skins crack and the nuts turn light golden brown and smell fragrant. You can also roast them at 350°F for 10 to 15 minutes, but check them periodically to be sure they don't burn.

Remove the nuts from oven and set aside to cool.

**3. Toasting hazelnuts loosens** their skins considerably. To remove the skins from toasted hazelnuts, place them in a colander with large holes. Put the colander in the sink and use a clean dishtowel to rub the nuts so the skins peel off. Shake the colander occasionally to encourage the skins to fall into the sink.

Another way to remove the skins is to put the warm nuts onto a clean dishtowel and gather it closed. Let the nuts steam for 4 to 5 minutes, then rub vigorously for 1 to 3 minutes. Rub longer to remove even more skin.

For recipes, like a cake, that require all the skins to be removed, blanch the nuts for 1 minute in boiling water spiked with baking soda (1 tablespoon per cup of water). Then plunge the nuts into cold water; the skins will slip right off. In this case, you would roast them after they were peeled, at the lower temperature.

## RED WINE–POACHED PEARS

RED WINE GIVES THESE PEARS A COMPLEX FLAVOR AND LOVELY GARNET HUE.
They're impressive sliced and served in this salad, or you can turn them into a quick
yet elegant dessert by drizzling them with syrup made from reducing the poaching
liquid (Love Note 2) and garnishing with whipped cream, crème fraîche, or vanilla ice
cream. They're perfect as a dessert for an elegant brunch.

| | |
|---|---|
| 1½ cups inexpensive dry red wine | 1 cup granulated sugar |
| 1½ cups water | 4 whole cloves |
| One 2-inch strip of lemon zest, removed with a vegetable peeler | 1 cinnamon stick |
| 2 tablespoons lemon juice (about 1 lemon) | 4 firm, ripe Bartlett or d'Anjou pears, peeled with stems intact (Love Note 1) |

1.  Combine the red wine, water, lemon zest, lemon juice, sugar, cloves, and cinna-
    mon stick in a narrow, deep saucepan that holds at least 3 quarts. Set the pot over
    medium-high heat and bring to a boil, whisking occasionally to dissolve the sugar.
    Reduce the heat and simmer for about 5 minutes.

2.  Stand the pears up in the liquid or lay them down so they are covered by the
    poaching liquid. Place a small heatproof plate on top to keep them submerged.

3.  Cover the pot and gently simmer the pears over low heat, turning them occasion-
    ally with tongs, until fork-tender, 10 to 15 minutes (Love Note, page 64, Belle's
    Chicken Noodle Soup).

4.  Remove the pot from the heat and allow the pears to cool in the liquid. Remove the
    spices and lemon zest. Refrigerate the pears in the poaching liquid for up to 3 days.
    Ideally, let the pears come to room temperature before serving.  *continued*

## LOVE NOTES

**1** **D'Anjou, red d'Anjou, and Bartlett pears** are probably the easiest varieties to find and are great for poaching as long as they're a bit underripe. Bosc pears also hold their shape well when cooked, but they can be slightly less flavorful.

**2** **To reduce the liquid to a syrup:** Bring the poaching liquid to a boil over medium-high heat in a shallow pan or sauté pan (the wider the pan, the more quickly liquids will reduce due to evaporation). Reduce the heat to low and continue to simmer until the liquid is reduced by three-quarters, 40 to 50 minutes. Allow the syrup to cool a bit.

To serve, let it drip off the end of a spoon as you move your hand back and forth over the salads or dessert pears, or pour it into a squeeze bottle and drizzle the syrup over. (Look for squeeze bottles at kitchen or restaurant supply stores. They're similar to ketchup and mustard bottles, and they give you more control so you can attempt interesting patterns and avoid blobs of sauce.)

# Perfect Caesar Salad

NEARLY EVERY ITALIAN RESTAURANT SERVES CAESAR SALAD, AND I WANTED Mama Mia Trattoria's Caesar to be the best. I experimented with the dressing for years, always tweaking it if a guest had a comment. I finally settled on what I believe is a recipe for a perfectly balanced salad. From the dressing to the croutons, all the ingredients work together to deliver a salad that's garlicky and savory yet bright—everything a Caesar should be.

1 (9-ounce) head romaine lettuce

⅓ cup Caesar Dressing (page 39)

1 cup Garlicky Croutons (page 38)

⅓ cup freshly grated Parmesan cheese, for garnish

1. Cut the head of romaine lengthwise and then crosswise into 2-inch pieces. Wash and dry the lettuce thoroughly and place in a large bowl (see Cleaning the Greens, page 8). Chill in the refrigerator while preparing the other ingredients.

2. Immediately before serving, add ⅓ cup of dressing to the lettuce. Toss until all of the leaves are coated. Taste and add more dressing, if desired. Add the Garlicky Croutons and toss again.

3. Evenly divide the salad between four plates and sprinkle with Parmesan cheese.

*continued*

## GARLICKY CROUTONS

THE DIFFERENCE BETWEEN FRESH-MADE AND STORE-BOUGHT CROUTONS IS STUNNING. Croutons are easy to make, and they're a great way to use up your stale French bread.

One (1-pound) loaf country or French bread with crust, cut into 1-inch cubes

¾ cup olive oil

5 large cloves garlic, finely chopped (about 2 tablespoons)

1 tablespoon finely chopped fresh Italian (flat-leaf) parsley

2 teaspoons kosher salt

1. Heat the oven to 350°F. Spread the bread cubes in a single layer on a rimmed baking sheet. Bake until dry and barely golden, 10 to 12 minutes (Love Note). Remove and allow to cool slightly.

2. Combine the olive oil, garlic, and parsley in a small bowl.

3. Sprinkle the salt over the bread and drizzle it with the olive oil mixture. Toss well to coat and return the pan to the oven.

4. Bake until golden brown, about 10 minutes. Remove from the oven and cool. Store in an airtight container for up to 2 weeks, or freeze for 6 months (be sure to defrost them before using).

### LOVE NOTE

**You must bake the croutons twice.** The bread dries out and gets a little color from the first baking and then gets crispy and golden the second time. If tossed in the oil mixture and then baked only once, the garlic would burn before the bread got crispy and golden.

## CAESAR DRESSING

I WORKED FOR YEARS TO GET THE DRESSING FOR MY CAESAR SALAD JUST RIGHT, and I believe I have found the perfect balance of lemon, garlic, and olive oil. However, it's all a matter of personal taste, so feel free to adjust these amounts as you see fit. If you are concerned about salmonella when using raw eggs, use pasteurized eggs instead.

2 to 3 large cloves garlic

4 anchovy fillets (Love Note, page 42, Mother's Greek/Italian Dressing)

½ teaspoon kosher salt

¼ cup lemon juice (about 2 medium lemons)

2 egg yolks

1 cup extra-virgin olive oil

1 cup vegetable oil

½ cup freshly grated Parmesan cheese

1½ teaspoons freshly ground black pepper

1.  In the bowl of a food processor, add the garlic, anchovies, salt, and lemon juice. (If whisking by hand, chop the garlic and anchovies before combining with the other ingredients.) Pulse to combine. Add the egg yolks and pulse until blended and thickened.

2.  With the motor running, very slowly drizzle the oils through the feed tube until they're fully incorporated and the dressing is thick and emulsified. Alternatively, you can use an immersion blender or whisk the dressing by hand.

3.  Transfer the dressing to a bowl and whisk in the Parmesan cheese and black pepper.

# Mother's Greek Salad

THE GREEK SALAD I SERVE AT MOTHER'S WAS INSPIRED BY A SIMILAR SALAD SERVED at Shish Kebob Restaurant in Port Washington, New York, where I lived for nearly 20 years. At Mother's we serve this by itself or on a "combo" plate with hummus (page 11) and warm pita—a heavenly combination.

1 head romaine, green leaf, or red leaf lettuce, cut into 1-inch strips, washed, and dried (about 6 cups)

3½ tablespoons Mother's Greek/Italian Dressing (facing page)

3 tablespoons chopped scallions (Love Note 1)

½ teaspoon chopped fresh dill

½ rib celery, finely chopped (3 tablespoons)

1 tomato, diced (½ cup)

½ cup crumbled feta cheese (about 3½ ounces)

½ small red onion, thinly sliced

12 pitted Kalamata olives (about ¼ cup; Love Note, Greek Macaroni & Cheese, page 243)

1. Put the greens in a large bowl. Add the dressing, scallions, dill, and celery; toss to coat.

2. Transfer the dressed salad to a serving bowl and top with the tomatoes, feta cheese, red onions, and olives.

3. Serve the salad immediately, on its own or with warm pita bread (Love Note 3, page 12, Hummus).

## LOVE NOTES

**1** When a recipe calls for **scallions,** use both the white and green parts unless otherwise instructed. Each part adds its own flavor. It's important to use a sharp, straight-edged knife for the job. A food processor, serrated knife, or dull knife will bruise the green part and make it mushy and slimy. Also, don't cut off the root (hairy) end first. Keep it on instead, so you have something to hold while you cut the very last bit of scallion.

**2** **Kalamata olives** are a Greek-style olive with a dark eggplant color and a rich, deep, tangy flavor. They're often slit open to absorb the vinegar marinade in which they're soaked.

## MOTHER'S GREEK/ITALIAN DRESSING

MAKES 1⅓ CUPS

UNDETERRED WHEN A RESTAURANT OWNER WOULDN'T SHARE HIS RECIPE FOR MY favorite Greek salad, I spent an afternoon devising my own and came up with this dressing as well. It is very delicious—and very garlicky. Make sure everyone with you has some of it so you won't chase anyone away. It also makes a great marinade for chicken or beef.

2 cloves garlic

3 tablespoons dried oregano

6 oil-packed anchovy fillets
(Love Note, page 42)

⅓ cup red-wine vinegar

½ cup olive oil

½ cup vegetable oil

¼ teaspoon kosher salt

½ teaspoon freshly ground black pepper

*continued*

1. Combine the garlic, oregano, and anchovy fillets in a food processor and pulse until finely chopped. Add the vinegar and pulse a few more times.

2. With the motor running, slowly drizzle the oils through the feed tube until they're fully incorporated and the dressing is emulsified. Alternatively, you can use an immersion blender, or mix by hand with a whisk (Love Note 2, page 31, Balsamic Vinaigrette). The dressing should be thick.

3. Season with the salt and pepper. (Anchovies are salty, so the dressing won't need much salt.) The dressing will keep covered and refrigerated for up to 2 weeks.

## LOVE NOTE

**Use leftover anchovies** in Caesar Dressing (page 39), or transfer to an airtight container, cover with 1 inch of olive oil, and refrigerate for up to a year. Don't use anchovy paste in a tube, which is made from bits and scraps and tastes about as appealing as it sounds.

# Mama's Italian Chopped Salad

THIS IS ONE OF THE MOST POPULAR SALADS AT MAMA MIA TRATTORIA. IT OFFERS the flavors of an antipasto platter—salami, cheese, and olives—all in one bite. A generous helping of romaine keeps it from being too heavy, and with a loaf of rustic bread on the side, it's a meal in itself.

I served this salad when I first opened Mother's and used sliced black California olives, thinking nothing of it. But a handful of guests did not approve, I guess because they thought them too bland. I changed to more flavorful Niçoise olives (from Nice, France), pitted but left whole because they're already tiny, and I haven't had a complaint since. Pitted Niçoise olives can be hard to find, and they're a pain to pit yourself, so feel free to experiment with your own favorite olives. You can even change up the cheese or meat. Harvey Gilbert, one of my regular guests as well as a friend, made a delicious variation using grilled chicken breast instead of salami and substituting Caesar dressing for the Italian.

The hardest part of this recipe is finely chopping everything, which is a great argument for investing in a good-quality, sharp knife (Love Note 1).

1 (9-ounce) head romaine lettuce, sliced crosswise into very thin strips, washed, and dried (about 6 cups)

1 cup drained and rinsed canned garbanzo beans (chickpeas)

1 cup pitted whole Niçoise or Kalamata olives or sliced canned black olives

1 medium tomato, cored and cut into ¼-inch dice

1 medium red onion, finely chopped (about 1 cup)

¼ pound provolone cheese, sliced into ⅛-inch-thick matchsticks (about 1 cup)

¼ pound Genoa salami, sliced into ⅛-inch-thick matchsticks (about 1 cup)

1 tablespoon thinly sliced fresh basil (Love Note 2)

¼ cup Mother's Greek/Italian Dressing (page 41)

Kosher salt

Freshly ground black pepper

*continued*

1. In a large bowl, combine the lettuce, garbanzo beans, olives, tomatoes, onions, provolone, salami, and basil.

2. Pour half of the dressing over the salad to moisten it. Mix gently, adding more dressing if necessary to make the salad moist but not soaked. Season with a pinch of salt and pepper and serve.

## LOVE NOTES

**1** **An 8-inch chef's knife** is probably the most useful cooking tool you'll ever own—but only if you keep it sharp. A sharp knife makes slicing and dicing faster and easier. Dull knives, on the other hand, require more effort to use, which also makes it easier to slip and cut yourself.

You don't need to spend tons of money on a big knife set. Get an 8-inch chef's knife for all-purpose work, a paring knife for detail work like coring and peeling, and a serrated knife to cut through things like bread and tomatoes without squishing them. Sharpen your knives at least once a year and hone the straight-edged knives each time you use them.

If you want to sharpen them yourself, I recommend a Chef'sChoice® knife sharpener, which is reliable and idiot-proof, so won't ruin your knives. You can also get your knives professionally sharpened at many cookware stores or hardware stores.

**2** **Tender leaves** like basil, spinach, and sage are hard to slice because they're so thin and bruise easily, which causes them to darken unappealingly. The best technique for thinly cutting these types of leaves is called "chiffonade." Stack 4 leaves, roll them up lengthwise like a jellyroll, and use a sharp knife to cut paper-thin slices across the roll. You can use this technique for any leafy herbs or lettuces that need to be very thinly sliced.

soups

**A steaming bowl of soup is warming, comforting, and filling, like a hug in a bowl.** Even if you're not ready to start a weekly soup-night tradition, you'll want to start incorporating some of these soups into your repertoire because they're just plain practical. They're economical because you can take advantage of seasonal produce, inexpensive staples like dried beans, and even leftovers from other meals. They're also easy to make, and you can stash some in the freezer for later. Even better, it only takes one bowl of something hearty to get the major food groups into your loved ones' bellies.

Whether you're cooking up something chunky or smooth, it's important to chop the ingredients the same size so they'll cook at the same rate. For chunky soups, make sure that size is small—about ¼ inch. Chopping ingredients for puréed soups is a little easier because they don't need to be tiny or look perfect since everything gets blended smooth in the end.

The most important ingredient, however, is love. That sounds like a cliché, but I'm talking about taking a few extra steps to add another layer of flavor to lift the dish from ordinary to extraordinary.

### LOVE STEP I: USE CLEAN, COLD WATER

A simple, and important, step is using fresh, cold water—it's the foundation of a stock, which is the foundation of a soup. Hot water comes from a tank that can have traces of metals and sediments, which in turn could create a bad taste in your soups. The heat can also leach heavy metals like lead from your plumbing into the water, which would then go into your soup.

### LOVE STEP II: MAKE THE STOCK

If the stock isn't good, your soup won't be, either. Ideally, you should make it with plenty of meaty bones (the meat gives it flavor and the bones give it "body" from their natural collagen). Cold homemade stock often has so much body that it can be scooped with a spoon, like Jell-O®, and body gives the stock a silky quality when heated into its liquid form. You can make a big batch of stock and freeze it in containers that can be defrosted later.

But you don't always have to buy bones for making stock. If you cut up your own chickens, keep the legs and thighs for a dish like Chicken Cacciatore (page 119), use the breasts for another recipe, and throw the remaining bones and carcass into a zip-top bag until you have enough to make stock. Then just cut up the aromatic vegetables (onions, garlic, celery, and carrots) that give stock extra flavor and you're ready to go.

If you have to start with a can of broth, be sure to use a low-sodium variety so that you can control the seasonings. Give low-sodium broth a little extra love by warming it with a few aromatic veggies, some leftover herbs, and a scrap or two of meat while you prep the rest of the ingredients. Even low-sodium broths have salt, so add only half of what's called for in the recipe, taste, and add more if needed.

### LOVE STEP III: SAUTÉ—THE *RIGHT* WAY

One way to provide love is by taking the time to sauté the aromatic vegetables, which slightly caramelizes their natural sugars, adding depth to an already magical combination.

To properly sauté, first make sure you have your ingredients—the fat (oil or butter) as well as the prepped veggies—at the ready. Second, make sure the pot is smoking hot before you put anything inside. Let it sit over medium-high heat for at least 2 minutes while you finish your final preparations. Check to make sure the pan is hot by holding your hand an inch away from the surface. You should feel the heat radiating onto your palm.

You'll also need fat for sautéing, but here's the dilemma: Vegetable oils have a high smoke point, making them ideal for high-heat cooking, but they lack flavor. They're best used with robustly flavored ingredients. Butter has loads of flavor and is the best choice for delicate or dairy-based soups, but it burns easily over high heat. If you want to sauté with butter, add the vegetables and butter at the same time. The vegetables will begin to sauté right away, and this will keep the butter from burning; just remember to keep stirring so the veggies don't burn.

### LOVE STEP IV: TAKE IT SLOW

Whenever you cook a soup or stock, bring it to a boil, then reduce the heat until you see small bubbles just around the rim, not rollicking bubbles across the surface. Boiling disintegrates the ingredients and makes the liquid cloudy. And ingredients often get scorched on the bottom if the heat is too high and you haven't stirred often enough.

Slow simmering and frequent stirring should keep your soup safe, but if you do burn the soup, pour the contents of the scorched pot into another clean pot immediately. But no scraping! Allow anything stuck to the bottom to stay there.

### LOVE STEP V: SEASON, SEASON, SEASON!

Many good dishes are ruined by not enough salt and pepper. I've included salt and pepper amounts in these recipes, but the amounts are only recommendations—you should season your food as you please. But first try one or two soups seasoned my way so you get an idea of what they should taste like and then make your determination.

A word of caution: If you are using canned broth or stock, only add half the recommended amount of salt and pepper listed in the recipe, then taste and add more as needed.

### LOVE STEP VI: ADJUSTMENTS

Even though I've given specific amounts in each recipe, nature isn't static. Vegetables contain water, and the levels vary based on freshness and storage. Vegetables have natural sodium, which can vary for many reasons. There are hundreds of different types of bacon, each with its own level of saltiness. And if you use iodized table salt instead of kosher salt, things will taste saltier with the same measured amounts.

You are the judge. If your soup is too thick, add more of the liquid used to make it. Too thin? Add beurre manié (Coq au Vin, page 127) a tablespoon at a time to any soup made with a roux to thicken it. Underseasoned? Add salt and pepper. Overseasoned? Sometimes lemon juice will do the trick, or throw a whole peeled potato into the pot, which might absorb the saltiness. Or make another half-batch of unseasoned soup and add it to the pot. Follow my directions, but trust yourself after you've made the soup a few times.

## PERFECTING CREAM SOUPS

Some of the cream soups in this chapter rely on a *velouté*, the French term for stock that has been thickened with a white roux (a mixture of equal parts fat and flour that has been cooked for 3 to 5 minutes). Making a velouté is an important technique to master so that you can make lump-free soups, sauces, and gravies. The trick is not to rush it. After blending melted butter and flour together in the pan (creating the roux), add room-temperature stock into the hot roux little by little, whisking constantly and letting the roux absorb the liquid after each addition. If lumps appear, just keep whisking over medium-high heat until the lumps disappear (they will, I promise).

Let the soup simmer so the starch molecules in the flour have a chance to swell and thicken the soup. Don't let the soup boil for too long, though, or the starch molecules will burst and the soup will thin out. If you end up getting lumps that won't go away, strain the velouté through a fine-mesh strainer into a clean pot and discard the lumps left behind.

Vegetables for cream soups need to cook for about 1 hour to be soft enough for puréeing. Don't undercook them or they won't purée smoothly and you'll end up with less soup after straining. An immersion blender makes quick work of puréeing the vegetables once you've added them to the velouté.

You can also use a blender or food processor, but only fill it halfway or the buildup of steam will cause the soup to spurt out as it's being blended and scald you. To keep the scalding risk low, vent the lid on the blender, put a kitchen towel over the top, and hold your hand on the lid to keep it from popping off. You might want to put a towel over the lid of the food processor, too.

Hold back some of the liquid (stock and/or cream) until after the soup has been puréed to adjust the final consistency of the soup. Add the last amount of liquid little by little, only until the soup is just thick enough to coat the back of a spoon (Love Note 3, page 98, Perfect Pot Roast).

**FILLING YOUR FREEZER**

Soups can be made in bulk, frozen for later, and reheated in minutes, so they're perfect for busy families. The yields in many of these recipes result in larger quantities than you might need for one meal. That's because I believe if you're going to spend your time and energy cooking something that freezes well, you might as well make extra just for that purpose.

When freezing, portion the soup into appropriately sized containers so that you can defrost only what you'll use at one time. If you're short on freezer space, use zip-top freezer bags and freeze the soup flat. Be sure to label your creations with the date, name, and any garnishing instructions. Soups will keep in the freezer for about 3 months without suffering a loss in quality.

**REHEATING**

Most soups are easily reheated in a saucepan over low heat. Creamy, puréed soups retain their silky texture best when defrosted in the fridge, which takes at least 24 hours. Soups that aren't dairy-based can be defrosted in the microwave to speed things up. Avoid putting a solid block of frozen soup in a saucepan—the outside may scorch before the rest has begun to defrost.

# Creamy Tomato Soup

THIS DREAMY SOUP IS THE PERFECT VERSION OF THE CLASSIC. ENJOY IT WITH A grilled cheese sandwich and be transported back to childhood. Or, top it with a dollop of unsweetened whipped cream for an entirely grown-up experience.

¾ cups plus 2 tablespoons (1¾ sticks) unsalted butter (divided)

3 medium yellow onions, coarsely chopped (about 3 cups)

7 ribs celery, coarsely chopped (a little less than 1 head)

1 bay leaf

1 sprig fresh thyme

2 (28-ounce) cans diced tomatoes in purée (Love Note)

2 (6-ounce) cans tomato paste

¾ cup flour

4 cups (1 quart) half-and-half

4 cups (1 quart) milk (or more to adjust consistency)

2½ cups heavy cream (divided)

3 teaspoons kosher salt

½ teaspoon freshly ground black pepper

1. Heat a large (8- to 10-quart), heavy stockpot over medium-high heat. When it's hot, add 2 tablespoons of the butter, the onions, and celery. (Don't worry about melting the butter first. It will continue to melt as the onions and celery start to cook.) Lower the heat if the vegetables start to show any sign of browning. Sauté until soft, about 20 minutes.

2. Add the bay leaf, thyme, tomatoes, and tomato paste, and cook over low heat until the vegetables are very soft, about 15 minutes more.

3. Meanwhile, in a 4-quart saucepan set over medium heat, melt the remaining butter. Add the flour, mixing until combined. Cook over low heat until the mixture turns pale yellow, resembles sand, and starts to give off a nutty aroma, 3 to 5 minutes.

4.  Slowly whisk the half-and-half and milk into the roux, allowing the roux to absorb each addition of liquid before adding more. Bring to a boil over medium-high heat, lower the heat, and simmer for about 15 minutes, stirring occasionally to ensure there are no lumps. (Simmering the soup after the flour has been added allows the starch to swell so that the soup thickens. Cooking the flour also gets rid of the raw flour taste.)

5.  Carefully pour the thickened cream mixture into the pot with the tomatoes and whisk well. Add 2 cups of the heavy cream and simmer over medium heat, stirring occasionally, for 10 minutes to meld the flavors. Remove the thyme and bay leaf.

6.  Purée the soup until smooth using an immersion blender, in batches in a blender or food processor, or with a food mill. (See Perfecting Cream Soups, page 50.) Strain through a fine-mesh strainer set over a clean pot, pressing on the vegetable solids with a rubber spatula to extract as much liquid as possible. Discard the solids.

7.  Bring the soup to a simmer, add more milk if it seems too thick, and season with the salt and pepper.

8.  Using a whisk or stand mixer fitted with the whisk attachment, whip the remaining ½ cup heavy cream until stiff peaks form.

9.  Ladle into bowls and serve topped with the whipped cream.

## LOVE NOTE

A **little extra tomato** in this soup won't hurt! Feel free to add leftover tomato paste, half a tomato you're not going to eat, or canned tomatoes from another recipe.

# Butternut Squash and Apple Soup

WE GET MORE RECIPE REQUESTS FOR THIS SOUP THAN ANY OTHER. ITS LIGHT, SILKY texture makes it an elegant way to start a meal, and it's perfect for fall and winter, when butternut squash and apples are at their peak and most affordable. The most time-consuming part of making this soup is peeling and seeding the squash and apples. Otherwise, it's really pretty easy.

5 pounds butternut squash, peeled, seeded, and diced (about 12 cups; Love Note 1)

1½ pounds (about 3 large) Granny Smith apples, peeled, cored, and diced (about 4 cups; Love Note 2)

1 (1-inch) piece cinnamon stick

1½ teaspoons finely minced fresh ginger

5½ cups Vegetable Stock (page 84), Chicken Stock (page 87), or canned low-sodium broth

4 tablespoons (½ stick) unsalted butter

¼ cup real maple syrup (any grade will do)

⅛ teaspoon freshly grated nutmeg (Love Note 3)

4 cups (1 quart) half-and-half

2½ teaspoons kosher salt

1 teaspoon freshly ground black pepper

½ cup unsweetened whipped cream, crème fraîche, or mascarpone, for garnish (optional)

1. In a large (8- to 10-quart), heavy stockpot, combine the squash, apples, cinnamon stick, ginger, and stock (Love Note 4). Bring to a boil over high heat. Lower the heat to a simmer and cook, covered, until the squash and apples are very soft, 30 to 40 minutes. (Don't undercook the vegetables or you won't have a silky soup.)

2. Remove the pot from the heat and remove the cinnamon stick. Add the butter, maple syrup, nutmeg, half-and-half, and salt and pepper, and purée until smooth with an immersion blender, in batches in a blender or food processor, or with a food mill. (See Perfecting Cream Soups, page 50.) *continued*

3. Pass the puréed soup through a fine-mesh strainer set over another clean pot, pressing on the vegetable solids to extract as much liquid as possible. Discard the solids.

4. Return the pot to the stove and bring the soup to a boil over medium heat, stirring now and then. Lower the heat and simmer for 5 minutes to meld the flavors. Taste and add more salt and pepper if needed.

5. Ladle into bowls and serve topped with a dollop of unsweetened whipped cream, crème fraîche, or mascarpone, if desired.

## LOVE NOTES

**1** **To prepare the squash,** cut in half widthwise, place the flat end on a cutting board, and remove the peel with a sharp knife or vegetable peeler. Cut the squash in half lengthwise and scoop out the seeds.

**2** **To prepare the apples,** peel with a vegetable peeler. Stand each apple stem-end up, and cut into quarters to expose the core, keeping as close to it as possible. (You can also use an apple corer.) Dice the quarters and discard the core.

**3** **Nutmegs** are large when whole, making them easy to hold while you grate them on a fine, rasp-style grater. Or buy a nutmeg grinder, which grates the nutmeg with a turn of the handle and stores the whole nutmeg, too.

**4** Add only **half the amount** of liquid called for and then check the consistency of the soup. If it looks like adding all the liquid might make the soup watery, don't add it.

# Hungarian Mushroom Soup

I AM A FIRM BELIEVER IN ROASTING OR SAUTÉING VEGETABLES TO COAX OUT THEIR flavors, and this soup is a prime example of that step. Slowly sautéing the onions (as any good Hungarian mother would!) makes the soup richer, the flavors deeper, and the taste a little sweeter. Sautéing the mushrooms correctly also adds another layer of flavor. Yes, good cooking takes patience, but the final result is worth it.

¾ cup plus 2 tablespoons (1¾ sticks) unsalted butter (divided)

4 medium yellow onions, finely chopped (about 4 cups)

1½ pounds mushrooms, thinly sliced (about 6 cups)

2½ teaspoons kosher salt (divided)

1 teaspoon freshly ground black pepper (divided)

2 tablespoons paprika

2 to 4 teaspoons chopped fresh dill (divided)

5 cups Chicken Stock (page 87), Vegetable Stock (page 84), or canned low-sodium broth (divided)

½ cup all-purpose flour

2 cups milk

2 teaspoons lemon juice (about ½ lemon)

1 cup sour cream

¼ cup chopped fresh Italian (flat-leaf) parsley (optional)

1. Heat a medium (6- to 8-quart), heavy stockpot over medium-high heat. When very hot, add 4 tablespoons of butter (don't wait for the butter to melt) and the onions, and sauté, stirring now and then, until very soft and just beginning to color, 10 to 15 minutes. (You might need to turn down the heat a bit if the onions start to color before they get soft.) Remove the onions to a bowl and set aside.

2. Increase the heat to high. When the pot is very hot, add another 4 tablespoons of butter (don't wait for the butter to melt) and immediately add the mushrooms (this way the mushrooms will sear before releasing their moisture, so they'll sauté better). Season with ½ teaspoon salt and ¼ teaspoon pepper, stir to combine, and sauté

*continued*

the mushrooms until they start to brown. (If they release their moisture, continue to cook over high heat until the liquid evaporates and the mushrooms start to sauté again.) Continue to cook over high heat, stirring occasionally, until the mushrooms are evenly golden, 6 to 8 minutes. (Lower the heat if necessary to prevent scorching.)

3. Lower the heat to medium (if you haven't already), add the paprika, and cook for about 1 minute while stirring. Return the onions to the pot. Add 2 teaspoons of the dill and 3 cups of the stock while stirring to combine. Cover and simmer over low heat for 15 minutes.

4. Meanwhile, in a 3- to 4-quart saucepan, melt the remaining 6 tablespoons of butter over medium heat and whisk in the flour. Cook, stirring occasionally, for about 3 to 5 minutes, until the mixture is light gold and looks like fine, wet sand.

5. Slowly whisk the milk into the roux, a little at a time, allowing the roux to absorb the liquid after each addition. Add the remaining 2 cups of stock and whisk again. Bring to a boil, then immediately reduce the heat to a gentle simmer and cook, whisking occasionally, for 10 minutes.

6. Pour the thickened milk into the pot with the mushrooms, being sure to scrape up the browned bits from the bottom of the pan. (If it's at all lumpy, pour it through a sieve rather than directly into the pot, and use a rubber spatula to push through every last drop.) Stir well to combine.

7. Cover and simmer for 10 to 15 minutes, stirring occasionally. Just before serving, add the remaining 2 teaspoons of salt and ¾ teaspoon of pepper, the lemon juice, sour cream, and another 2 teaspoons of dill, if desired.

8. Ladle into bowls and serve garnished with chopped fresh parsley, if desired.

# Cream of Spinach Soup

CREAMED SPINACH IS ONE OF MY ALL-TIME FAVORITE VEGETABLE DISHES, AND turning it into soup seemed like a natural progression. This has the exact same flavors of the classic side dish, just creamier so that you can eat it with a spoon. Topped with finely shredded spinach leaves, this makes a nice first-course alternative to salad, especially during the winter. It's healthy, not too heavy, and warms you up from the inside.

¾ cup (1½ sticks) unsalted butter (divided)

4 medium yellow onions, thinly sliced (about 4 cups)

4 cloves garlic, chopped (about 2 tablespoons)

2½ pounds (about 3 large) russet potatoes, peeled and sliced into ¼-inch-thick slices (about 8 cups)

6 cups Vegetable Stock (page 84), Chicken Stock (page 87), or canned low-sodium broth

½ cup all-purpose flour

8 cups (2 quarts) half-and-half

5 tightly packed cups fresh spinach leaves (about 8 ounces or 2 bunches), stems trimmed

5 teaspoons kosher salt

2 teaspoons freshly ground black pepper

20 spinach leaves, cut into chiffonade (Love Note 2, page 44, Mama's Italian Chopped Salad; optional)

1.  Heat a medium (6- to 8-quart), heavy stockpot over medium-high heat. When hot, add 4 tablespoons of the butter (don't wait for the butter to melt) and the onions. Stir well and sauté until they start to color around the edges, lower the heat to medium, and continue to sauté until soft but not browned, about 10 minutes. Add the garlic and sauté for 2 minutes more.

2.  Add the potatoes and stock to the onions, cover, and simmer until the potatoes are very tender, about 20 minutes.

*continued*

3. Meanwhile, in a medium (4- to 6-quart) saucepan, melt the remaining ½ cup (1 stick) butter over medium heat. Add the flour and stir well to make a roux. Cook over medium heat for 3 to 5 minutes, or until the mixture is pale yellow and resembles sand.

4. Add the half-and-half, a little at a time while whisking, allowing the roux to absorb the liquid after each addition. (Don't give up if there are lumps; keep whisking and they should eventually go away.) Whisk over medium heat until the mixture comes to a boil. Lower the heat and simmer for 15 minutes, stirring occasionally.

5. Add the 5 cups of spinach leaves to the potato-onion mixture and season with the salt and pepper. Bring to a boil, lower the heat, and simmer uncovered for about 5 minutes. Add the thickened half-and-half to the pot with the vegetables and stir well. Remove the pot from the heat and purée the soup using an immersion blender, in batches in a blender or food processor, or with a food mill. (See Perfecting Cream Soups, page 50.) Strain through a fine-mesh sieve into a clean pot (discard any solids) and keep warm over low heat until ready to serve.

6. Ladle into bowls and serve topped with the fresh spinach leaves cut into chiffonade, if desired.

# Belle's Chicken Noodle Soup

MY MOTHER, BELLE, ALWAYS MADE THIS SOUP FOR THE JEWISH HOLIDAYS, SO THERE was no question about what would be the signature soup at Mother's. We offer it with egg noodles or matzo balls, and it can easily become Chicken and Dumplings with a few more steps (page 129). Sometimes called "Jewish penicillin," this soup is simple to make, and devotees know when it's time for their fix—a sniffly nose, a rough day, or just because.

Whenever my daughter Stephanie got sick, we had our routine: First stop was the doctor, then to the pharmacy to get the prescribed medicine, and finally to the supermarket to pick up the ingredients for this soup. Once home, the soup was simmering on the stove within 15 minutes.

**FOR THE BROTH**

2 whole chickens, plus other carcasses if available (see page 123 for information about cutting up your own chickens)

2 yellow onions

4 ribs celery (cut in half to fit the pot, if necessary)

4 carrots, peeled (cut in half to fit the pot, if necessary)

4 parsnips, peeled (cut in half to fit the pot, if necessary)

1 bunch fresh Italian (flat-leaf) parsley, with stems (about 20 sprigs)

4½ teaspoons kosher salt (divided)

2 teaspoons freshly ground black pepper (divided)

**FOR THE SOUP**

2 cups finely diced carrots (about 3 large, peeled)

2 cups finely diced celery (about 4 large ribs, ends trimmed)

2 cups cooked chicken (reserved from making the broth)

1 pound egg noodles, cooked

1 bunch fresh dill, chopped, for garnish

**TO MAKE THE BROTH**

1. In a narrow, deep pot just large enough to hold the chickens (10- to 12-quart capacity), place the chickens, onions, celery, carrots, parsnips, and parsley. (Make

*continued*

sure you use a narrow pot rather than a wide one. Otherwise, you may have to use too much water to cover the chickens.) Add just enough cold water to barely cover the chickens (ideally, not more than 5 quarts, or 20 cups). Bring to a boil over high heat, skimming off any scum that rises to the surface. Reduce the heat to a simmer (rapidly boiling soup or stock often makes it look cloudy instead of clear) and season with 2 teaspoons of salt and 1 teaspoon of pepper. (You're seasoning here because you want the chicken to have some flavor when you use it later in other dishes. The soup will be seasoned again later.)

2. Simmer the broth, uncovered, for at least 3 hours. Season again with 2½ teaspoons salt and 1 teaspoon pepper. Taste; if it tastes like chicken, it's ready. If not, let it cook a bit longer and taste again. It can cook for another hour as long as it is barely simmering, but no more than 4 hours total or the chicken will dry out.

3. When the broth is done, turn off the heat, lift the chicken from the pot with slotted spoons or a spider (Love Note 1, page 223, Spaetzle), and set aside in a large bowl or on a rimmed baking sheet until cool enough to handle.

4. Strain the broth into a clean 6- to 8-quart pot, and discard the solids. If you're not making the soup right away, cool and refrigerate the broth so you can scrape off the solidified fat from the surface before continuing (you can save it to make Belle's Chopped Liver, page 14). Otherwise, allow the stock to sit undisturbed for at least 10 minutes, and spoon off the fat that rises to the surface.

**TO MAKE THE SOUP**

1. Set the pot of broth over medium heat and bring to a simmer.

2. Add the diced carrots and celery to the simmering broth, and cook until just fork-tender, about 8 minutes (Love Note).

*continued*

3. Taste the soup and adjust the seasoning with more salt and pepper, if necessary.

4. While the vegetables are cooking, pick the meat from the chicken, leaving the pieces as large as possible, and set aside. Discard the bones.

**TO SERVE**

1. Add the 2 cups of cooked chicken to the soup.

2. Divide the cooked noodles among the serving bowls. Ladle the soup over the noodles, sprinkle with the fresh chopped dill, and serve.

### LOVE NOTE

My favorite tool for **checking the doneness of vegetables or fruit** is a thin, two-pronged fork. It has long, narrow tines that allow me to pierce the cooking vegetables without leaving a trace. When vegetables offer no resistance, I know they are cooked to perfection, so I stop the cooking immediately before the vegetables get overcooked. If the tines of the fork don't slide in and out easily, the vegetables are not done and need to be cooked some more.

# M.O.M.

## Belle Cohen Schroeder
{ BELLE'S CHICKEN NOODLE SOUP }

Belle is an extra-special mom because she's my mother. She was born to Russian-Jewish parents in 1920 in Philadelphia (her dad died just before she was born). Raised during the Depression, Belle began working as a waitress when she was 16, and then married her boss and became a restaurateur herself. She and her first husband, Roy, owned a number of different restaurants where Belle was the cook, waitress, hostess, and manager (kind of like I am today).

When they divorced, Belle opened up her own luncheonette, called The Little Spot—with only 3 booths and 13 stools. She made everything from scratch every day and waited on the customers, too. She was a trailblazer—a single mother of two running a successful business back in the '50s. She met my dad in 1955, they married in 1956, she sold her restaurant, and I was born a year later.

Belle passed away when I was only 21, but the memories of her cooking live on. There's no doubt that I inherited my cooking abilities from her. She hosted numerous family dinners and fancy French buffets for 30 friends, and she cooked every night for her family. I still remember the *kvell* (oohing and ahhing) of the family while they were sipping her matzo ball soup or eating her made-from-scratch gefilte fish, and only wish she were alive today to taste mine.

# Mama's Minestrone

I DECIDED TO OFFER JUST ONE SOUP AT MAMA MIA TRATTORIA, SO I KNEW IT HAD to be the best of the best. I also wanted it to appeal to both carnivores and vegetarians. These were lofty goals, but I think I achieved them with this delicious soup. The secret is in how the vegetables are cooked. I coax deep flavors out of the vegetables by giving each one the attention it deserves.

My boyfriend, Rob, has created a fabulous variation (of which he's very proud) by sautéing spicy Italian pork or chicken sausage, using some of the soup to scrape up the fond (see page 90) left in the pan from the meat and adding it back to the soup for extra flavor. With a loaf of crispy bread and a bowl of pecorino romano cheese nearby, this soup is nirvana!

**FOR THE BEANS**

½ pound dry white beans, rinsed, soaked, and drained (Love Note 1, page 72, Black Bean Soup)

1 small yellow onion, quartered

1 small carrot, peeled and coarsely chopped

1 small rib celery, coarsely chopped

1 bouquet garni (1 bay leaf, 2 sprigs thyme, 3 sprigs Italian parsley, tied together with string)

½ teaspoon kosher salt

¼ teaspoon freshly ground black pepper

**FOR THE SOUP**

¼ cup extra-virgin olive oil (divided)

2 medium yellow onions, cut into ¼-inch dice (about 2 cups)

1 large carrot, peeled and cut into ¼-inch dice (about ¾ cup)

1 large rib celery, cut into ¼-inch dice (about ½ cup)

3 cloves garlic, minced (about 1 tablespoon)

2 medium zucchini, cut into ¼-inch dice (about 2 cups)

1 cup shredded Savoy cabbage (about ⅓ pound; Love Note 1)

¼ pound green beans, sliced into 1-inch pieces (about 1 cup)

¼ pound red potatoes, cut into ½-inch dice (about 2 cups)

1 (28-ounce) can whole plum tomatoes, drained and squished

8 cups Vegetable Stock (page 84) or canned low-sodium broth

1½ teaspoons kosher salt

½ teaspoon freshly ground black pepper

1 tablespoon chopped fresh Italian (flat-leaf) parsley

1½ cups cooked elbow macaroni (about 3 ounces dry, or ¾ cup; Love Note 2; optional)

½ cup grated pecorino romano cheese

**TO PREPARE THE BEANS**

1. Place the soaked beans in a medium (6- to 8-quart) stockpot, and cover with cold water. Add the onions, carrots, celery, and bouquet garni. Bring to a boil over medium-high heat, and then lower the heat to a simmer and continue to cook, covered, until the beans are tender, about 1 hour. Season with the salt and pepper and stir well to combine. Simmer for another 15 minutes.

2. Remove the onions, carrots, celery, and bouquet garni and discard. Drain the beans through a strainer set over a bowl, reserving the liquid. (You can make the beans several days ahead; refrigerate the cooking liquid and beans separately.)

3. Using an immersion blender, food processor, blender, or food mill, purée one-third of the beans (you'll need some of the bean liquid to get the beans to move around, especially in a blender), and set aside.

**TO MAKE THE SOUP**

1. While the beans are cooking, heat a medium (6- to 8-quart), heavy, wide stockpot (the wider the better to ensure the vegetables have plenty of room while they're sautéing) over medium-high heat. When hot, add the olive oil and onions and sauté, stirring now and then, until soft, about 10 minutes. Lower the heat to medium if the onions start to turn brown. (The onions should be evenly golden, not brown, or they will be bitter and add dark spots to the soup.) Add the carrots and celery and continue to cook, stirring occasionally, until very soft, another 10 to 15 minutes. Add the garlic, stir, and cook until fragrant, about 1 minute (don't let it brown).

*continued*

2. Add the zucchini, stir to combine, and sauté for a few minutes. Add the cabbage, stir, and cook for a few minutes until wilted. Add the green beans, potatoes, tomatoes, and stock, and stir to combine. Bring to a boil over high heat, lower the heat, and simmer, covered, for 1 hour. (Lift the lid to check and stir it now and then.)

3. After the soup has simmered, stir in the bean purée and whole cooked beans. Season with the salt and pepper. Simmer, uncovered, for 15 minutes to meld the flavors. Stir in the parsley. If necessary, thin the soup with the reserved bean liquid.

**TO SERVE**

Just before serving, divide the cooked macaroni, if using, among serving bowls (adding the macaroni just before serving keeps it from getting too mushy). Ladle the soup over the macaroni and sprinkle each serving with a heaping tablespoon of cheese.

## LOVE NOTES

**1** **There are several varieties of cabbage:** red, green (smooth and round), napa (elongated rather than round), and Savoy, which has pretty, crenulated leaves. Green and red cabbage taste almost identical, but red cabbage has a way of bleeding its color into whatever it's cooked with, so I wouldn't use it here. I prefer Savoy cabbage for this soup because it has a deep flavor and wonderful texture, but feel free to substitute green cabbage if that's what's available.

**2** **The macaroni is optional.** The soup is hearty on its own and doesn't need it, but some people expect macaroni in their minestrone, so I've given you the amount needed, should you want to include it in the final dish.

# Black Bean Soup

THIS SOUP KEEPS REALLY WELL IN THE FREEZER, AND IT'S DELICIOUS REHEATED.
IT'S also versatile. If you reduce the liquid a bit, you can use it in a breakfast burrito
with scrambled eggs and cheese. The flavors in this soup go just as well with lentils
(which cook in about an hour and don't need to be presoaked) as with the black beans,
so feel free to substitute if you're short on time or looking for a change of pace.

4 cups dried black (turtle) beans, rinsed, soaked, and drained (Love Note 1)

12 cups (3 quarts) Chicken Stock (page 87), Vegetable Stock (page 84), or canned low-sodium broth

1 (2-pound) ham hock

2 small bay leaves

1½ teaspoons kosher salt

½ teaspoon freshly ground black pepper

3 tablespoons unsalted butter or vegetable oil

2 medium yellow onions, diced (about 2 cups)

3 ribs celery, diced (about 1½ cups)

2 large carrots, peeled and diced (about 1½ cups)

1 tablespoon finely chopped garlic (about 3 cloves)

¾ teaspoon ground cumin (Love Note 2)

½ teaspoon dried thyme, or 1 teaspoon chopped fresh thyme

1 cup tomato purée

¼ cup finely chopped fresh Italian (flat-leaf) parsley

Tabasco sauce, to taste

½ cup sour cream, for garnish

½ cup sliced scallions, for garnish

½ cup grated Cheddar cheese, for garnish

1.  In a medium (6- to 8-quart), heavy stockpot, combine the soaked beans, stock,
    ham hock, and bay leaves. Cover the pot and bring the mixture to a boil over
    medium-high heat. Reduce the heat to medium-low and gently simmer, covered,
    for 2 hours, stirring now and then. Add the salt and pepper and continue cooking
    for about 30 minutes more. (Black beans take longer to cook than most other beans;

they may need as much as 4 hours. Taste one—if it doesn't melt in your mouth, continue to simmer until the beans are done, checking them now and then.)

2. While the beans are cooking, heat a 4-quart pot over medium-high heat. When it's hot, add the butter or oil, onions, celery, and carrots and sauté until the vegetables soften and color slightly, 10 to 15 minutes. (Lower the heat to medium if the vegetables are taking on too much color too fast.) Add the garlic and sauté for another minute. Push the vegetables aside to clear a spot in the pot. Add the cumin and thyme and sauté slightly, and then stir into the vegetables. Remove from the heat.

3. Remove the ham hock from the pot of beans and set aside to cool. Remove the bay leaves and discard. Purée half the beans with an immersion blender, food processor, blender, or a food mill. (You'll need some of the cooking broth to get the beans to move around, especially in a blender.) Return the purée to the whole beans in the pot.

4. Add the sautéed vegetables to the beans along with the tomato purée, parsley, and Tabasco. Simmer over low heat for about 30 minutes. During this time, trim and discard any fat or rind from the ham hock. Pull the meat from the bone, shred or cut it into ½-inch cubes, and add it to the soup, stirring to incorporate. Season the soup with more salt and pepper, if necessary.

5. Ladle into bowls, top with a dollop of sour cream, scallions, and Cheddar cheese, or a combination of your choice. Leave the bottle of Tabasco on the table for those who like their soups hot and spicy.

*continued*

## LOVE NOTES

**1** Before soaking, **check your beans** carefully for pebbles and debris and rinse them well. Typically, you want to soak beans overnight in cold water, changing the water once or twice during the soak. If you forget or didn't plan ahead, you can do the quick-soak method: Bring a pot of water to a boil. Add the beans and boil for 1 minute. Turn off the heat, cover, and let the beans sit for 1 hour. Drain, discarding the soaking water, which has a lot of the compounds that can cause flatulence.

**2** **Buy fresh spices** in small amounts—only what you can use in about 6 months. Their flavor will be even stronger if you use whole spices that you grind yourself before using, some of which should be toasted before grinding to bring out their flavor.

Toasting spices is a common practice in many of the world's cuisines, such as Indian and Thai. To understand why toasting spices is so important, think of coffee beans. A pot of coffee made with green, unroasted beans sounds awful; it's the same principal with spices like cumin. The flavors develop with a little heat.

For this dish, if you have whole cumin seeds, use ¾ teaspoon and toast them lightly before using. Place the seeds in a small, dry sauté pan over medium heat. Cook, stirring occasionally to keep them from burning, until they begin to release their aroma and smoke slightly, about 3 minutes. Grind the toasted seeds into a powder with a spice mill or a mortar and pestle.

# Manhattan Clam Chowder

THIS CHOWDER IS A GREAT CHANGE OF PACE FROM THE CREAMY NEW ENGLAND version. With its base of stock and tomatoes, rather than roux and cream, it's lighter and a bit healthier. It's still a chowder, though, because it has bacon and potatoes. We use canned clams because we make 5 gallons at a time, but I highly recommend fresh for this recipe.

2 strips bacon, finely diced (chill for 10 minutes in the freezer to make it easier to cut; about ¼ cup)

2 tablespoons vegetable oil

1 large yellow onion, finely diced (1½ cups)

1 large carrot, peeled and finely diced (about ¾ cup)

2 ribs celery, finely diced (about ½ cup)

1 leek, white part only, thinly sliced into half-moons and washed (about ½ cup)

1 medium green bell pepper, stemmed, seeded, and finely diced (about 1 cup)

1 clove garlic, minced (1 teaspoon)

1 (14.5-ounce) can diced tomatoes, with juice

1 (10.75-ounce) can tomato purée

1 bay leaf

½ teaspoon chopped fresh thyme

1 pound russet potatoes, peeled and cut into ½-inch dice (about 3 cups)

3½ cups Fish Stock (page 86) or 2 (14-ounce) cans clam juice

2 (10-ounce) cans baby clams in juice (Love Note 1)

1½ teaspoons kosher salt

1 teaspoon freshly ground black pepper

5 dashes Tabasco sauce, or to taste (Love Note 2)

3 dashes Worcestershire sauce, or to taste

1. Place a medium (6- to 8-quart), heavy soup pot over medium-high heat. When hot, add the bacon. When it starts to brown in spots, lower the heat to medium and

*continued*

continue to cook until most of the fat has been rendered and the bacon is almost crisp, about 4 minutes.

2. Add the vegetable oil, onions, carrots, celery, leeks, and green bell peppers. Sauté, stirring occasionally, until very soft, 10 to 15 minutes. Add the garlic and sauté for another 2 minutes.

3. Add the diced and puréed tomatoes, bay leaf, thyme, and potatoes.

4. Add the stock or clam juice to the pot. Stir to mix well. Bring to a boil over high heat, and then lower the heat to a simmer and cook for 30 minutes, stirring occasionally, or until the potatoes are fork-tender (Love Note, page 64, Belle's Chicken Noodle Soup).

5. Add the clams with their juice and season with the salt and pepper. Add the Tabasco and Worcestershire (Love Note 2). Bring back to a simmer for several minutes.

6. Ladle into bowls and serve with crusty bread or crackers.

*continued*

# LOVE NOTES

**1** **Any clam chowder** is best made with fresh clams, although it's definitely more time-consuming to use fresh than canned. There are all kinds of fresh clams (littleneck, steamer, and Manila, to name a few), and availability depends on where you live. On average, 1 pound of fresh Manila clams, which are pretty small, yields about 20 clams with ¾ cup of meat. So for this soup, which uses about 1½ cups of canned clam meat, you'd need about 2 pounds of fresh clams.

To prepare clams, sort through and discard any that are open and do not close when you tap on the shell. Place a large bowl in the sink and fill it with cold water. Add the clams and swirl them around. Lift them out into another bowl (this way the sand remains in the bowl instead of getting poured back onto the clams). Fill the second bowl with cold water and let the clams soak for 20 minutes to expel any sand inside the shells. Repeat this process, if necessary, until there's no more sand.

To cook, place the clams in a medium saucepan with 1 cup of water. For a little extra flavor, add a chopped shallot.

Cover the pot and place over medium-high heat. Steam the clams just until they open, 5 to 10 minutes. Remove the pot from the heat and pour the clams into a strainer set over a bowl to catch the cooking liquid. Discard any clams that did not open. Remove the rest of the clams from their shell, add the clams to the soup, and reserve some shells to add to the soup as a picturesque garnish (kids love them).

Strain the clam cooking liquid through a coffee filter or cheesecloth-lined strainer (to catch any sand and debris) set over a measuring cup. Add enough additional fish stock or clam juice to equal the 4 cups of liquid called for in the recipe which includes the juice in the canned clams.

**2** **Customize your chowder** to make it yours. Make it as hot as you like with Tabasco and black pepper or a little more savory with extra Worcestershire sauce. Just remember to go light and slow, tasting after each addition. You can always add, but taking away isn't that easy.

# Salmon Chowder

OREGONIANS CHERISH PACIFIC NORTHWEST SALMON. ANYONE'S WHO'S TASTED IT knows why—it is rich without being fatty, delicate yet complex in flavor, and beautiful in color. If wild salmon is not readily available or is prohibitively expensive, substitute farm-raised salmon for an equally tasty soup. If you have fresh—or grilled—corn on hand, add the kernels to the soup just a few minutes before the potatoes are done.

1 pound salmon fillets (skin and bones removed)

½ pound bacon, finely diced (chill for 10 minutes in the freezer to make it easier to cut; about 1 cup)

¾ cup (1½ sticks) unsalted butter (divided)

2 medium yellow onions, finely diced (about 2 cups)

2 carrots, peeled and finely diced (about 1½ cups)

3 ribs celery, finely diced (about 1½ cups)

1 cup all-purpose flour

8 cups (2 quarts) Fish Stock (page 86)

½ cup dry white wine, such as Chardonnay

1 tablespoon chopped fresh thyme, or 2 teaspoons dried thyme

1 bay leaf

1 pound (about 4 medium) red potatoes, finely diced (2 cups)

1 cup heavy cream

1 tablespoon finely chopped fresh dill

3 teaspoons kosher salt

1 teaspoon freshly ground black pepper

1. Cut the salmon into 1-inch cubes, and run your fingers over it to make sure there are no tiny bones embedded in the flesh. Refrigerate until ready to use.

2. Heat a medium (6- to 8-quart), heavy stockpot over medium-high heat. When hot, add the bacon and cook until it begins to brown in spots. Lower the heat to medium and cook, stirring, until the fat has rendered, about 10 minutes.

*continued*

3. Turn the heat up to high, and add 2 tablespoons of butter, the onions, carrots, and celery. Sauté until they start to color around the edges, then lower heat to medium and continue to sauté until soft, at least 20 minutes. Remove the bacon and vegetables from the pot and set aside.

4. Add 10 tablespoons of butter and melt. Stir in the flour with a wooden spoon to make a blond roux; cook, stirring occasionally, for 3 to 5 minutes, until the mixture looks like fine, wet sand.

5. Slowly add the stock, a little at a time, whisking constantly and letting the roux absorb the liquid after each addition. (Take your time here. The best defense against lumps is steady whisking and slow pouring. Add the stock in stages, letting the roux absorb each addition before whisking in more.) Bring the mixture to a boil, reduce the heat, and simmer for 10 minutes. (This mixture is called a *velouté*, the French culinary term for stock that has been thickened with roux.)

6. Return the vegetables and bacon to the pot with the fish velouté. Add the wine, thyme, bay leaf, and potatoes.

7. Bring to a boil, reduce the heat, and simmer until the potatoes are soft, 20 to 30 minutes.

8. Add the salmon and cook until opaque throughout, about 10 minutes.

9. Remove the pot from the heat and gently stir in the cream, dill, salt, and pepper (be careful not to break up the salmon as you stir). Taste and adjust the seasoning with more salt and pepper as needed. Ladle into bowls and serve.

# Seafood Gumbo

THERE ISN'T A MOTHER IN LOUISIANA WHO DOESN'T HAVE HER OWN VERSION OF gumbo. Each has her own special way of making it and uses her favorite seafood, thickeners, and other ingredients. However, among all the variations there's always one thing in common—a brown roux (Love Note 1). Knowing how long to cook the roux and what color it should be is very important for a good gumbo.

Because the roux cooks for a very long time (at least 45 minutes), it loses much of its thickening power. That's why you need more of it than you would of a blond roux for a sauce or soup. My recipe is an amalgam of the best gumbos I've tasted and uses all three gumbo thickeners—roux, okra, and filé powder (ground sassafras leaves).

Traditionally, gumbo is made with a combination of crab, crawfish, and/or oysters, but you can vary the seafood according to your taste and what's available (just make sure to use equivalent amounts to what's listed in the recipe). At Mother's, I often use shrimp and local fresh fish such as snapper or salmon.

**FOR THE ROUX**

⅓ cup vegetable oil

½ cup all-purpose flour

**FOR THE GUMBO**

4 tablespoons (½ stick) unsalted butter

1 large yellow onion, finely chopped (1½ cups)

3 ribs celery, finely chopped (1½ cups)

1 large green bell pepper, seeded and finely chopped (1½ cups)

2 cloves garlic, chopped (2 teaspoons)

1 teaspoon cumin seeds, toasted and ground (or just use ground; Love Note 2, page 72, Black Bean Soup)

¼ teaspoon cayenne pepper

¼ teaspoon dried thyme

8 cups (2 quarts) Fish Stock (page 86), shrimp stock, or bottled clam juice

1 (14.5-ounce) can whole or diced tomatoes

1 (6-ounce) can tomato paste

1 bay leaf

¼ cup Worcestershire sauce

*continued*

1 cup dry white wine, such as Chardonnay

5 dashes Tabasco sauce or to taste

4 teaspoons kosher salt

¾ teaspoon freshly ground black pepper

½ pound fresh okra, or 5 ounces frozen okra (Love Note 2)

½ pound miniature (70 to 90) shrimp (Love Note 3; also Love Note 1, page 26, Shrimp Rémoulade)

½ pound salmon, snapper, or cod, cut into ½-inch cubes

¼ cup chopped fresh Italian (flat-leaf) parsley

2 cups cooked white rice (Love Note 4)

Filé powder (Love Note 5; optional)

### TO MAKE THE ROUX

Heat the oven to 350°F. In a small, heavy sauté pan with an ovenproof handle, heat the oil over medium heat. Add the flour, a little at a time, while whisking well to ensure there are no lumps. Place the sauté pan in the oven and bake the roux until it almost looks milk-chocolate brown in color, stirring periodically, about 45 minutes. (I prefer using the oven to make a dark roux. It cooks more evenly and there's no scorching.) Remove the pan from the oven and set on the stove (no heat) until needed. It will continue to cook, turning a little darker as it cools. Alternatively, you can cook the roux on the stovetop over low heat, stirring frequently with a wooden spoon until it turns milk-chocolate brown, 30 to 45 minutes—but make sure you keep a close eye on it!

### TO MAKE THE GUMBO

1. Heat a medium (6- to 8-quart), heavy stockpot over medium-high heat. When hot, add the butter, onions, celery, and green bell peppers. Sauté the vegetables until they start to color around the edges, stirring now and then. Lower the heat to medium and continue to sauté until very soft, about 15 minutes.

2. Add the garlic and sauté for 1 minute more (don't let it brown). Add the ground cumin, cayenne, and thyme. Sauté for about 1 minute more.

*continued*

3. Scrape the roux into the pot with the vegetables and stir to mix well. Whisk in the fish stock, tomatoes (if whole, cut them with scissors while in the can or squish them with your clean hands as you add them to the pot), tomato paste, bay leaf, Worcestershire, wine, Tabasco, salt, and pepper. Bring to a boil, stirring occasionally to make sure the ingredients are well combined and there's no scorching.

4. Reduce the heat to low. Partially cover (not totally, because you want some evaporation and concentration of flavors in the soup), and simmer for 1 hour. (Remember to stir the soup occasionally so the heavier ingredients don't settle to the bottom of the pot and burn. There is no amount of spice or seasoning that can hide a burnt flavor!)

5. Add the okra, shrimp, and fish; simmer until cooked through, about 15 minutes. Add the parsley and stir.

**TO SERVE**

Place 2 tablespoons of rice in each bowl (if you like a lot of rice, feel free to add more). Ladle the gumbo over the rice, sprinkle each serving with about ⅛ teaspoon filé powder, if using, stir, and serve.

**1   Roux, a mixture** of relatively equal parts butter and flour, is used to thicken soups and sauces but can also add flavor and color. The function depends on how long the roux is cooked—the longer it cooks, the less thickening power it has but the more color and flavor it adds. A "white" roux is cooked over low heat for 3 to 4 minutes until it has a sandy consistency and a beige color. A "blond" roux is cooked a minute or two longer for a light gold color. You only need 2 tablespoons of roux for every cup of liquid to thicken sauces or soups.

A "brown" roux is usually made with oil or lard instead of butter and cooked for nearly an hour over low heat to achieve the consistency of clay and a specific shade of brown, from peanut butter to light coffee or even a mahogany color. This roux adds depth of flavor and color to gumbo and étouffées but has only one-third the thickening power of a blond roux.

**2   Fresh okra** can be slimy. If you add it to the gumbo early and let it simmer with the stock, the sliminess will cook away, but so will most of the okra. If you want gumbo with discernible pieces of okra without the sliminess, cook it first before adding it to the gumbo. To precook okra, melt 2 tablespoons butter in a sauté pan over medium heat. Add trimmed, sliced okra and cook for 15 to 20 minutes, or until slightly browned and you don't see any stringiness. Or use frozen okra and add it just before the soup is done.

**3   I use miniature shrimp** (size 70–90)—they are small enough to fit on a spoon and come peeled and deveined.

**4   Cook the rice separately** and add it just before serving, so that it doesn't break down and get too mushy. If freezing gumbo, put the cooked rice in before freezing. If storing the soup in the refrigerator, keep the rice separate. To serve refrigerated gumbo, reheat the soup, place cold rice in bowls, ladle hot gumbo on top, and serve—the hot gumbo will warm the rice quickly.

**5   Filé powder** comes from dried and ground sassafras leaves and is a traditional seasoning and thickening agent for gumbo. Filé's thickening power is temporary, so sprinkle on top of each portion just before serving.

# Vegetable Stock

THIS STOCK IS PERFECT WHEN YOU ARE COOKING SOMETHING VEGETARIAN AND don't want to use just water. It's a great opportunity to add another layer of flavor to a dish. It takes less than an hour to infuse a pot of water with a medley of aromatic vegetables, which can then be used to add depth to even delicate soups. When making stock, there's no need to tie the herbs in the bouquet garni together, since they'll be strained out at the end.

¼ cup canola oil

1 large yellow onion, coarsely chopped

2 leeks (white and light green parts), coarsely chopped and rinsed well

¼ pound green cabbage, coarsely chopped (about 1 cup)

2 carrots, coarsely chopped

1 large turnip, coarsely chopped (Love Note 1)

3 ribs celery, coarsely chopped

1 large tomato, coarsely chopped

18 cups (4½ quarts) cold water

1 bouquet garni (1 bay leaf, 2 sprigs thyme, 3 sprigs Italian parsley)

6 cloves garlic, in their skins

1.  Heat the oil in a large (8- to 10-quart), heavy stockpot over medium-high heat. When hot, add the onions, leeks, cabbage, carrots, turnips, celery, and tomatoes. Cook, stirring occasionally, until the vegetables start to release moisture, about 5 minutes.

2.  Add the water, bouquet garni, and garlic (Love Note 2). Bring to a boil over high heat, then reduce the heat to low and simmer, uncovered, for 45 minutes.

3.  Turn off the heat. Set a fine-mesh strainer over another large pot or bowl. Pour the stock through, pressing on the vegetable solids to extract all the liquid; discard the solids. Allow the stock to cool (Love Note 2, page 88, Chicken Stock) before refrigerating or freezing (Love Note 2, page 91, Brown Veal Stock).

## LOVE NOTES

**1** **Turnips are easily confused** with rutabagas. And if you end up with a rutabaga in this recipe, that's fine (rutabagas are a cross between cabbage and turnips). Turnips are smaller, smoother, and whiter, with a reddish top. Rutabagas are often called yellow turnips because they're similarly shaped (kind of like a beet) but bigger, woodier, and more yellow.

**2** You might notice **there is no salt in this recipe.** Stock is meant as an ingredient for other dishes, not something that's supposed to stand on its own, which is why I don't call for any salt and pepper in my stock recipes. If salt and pepper were added now, it would skew the seasonings in any dishes that use it.

# Fish Stock

CALL AHEAD AND ASK YOUR FISHMONGER TO SAVE FISH HEADS AND BONES FOR YOU. They are great for chowders and fish stews like Mama's Cioppino (page 167).

5 pounds fish bones or heads from white fish (do not use strong-flavored fish like salmon)

1 large yellow onion, coarsely chopped

1 carrot, coarsely chopped

1 rib celery, coarsely chopped

1 bouquet garni (1 bay leaf, 2 sprigs thyme, 3 sprigs Italian parsley)

6 cloves garlic, in their skins

1 cup dry white wine (such as Chardonnay)

18 cups (4½ quarts) cold water

1. Place the fish bones or heads in a large pot, bowl, or bucket, cover them with cold water, swish them around, and drain. Repeat twice.

2. Place the fish, onions, carrots, celery, bouquet garni, garlic, white wine, and water in a large (8- to 10-quart) stockpot (cut the fish bones into smaller pieces to fit if necessary; a cleaver or poultry scissors works great for this).

3. Bring to a boil over high heat, then reduce the heat to medium-low and simmer for 40 minutes, skimming off any foam that rises to the surface.

4. Remove the pot from the heat. Use tongs or a spider to remove the fish bones; discard. Set a fine-mesh strainer over another large bowl or pot. Pour the stock through, pressing on the vegetable solids to extract all the liquid; discard the solids. Allow to cool (Love Note 2, page 88, Chicken Stock) before refrigerating or freezing (Love Note 2, page 91, Brown Veal Stock).

# Chicken Stock

YOU MIGHT WONDER WHY IT'S WORTH MAKING STOCK WHEN THERE ARE SO MANY cans of broth at the store. I urge you to buy several cans and taste them. Look at them, too. Are they a rich yellow or a wan gray? Do they taste of meat and fresh vegetables or like salty water? I think you'll find that most store-bought broth doesn't compare to the rich flavor and silky texture of homemade stock (Love Note 1).

Chicken stock is easy to make. Just work the cooking into your normal routine— throw the ingredients in a pot on a weekend morning and let it simmer while you go about your day. Or put the pot on when you get home from work and let it simmer until bedtime. This recipe makes a lot, so you'll have plenty to freeze.

6 pounds chicken bones, such as necks, backs, legs, feet, and wings

18 cups (4½ quarts) cold water

1 large yellow onion, coarsely chopped

1 carrot, coarsely chopped

1 rib celery, coarsely chopped

1 bouquet garni (1 bay leaf, 2 sprigs thyme, 3 sprigs Italian parsley)

6 cloves garlic, in their skins

1. Rinse the bones. Place them in a large (8- to 10-quart) stockpot and add enough cold water to cover. Bring to a boil, then reduce the heat immediately to a low simmer. Skim off any scum that rises to the surface.

2. Add the onions, carrots, celery, and bouquet garni; continue to simmer, uncovered, for at least 4 hours. Remove from the heat and use tongs or a spider to remove the chicken bones; discard. Set a fine-mesh strainer over another large clean bowl or pot. Strain the stock through, pressing on the vegetable solids with a rubber spatula to extract all the liquid; discard the solids.

3. Allow the stock to cool (Love Note 2) before refrigerating or freezing (Love Note 2, page 91, Brown Veal Stock).

*continued*

**1** **Stock-making** allows you to use up all sorts of odds and ends that would normally go into the trash: leftover carcasses and backs from roasted chickens, carrots and celery that have gone rubbery, parsley stems, and onion ends. All of these things have flavor that shouldn't be wasted when you can simply simmer them in water and get an elixir that enhances so many dishes. Just store these odds and ends in a zip-top bag in the freezer until you have enough to make stock.

**2** It's important to **cool large batches of stocks and soups** before refrigerating because a large amount of hot liquid can throw off the temperature of your fridge, making it too warm and therefore a potential breeding ground for bacteria. But you need to cool those liquids quickly so that they, too, don't become unsafe in the process.

The easiest way to do this is to purchase what's called an ice wand or cold paddle from a restaurant supply store. Fill the heatproof plastic container with water, freeze, and then use it to stir the liquid until cool without diluting it. Don't be tempted to use a 2-liter bottle or zip-top bag instead, since the plastic those items are made from isn't meant to be heated and may leach chemicals into your food.

Alternatively, you can place the pot in a sink filled with ice water (make sure the water doesn't come more than three-quarters of the way up the sides or else the water might slosh into the pot) and stir the stock to make sure as much of it comes into contact with the cooling sides of the pot as often as possible. Decanting the stock into a very wide bowl or roasting pan will help give it more surface area, which speeds cooling, too.

The best way to remove fat from stock is to refrigerate it in large containers overnight. By the next morning, all the fat will have risen to the surface and solidified. All you need to do is scrape it off, and then portion the stock into containers for freezing. Don't be alarmed if your stock has the consistency of Jell-O—that just means you did a good job! When a stock has body and jiggles, it's because it has plenty of collagen (which comes from the bones), and collagen enhances the flavor and mouth-feel, giving the stock a richness canned broth doesn't have.

# Brown Veal Stock

ROASTING BONES GIVES THIS STOCK A RICH, DEEP FLAVOR AND DARK COLOR. DON'T worry if you can't find veal bones: Just use beef bones instead and make beef stock. Veal and beef stocks are essentially interchangeable; it's just the extra collagen in the veal bones that give this stock a little extra body.

| | |
|---|---|
| 4 pounds meaty veal or beef soup bones (preferably with marrow; Love Note 1) | 2 ribs celery, coarsely chopped |
| | 1 medium carrot, coarsely chopped |
| 1 pound beef short ribs (Love Note 1; optional) | 3 tablespoons tomato paste |
| | 20 cups (5 quarts) cold water |
| Vegetable oil | 1 bouquet garni (1 bay leaf, 2 sprigs thyme, 3 sprigs Italian parsley) |
| 1 medium yellow onion, coarsely chopped | |
| | 3 cloves garlic, in their skins |

1. Heat the oven to 400°F. Lightly oil a baking sheet or roasting pan. Place the bones and short ribs, if using, in a single layer in the pan and place the pan in the oven. Roast until the bones and ribs are very brown, 1 to 1½ hours.

2. Remove the bones and ribs from the oven and place in a large (8- to 10-quart), heavy stockpot just big enough to hold them.

3. Place the roasting pan used to brown the bones on the stovetop. Remove all but 2 tablespoons of fat from the pan. If there isn't 2 tablespoons of fat, add enough vegetable oil to equal 2 tablespoons. Place over medium-high heat. When hot, add the onions, celery, and carrots. Sauté until the vegetables are caramelized and almost brown, 10 to 15 minutes. Add the tomato paste and cook until the paste turns dark brown, about 2 minutes.

4. Pour about 1 cup of the water into the roasting pan to deglaze it and scrape up the browned bits on the bottom of the pan (see "Fond," page 90). Pour the vegetables

*continued*

and liquid into the stockpot with the bones. Add the rest of the water, plus more if necessary to just cover the bones, the bouquet garni, and garlic.

5. Bring to a boil over high heat, then immediately reduce the heat to a gentle simmer, skimming off any scum that rises to the surface. Continue to simmer over very low heat, uncovered, for at least 6 hours.

6. Turn off the heat. Use tongs to remove the bones from the stock and discard them (or find a dog to give them to). Pour the stock through a fine-mesh strainer set over another large bowl or pot. Press on the solids to remove as much liquid as possible. Discard the solids and let the stock cool (Love Note 2, page 88, Chicken Stock) before refrigerating or freezing (Love Note 2).

 Fond

The French word *fond* means "base," "foundation," or "stock." It is also used to refer to the browned residue left in the bottom of a pan after sautéing meats and vegetables. Fond has a lot of flavor that should always be captured and incorporated into whatever you're cooking. And that's why it's very important that you don't burn the bottom of your pan when sautéing vegetables. You want heat high enough to make sure the vegetables actually sauté, but not so high that the bottom of the pan burns and you therefore lose the ability to use the precious fond.

Sometimes all you have to do is use a wooden spoon or heatproof rubber spatula to scrape the bottom of the pot as the vegetables sauté. Other times, you have to deglaze the pan with a small amount of liquid, such as stock, wine, or another cooking liquid called for in the recipe. Adding the cool liquid to the hot pan will cause the liquid to immediately steam and bubble up, loosening the fond and dissolving it into the liquid. Scrape the pan with a wooden spoon or rubber spatula until the bottom is clean and all the browned bits are incorporated into the liquid.

## LOVE NOTES

**1** It is important to get **meaty bones** for stock, otherwise the result of your efforts will taste thin instead of rich. Sometimes you can find soup bones in the freezer section at the supermarket; or ask someone at the butcher counter for bones (it helps to call a day or two ahead).

Good stock bones are the femur (ask the butcher to cut it into pieces to expose the marrow and to help the pieces fit in your pot), knuckle bones, and neck bones. Make sure there's still some meat on them. To ensure you get enough beefy flavor, you can add a pound of oxtails (usually available only in fall and winter) or short ribs (but not the thin flanken cut), which are avail-

able year-round. (If not using oxtails or beef ribs, increase the amount of bones by 1 pound, to 5 pounds.)

**2** If you **make a lot of soups** and stews, freeze the stock in quart-size containers so that you can defrost just what you need. Zip-top freezer bags allow you to freeze the stock flat to take up less freezer space.

To make filling the bags easier, line a large bowl with the bag, folding the top over the edge of the bowl. The bowl will keep the bag open and supported while you ladle the soup into the bag. You might want to freeze a few 1- or 2-cup portions as well, to use in sauces and gravies.

entrées

**Once upon a time, mothers would spend almost an entire day cooking.** They'd put something on the stove or in the oven and let it simmer slowly while they went on with their day.

Compared with modern life, those days have more in common with fairy tales than reality. Our lives are busier than ever, and many of us don't have the time—or the inclination—to spend all day in the kitchen. And that's why when we do fire up the stove, we want to make something with a big payoff—in either flavor, time savings, or both. Throughout this chapter you'll find dozens of recipes that have those two things in common. From Perfect Pot Roast (page 95) to Jan's Stuffed Eggplant (page 183), each dish is as yummy as it gets, and you'll find that most can save you time in the long run.

I know what you're thinking: How can pot roast be a time-saver? Because it's all about the leftovers. If I'm going to make a mess in the kitchen, I might as well make a lot of food. I'll have the same number of bowls and dishes to clean and use the same amount of time and effort, but I'll have more than one night's dinner as the result. That's why many of these recipes can serve a crowd. You can either invite family and friends over or save the leftovers for another time.

### MAKE LEFTOVERS COUNT

The term *leftovers* isn't exactly appealing, but when you cook with them in mind, it's like money in the bank. Eat them for a fast lunch or dinner later in the week, or portion them into quart-size containers, freeze, and enjoy them next month, when they'll seem new again. Just make sure to label the containers. In the restaurant biz we don't use fancy preprinted labels; we just use good-quality masking tape and a permanent marker. Write the contents and date on the tape, and adhere it to the *front,* not the top, so when things are stacked, you don't have to move things around to find out what's inside.

But leftovers don't have to duplicate the original meal—transform them into something completely different with little effort: Brisket is great as a sandwich, poached salmon can become hash, and pot roast can be turned into a meaty ragù sauce, perfect on fettuccine.

### LONG-SIMMERING VS. QUICK-COOKING

Admittedly, some of these long-simmered dishes take too long to cook to be practical for a busy weeknight. So save the braises and stews for the weekend. They don't take long to assemble, and you can let them simmer while you putter around the house. Plus, they're filling, nutritious, and rely on cheap cuts of meat. Unlike pricey steaks and tenderloins (which start out tender and need just minutes to cook), chuck roasts and pork shoulders have lots of connective tissue because they're well-worked muscles. But after hours of gentle simmering, the muscle fibers become tender and the connective tissue melts into delicious silkiness—all for just a few dollars per pound.

Best of all, this transformation takes little effort. After searing to add a layer of flavor, the meat is covered three-quarters of the way by a flavorful liquid (such as herb-and-vegetable-spiked wine or broth). Stews are essentially the same thing, but the meat is cut into smaller chunks and submerged completely.

Interspersed throughout this chapter are speedier dinners you can accomplish on any weeknight, like Parisian Chicken (page 146) and Pan-Seared Cod Puttanesca (page 164). The prep work on these dishes is quick, and the food cooks in minutes instead of hours. Plan your weekly menu around these dishes and you'll never want to go back to take-out!

# Perfect Pot Roast

THIS IS BY FAR THE MOST POPULAR DISH ON OUR MENU AT MOTHER'S BISTRO & bar, and it typifies what we do best—slow-cooked foods. I like to braise in the oven because the heat is indirect, so foods cook more evenly and there's less chance of a hot spot in the pan scorching the food. Like most braised dishes, pot roast freezes and re-heats well, so if you want leftovers, double the recipe. (Take a look at the Love Notes for more braising tips.) Mother's Smashers (page 212) are a great foil for the rich, deep flavors of the gravy.

4 pounds beef chuck (Love Note 1), tied if desired

3 teaspoons kosher salt

1 teaspoon freshly ground black pepper

¼ cup vegetable oil

3 medium yellow onions, coarsely chopped (about 3 cups)

½ pound (about 4) carrots, peeled and coarsely chopped (about 3 cups)

3 ribs celery, coarsely chopped (1½ cups)

3 cloves garlic

¾ cup tomato purée

¼ cup all-purpose flour

1 cup dry red wine, such as Cabernet Sauvignon, Zinfandel, or Côtes du Rhône

1 bouquet garni (1 bay leaf, 2 sprigs thyme, and 3 sprigs Italian parsley; Love Note 2, page 112, Meatloaf Gravy)

6 to 10 cups Brown Veal Stock (page 89), or canned low-sodium beef broth

1. Heat the oven to 350°F, and place a rack in the center. Using a sharp knife, trim any excess fat or gristle from the meat. Season with the salt and pepper (you might need to use less salt if you're using canned broth, which already has salt).

2. Choose a Dutch oven or stockpot just large enough to hold the meat flat. (If it's too big, you'll need too much liquid, which will dilute the flavors of the dish; too small, and the meat won't cook evenly.) Place the pan over high heat for several

*continued*

minutes, until hot. When hot, add the oil and heat until shimmering (adding the oil *after* the pan is hot keeps it from breaking down and getting smoky while the pan heats). Add the beef and brown on all sides (Love Note 2). Transfer the meat to a plate or baking sheet and set aside.

3. Reduce the heat to medium-high. Add the onions, carrots, celery, and garlic (since they will cook for a few hours, these larger pieces will have plenty of time to get tender); cook until lightly browned, stirring occasionally. Adjust the heat to medium and continue cooking until very soft, about 20 minutes. Stir in the tomato purée, increase the heat to medium-high, and cook until slightly browned, about 5 minutes (this deepens the tomato flavor).

4. Lower the heat to medium, add the flour, and mix well with a wooden spoon to make a roux. Cook, stirring frequently, for 3 to 4 minutes. Stir the wine into the roux a little at a time, allowing the roux to absorb the liquid before adding more. (This helps prevent lumps.) Be sure to scrape up any browned bits from the bottom of the pot (see "Fond," page 90). Return the meat to the pot. Add the bouquet garni and enough stock to rise two-thirds of the way up the meat (the amount will vary with the size and type of pot you are using, but don't cover the meat entirely). Bring to a boil over high heat. Remove from the heat, cover the pot tightly with a lid or aluminum foil, and place on the center rack (or lower, if need be, to accommodate your pot) of the oven. Braise until the beef is fork-tender (it should fall right back into the pan when pierced with a two-pronged fork), about 2 hours.

5. If serving immediately, lift the beef out of the pot using tongs or a spatula and keep warm on a plate tented with foil. Strain the sauce through a strainer into another pot (if you like, pick out the carrots and serve alongside the beef, but discard the rest of the solids). Let the sauce sit for a few minutes. Then degrease the sauce by dragging a ladle or spoon over the top to catch any fat that has risen; discard. Repeat until most of the fat is removed. If the sauce is too thin (Love

Note 3), set the pot over medium-high heat and simmer, stirring occasionally, until the liquid reduces and is slightly thicker. Taste and adjust the seasonings as needed.

6. Using a sharp slicing knife, cut the beef across the grain into thick slices and serve with the sauce. (Don't worry about getting beautiful slices—chunks of this meat are just as delicious.)

7. If making this ahead of time (it keeps well in the refrigerator for 3 to 4 days), remove the meat from the pan and let cool, and then place it in an airtight container and refrigerate. Strain the sauce into another container and refrigerate (you don't have to defat it first). One hour before serving, remove the sauce from the refrigerator, scrape off any fat that has congealed on top, and discard. Slice the beef and put it in an ovenproof serving dish, pour the sauce over it, cover with foil, and heat in a 350°F oven for about 45 minutes. Serve hot.

*continued*

# LOVE NOTES

**1.** **Braised dishes** are meant to be made with less-expensive cuts of meat such as chuck. With long, gentle cooking, these tougher, fattier cuts become more tender, whereas lean, more-expensive cuts actually toughen with long cooking times. If the roast is tied at 1½-inch intervals, it will hold together better for slicing.

**2.** **Browning meat is a vital step** in all braised dishes and stews. Contrary to popular belief, browning doesn't lock in juices, but it does caramelize the outside of the meat, which develops many different flavor compounds, each contributing depth to the final dish. The key to browning is a *very* hot pan—smoking hot. It should always be heated over high heat for several minutes *before* adding the oil and the meat. Keep the heat high while searing the meat or it will start to boil rather than brown.

**3.** How can you tell **when a sauce is the proper thickness?** When it coats the back of a spoon. How can you tell when it coats the back of a spoon? It's easy: Dip the spoon into the sauce. Hold it horizontally, with the back facing you, and run your finger through the center from the tip to the handle. If a line remains, your sauce is thick enough. If the sauce immediately blends through the line, then it is too runny and should cook a bit longer.

# Mother's Beef Brisket

THIS BRISKET IS JUST LIKE MY MOM USED TO MAKE—LITERALLY. AND IT'S ONE OF the dishes we featured when I made my mother the M.O.M. (see her story on page 65). At the time, she had already passed away several years before, but I decided mothers can be honored even if they are only with us in spirit. The only change I've made to her recipe is substituting veal stock for water to give the dish a little more flavor. Although there are hundreds of recipes for brisket, I never stray from this one. To me it always will be the best.

Braised brisket is perfect for holidays or parties because it reheats so well. Cook it and slice it a day ahead without the complication of guests and hosting duties, and then rewarm it in the oven for the main event.

1 whole beef brisket (about 10 pounds; Love Note 1)

2 tablespoons plus 2 teaspoons kosher salt (divided)

1 tablespoon plus 2 teaspoons freshly ground black pepper (divided)

1½ tablespoons plus 2 teaspoons Hungarian sweet paprika (divided)

⅓ cup vegetable oil

10 medium yellow onions, finely diced (about 10 cups)

about 8 cups (2 quarts) Brown Veal Stock (page 89) or canned low-sodium beef broth

4 pounds (about 12) red potatoes, with skins

1. Using a long, sharp knife, trim the excess fat from the brisket to about ⅛ inch. Evenly season the meat all over with 2 tablespoons of the salt (use less if using canned broth), 1 tablespoon of the pepper, and 1½ tablespoons of the paprika.

2. Heat the oven to 350°F, and place a rack in the center. Place a Dutch oven or deep roasting pan over high heat for several minutes (make sure the pan is large enough to keep the brisket flat). You may need to cut the meat to fit into the pan. If so, be sure to cut it at the obvious, natural seam, which separates the fattier point cut

*continued*

from the lean first cut. This will make it easier to cut in the right direction for serving (Love Note 2). When hot, add the oil and heat until shimmering. Add the brisket and brown for 3 to 4 minutes on one side, and then turn over and brown the other side, 3 to 4 minutes more. Remove from the pan and set aside on a baking sheet or large plate.

3. Reduce the heat to medium-high and add the onions to the pan. Sauté until they start to brown slightly. Lower the heat to medium, and continue to cook until they are very soft and slightly browned, about 15 minutes.

4. Return the brisket to the pan with the onions and pour in enough stock to barely cover the meat (you may need more or less depending on the size of the brisket and dimensions of the pot). Bring to a boil over high heat. Remove from the heat, cover the pan tightly with either aluminum foil or a lid, and place in the oven.

5. While the brisket is cooking, cut the potatoes into 1-inch chunks. Keep them in cold water until ready to use.

6. After the brisket has cooked for 1½ hours, drain the potatoes in a colander and place in a large bowl. Toss the potatoes with the remaining 2 teaspoons salt, 2 teaspoons pepper, and 2 teaspoons paprika.

7. Remove the lid from the brisket and flip the meat so the top is now the bottom and is submerged in the cooking liquid. Arrange the potatoes around the meat, making sure that most are submerged in the liquid rather than on top of the meat. Cover the pan and return it to the oven for another 45 minutes.

8. Remove the cover from the pan (but if a lot of the meat is above the liquid, throw a piece of aluminum foil just on top the meat) and continue to cook until the potatoes are fork-tender (the fork should slide in and out without resistance), some of the liquid has reduced, and the brisket is done, about another 45 minutes. To

check the doneness of the brisket, pierce it with a two-pronged fork. If the meat falls away and back into the pan, it is done. If the meat offers resistance or clings to the fork, return it to the oven and continue to cook for another 30 minutes (or until it's done, checking occasionally).

9. Remove the pan from the oven. Using a wide spatula or tongs, lift the brisket out and place it on a cutting board. Use a slotted spoon or spider to lift the potatoes out of the liquid and transfer to a serving bowl. Cover with foil to keep the potatoes warm while you cut the brisket.

10. Using a thin, sharp slicing knife, cut the brisket against the grain (Love Note 2) into ¼-inch-thick slices. (The grain pattern shifts from one direction in the thinner flat end to a slightly different direction in the thicker, fattier point end. Just keep an eye on the meat and shift the angle of your knife to accommodate. If you had to cut the meat to fit it in the pan, you can slice the sections separately, making sure everyone gets a little of each.) Place the slices on a serving platter. Pour a small amount of the gravy onto the meat and the rest into a gravy boat to pass with the potatoes and meat.

*continued*

 **Uses for Leftover Brisket**

Leftover beef brisket makes excellent sandwiches—add some horseradish to mayonnaise, then spread it on some rye or rustic French bread, and top the brisket with lettuce, tomato, and red onion. Or brown the brisket in a sauté pan, top with Cheddar cheese, and place under a broiler to melt. Serve on French bread topped with sautéed or caramelized onions, with a schmear of horseradish mayonnaise.

# LOVE NOTES

**1** **A whole brisket** is a really large piece of meat and can be hard to find, since most families don't need that much meat at a whack. Plan ahead and order one in advance from the meat counter.

Brisket cuts go by several different names: first cut, second cut, point, flat, round, and deckle. The whole brisket is two muscles connected by a layer of fat and connective tissue that you can trim off after cooking (leave some of it on during the cooking for added flavor). The outer one is smaller, fattier, and has a pointed end; the inner one is leaner, flatter, and has a squared-off end. The extra fat and untidy appearance make the outer muscle less desirable (even though it's more flavorful); it's called either point cut or second cut. The tidy inner muscle usually is called flat cut or first cut.

I think cooking the whole brisket is best—it's cheaper by the pound and gives you the best of both worlds: all the delicious fat and connective tissue of the point cut that make the meat

succulent, tender, and flavorful, as well as the volume of meat in the flat cut so that you'll have plenty for everyone— and leftovers for sandwiches, too. If you really don't want that much meat, look for (or ask for) a cut labeled "front cut," which is half of a brisket that includes both the outer and inner muscles.

**2** **Always cut meat across the grain,** regardless of whether you're carving a turkey or slicing brisket. This shortens the muscle strands, which makes the meat easier to chew and makes it seem more tender.

After cooking, slice the brisket and place slices in a roasting pan to be reheated later. If reheating potatoes also, put them on one side of a roasting pan and the sliced meat on the other. Pour some of the gravy over the meat and a little over the potatoes, cover well with aluminum foil (so they don't dry out), and place in a 350°F oven to heat for about 1 hour.

# Boeuf Bourguignonne

THIS CLASSIC DISH FROM BURGUNDY, FRANCE, SOUNDS FANCY, BUT IT'S JUST A WINE-based beef stew. This recipe came from a Mother of the Month who isn't a mother to children but is a mother to many animals and who used to be a mother hen to many chicks (figuratively speaking) during her rock and roll days, when she was known as Penny Lane (see her story on page 108).

5 pounds beef chuck, cut into cubes (Love Note 1)

2½ teaspoons plus a pinch kosher salt (divided)

1½ teaspoons plus a pinch freshly ground black pepper (divided)

½ pound bacon, sliced crosswise into ¼-inch pieces (chill for 10 minutes in the freezer to make it easier to cut; Love Note 2)

¼ cup vegetable oil

3 medium yellow onions, finely diced (3 cups)

3 large carrots, peeled and finely diced (about 2½ cups)

4 cloves garlic, finely chopped (about 2 tablespoons)

¼ cup brandy

⅓ cup all-purpose flour

1 (750-ml) bottle dry red wine, such as Burgundy or Pinot Noir

4 cups (1 quart) Brown Veal Stock (page 89) or canned low-sodium beef broth (divided)

1 bouquet garni (1 bay leaf, 2 sprigs thyme, 3 sprigs Italian parsley, tied together; Love Note 2, page 112, Meatloaf Gravy)

3 tablespoons unsalted butter (divided)

10 to 12 ounces pearl onions, peeled (about 1½ cups; Love Note 3)

1 pound button or cremini mushrooms, sliced (4½ cups)

2 tablespoons chopped fresh Italian (flat-leaf) parsley

1. Heat the oven to 350°F. Arrange the beef in a single layer on a rimmed baking sheet (a great tool for spreading out ingredients to be seasoned and to hold cooked

*continued*

meat while browning) and season generously with 2 teaspoons of the salt (use less if using canned broth) and 1 teaspoon of the pepper.

2. Heat a large (8- to 10-quart) Dutch oven or stockpot over medium-high heat for several minutes. When hot, add the bacon and cook until almost crisp and the fat is rendered. Remove with a slotted spoon to a paper towel–lined plate, leaving behind as much fat as possible.

3. Increase the heat to high. Add just enough beef to cover the bottom of the pot without crowding. Brown the pieces on all sides, using tongs to turn them, transferring them back to the baking sheet as they finish browning and adding more meat to the pot as room allows (it's OK to use the baking sheet that had the raw meat, because the meat will be fully cooked later).

4. When all the meat is browned and removed from the pot, add the oil, and then the diced onions and carrots, and cook for 2 to 3 minutes. Lower the heat to medium-high and continue to sauté until they begin to soften, about 10 minutes. Add the garlic and sauté for another 3 minutes. Add the brandy and flambé. (To flambé, pour the brandy into the pot and light it immediately by holding a long match or barbecue lighter just above the surface of the liquid. Try to keep the flames going for as long as possible to burn off the alcohol; Love Note 4.)

5. Reduce the heat to medium and stir in the flour to make a roux. Cook the roux, stirring, for about 3 minutes.

6. Stir in the wine, a little at a time, allowing the roux to absorb the liquid before adding more (this will help prevent lumps) and scraping up any browned bits at the bottom of the pot. Add 3¾ cups stock, the browned meat, and the bouquet garni. Bring to a boil over high heat. Remove from the heat, cover, and place in the oven for about 2 hours. Test for doneness by piercing the meat with a two-pronged fork.

*continued*

If it falls away from the fork easily, it is done. If the meat offers resistance or clings to the fork, return it to the oven and continue to cook for another 20 minutes, or until done.

7.  While the stew is cooking, glaze the onions: Place a medium (8- to 10-inch) sauté pan over medium-high heat for several minutes. When hot, add 1 tablespoon butter and the onions at the same time. Season with a pinch of salt and pepper and sauté until lightly browned. Add the remaining ¼ cup stock, cover, reduce the heat to medium-low, and continue to cook until the onions are soft and glazed, 15 to 20 minutes, shaking the pan now and then (they should be a bit shiny). If there is still liquid in the pan by the time the onions have softened, remove the cover and continue cooking (while gently swirling the pan to keep the onions from scorching) until all the liquid has evaporated. Transfer to a bowl and set aside.

8.  Return the sauté pan to high heat. When very hot, add the remaining 2 tablespoons butter and enough mushrooms to cover the bottom of the pan (the mushrooms need to be seared at high heat so they'll brown instead of steam). Season with ½ teaspoon salt and ¼ teaspoon pepper, and cook over high heat until slightly browned, about 5 minutes. Transfer the mushrooms to the bowl with the onions. Repeat if necessary with any remaining mushrooms. (Cooking the mushrooms and onions separately and adding them to the stew at the end helps to keep their flavors from becoming muddled so that they're more pronounced in the finished dish.)

9.  Remove the stew from the oven, and gently stir in the sautéed mushrooms, onions, and bacon. Taste and adjust the seasoning as necessary with more salt and pepper; sprinkle with the parsley and serve with steamed new potatoes, Mother's Smashers (page 212), or rice.

*continued*

**1  Beef chuck** is meat from the neck and shoulder, and although there are several cuts to choose from, the cuts all have the same qualities in common—they're inexpensive and tough. Chuck meat is laced with fat, collagen, and connective tissue, which require long, slow cooking to break down. But when that happens, they melt into the meat and make it incredibly tender, moist, and delicious.

Look for cuts called chuck roast or pot roast, or, if you want to save a little time, get stew meat, which is already cubed. Even though these cuts are called roasts, they're usually best in braises and stews, where the cooking liquid keeps them from drying out.

**2  *Lardons* is the French term** that refers to small strips or cubes of fatty bacon or pork. In French cuisine, they are frequently used to flavor salads, stews, quiches, and potatoes.

**3  Blanching** is the fastest way to peel a large batch of pearl onions: Prepare a large bowl of ice water and set it near the stove. Bring a pot of water to a boil, add the onions, and cook for 2 minutes. Remove them with a slotted spoon and then plunge into the ice water to stop the cooking. Cut off the root ends and slip the skins right off.

**4  Flambéing is a dramatic** and fun way to burn off the harsh alcohol flavor of a liquor while leaving its more pleasant flavors behind. But you do need to use caution and common sense. Follow these rules: Don't carry the pan around while it's flaming. Keep a large metal lid at hand in case you need to extinguish the flames. Don't pour any liquor directly from the bottle into the flaming pan (the flames can migrate up the stream into the bottle). Make sure the alcohol is hot enough to start vaporizing but not so hot that it's boiling, which will burn off the vapors before you have the chance to ignite them.

Once the alcohol is hot, light just the vapors at the edge of the pan—not the actual liquid—using a long match or barbecue lighter. Liquors that are 80 proof work best. Beer and wine don't have enough alcohol, and anything above 120 proof is dangerous.

If igniting the brandy makes you nervous, just add it to the pot after whisking in the wine in Step 6.

## Pennie Trumbull *(aka Penny Lane)*
{ BOEUF BOURGUIGNONNE }

Pennie was born in Portland, Oregon, and grew up on amazing home cooking—her mother made a fresh pie every day, canned tons of fruits and vegetables, and never let anyone leave her house without a jar of something. Pennie made her first lasagne at 10 years old (but she forgot to turn on the oven). She took cooking classes for four years while still in high school, making elaborate, multi-course French dinners every Wednesday night. By the time she was 17, Pennie had read every book in the library about famous hostesses and entertaining and frequently tried to practice what she read.

If Pennie's name sounds a bit familiar, it might be because a slice of her early life was loosely portrayed in Cameron Crowe's Academy Award®–winning film *Almost Famous,* based on the period when Pennie became a popular muse and companion to famous rock stars in the 1970s. When she was 19 she "retired," began studying journalism, and attended California State University, Northridge, on a full fencing scholarship. She went on to have a successful business career in southern California but eventually relocated back to Portland.

Today, Pennie lives on her family's farm and credits her parents for inspiring her love of good friends, fresh quality food, and impromptu entertaining. She's thankful her neighbors no longer raise an eyebrow when famous and/or almost famous friends show up in tour buses or helicopters.

# Mother's Meatloaf

MEATLOAF IS EASY TO MAKE—BUT IT'S ALSO EASY TO MAKE WRONG, EITHER DRY AND tasteless or heavy and greasy. There are a few things we do at Mother's to make sure our meatloaf is perfect: We sauté plenty of aromatic vegetables so they are soft and slightly caramelized; we use oats instead of breadcrumbs to absorb and retain more of the meat's natural juices; and we use ketchup on top and inside, too, for more moistness and zing. Strips of bacon on top baste the loaf as it cooks while adding another layer of flavor in the process. To keep all that moisture and fat from weighing things down, we bake the loaf on a rack instead of in a loaf pan, so excess grease can drip right off.

You can serve the meatloaf plain, but we like to serve ours with gravy for an even richer, saucier dish. Plus, it makes the mashed potatoes happy—and you know you're going to want a big pile of Mother's Smashers (page 212) with this dish.

2 tablespoons unsalted butter

1 large yellow onion, finely chopped (about 1¼ cups)

1 medium green bell pepper, finely diced (about 1 cup)

1 large rib celery, finely diced (about ½ cup)

2 large eggs

2 pounds 80 percent lean ground beef, preferably all-natural (Love Note 1)

2 teaspoons dried thyme

¼ cup rolled oats (quick cooking is fine, but not instant)

½ cup ketchup (divided)

2 teaspoons kosher salt

1½ teaspoons freshly ground black pepper

3 strips bacon

2 cups Meatloaf Gravy (page 111)

1.  Heat a large (12- to 14-inch) sauté pan over medium-high heat for several minutes. When hot, add the butter, onions, green peppers, and celery. Cook until the vegetables start to brown slightly, about 5 minutes. Continue to cook until they are very tender, about 15 minutes (lower the heat to medium if the vegetables are browning too much). Transfer the vegetables to a plate or baking sheet and cool to room temperature (they can be cooked a day ahead and refrigerated).  *continued*

2. Heat the oven to 350°F. Grease a standard-size loaf pan or spray it generously with nonstick cooking spray. Whisk the eggs in a large bowl. Add the cooled sautéed vegetables, ground beef, thyme, oats, ¼ cup of the ketchup, the salt, and pepper. Mix thoroughly but gently (Love Note 2).

3. Press the ground beef mixture into the prepared pan. Pound the pan a couple of times on the counter to get rid of the air pockets. Spray a rack with nonstick cooking spray and set it on a rimmed baking sheet. Turn the loaf out onto the rack. (Sometimes the loaf sticks in the pan, and you might have to bang the pan a couple of times to coax the meat out. Pat the loaf back into shape if necessary.) Spread the top of the loaf with the remaining ¼ cup ketchup. Arrange the bacon strips lengthwise on top.

4. Bake for 1 hour, or until an instant-read thermometer inserted in the center registers 155°F.

5. Remove from the oven and let rest for 10 minutes. (While it rests it will continue to cook, and the temperature will rise another 10°F. Also, resting helps the meat reabsorb the juices before being sliced.) Slice the loaf and serve topped with Meatloaf Gravy, or refrigerate and serve in sandwiches.

## LOVE NOTES

**1.** There is a **flavor difference between naturally raised beef** and factory-farmed beef. Taste for yourself: Buy a small amount of both, season with just salt and pepper, and grill two burgers. You'll understand in one bite.

**2.** **Use a gentle hand when mixing** ground meat. The more you mix it, the more you break down the fat, which means the end product will be tough.

## MEATLOAF GRAVY

MAKES ABOUT 4 CUPS

THIS GRAVY IS ONLY AS GOOD AS THE STOCK YOU USE. EITHER START WITH YOUR own veal stock, or buy the best low-sodium broth you can afford.

This gravy freezes well and can be reheated on the stove over low heat. You can use this recipe to make chicken or turkey gravy for a roast bird, substituting chicken or turkey stock for the veal stock (Love Note 1).

4 tablespoons (½ stick) unsalted butter

1 medium yellow onion, chopped (about 1 cup)

½ carrot, peeled and chopped (about ⅓ cup)

1 rib celery, chopped (about ½ cup)

3 cloves garlic, minced

⅓ cup all-purpose flour

4 cups (1 quart) Brown Veal Stock (page 89) or canned low-sodium beef broth

1 bouquet garni (1 bay leaf, 2 sprigs thyme, 3 sprigs Italian parsley, tied together; Love Note 2)

1½ teaspoons kosher salt

½ teaspoon freshly ground black pepper

1. Place a medium saucepan over medium-high heat for several minutes. Add the butter, onions, carrots, and celery at the same time (don't wait for the butter to melt or it might burn) and sauté until the vegetables start to brown around the edges, about 5 minutes. Add the garlic, reduce the heat to medium so the garlic doesn't burn, and continue to cook until the vegetables are soft, another 5 minutes. Add the flour and mix well to make a roux (Love Note 3). Cook, stirring frequently, for about 3 minutes.

2. Stir the stock into the vegetables, a little at a time, letting the roux absorb the liquid before adding more (this will help prevent lumps). Bring the gravy to a boil over

*continued*

high heat, then reduce the heat to medium so it simmers (you don't want to boil a cornstarch- or flour-thickened sauce for long because the heat will cause the starch granules to burst and the sauce will become thin). Add the bouquet garni, cover, and simmer for about 45 minutes; skim off any scum that rises to the surface.

3.   Season with the salt and pepper (use less salt if using canned broth). Serve with the meatloaf or any other red meat.

## LOVE NOTES

**1** When making **turkey or chicken gravy** to go with a roast bird, be sure to deglaze the roasting pan with the stock to get all the flavorful browned bits. Then whisk the stock into the roux. Alternatively, pour the finished gravy into the roasting pan, scraping with a rubber spatula to deglaze, then strain the gravy before serving.

**2** **A bouquet garni** infuses cooking liquid with flavor without adding unwanted texture, since you can pull it out before serving. To tie the herbs in a bundle so you don't have to hunt around for them when it's time for their removal, use cotton or linen kitchen twine, not the stuff made with jute. If using whole spices like peppercorns, cloves, or coriander, use a small square of cheesecloth to wrap the ingredients in a bundle and tie with kitchen twine. If you're going to strain the liquid, don't bother tying the herbs together or using cheesecloth.

**3** **White, or blond, roux** is used to thicken soups, stews, sauces, and gravies. Roux should always be cooked over even, moderate heat so that it doesn't burn. If it's going to be used as a thickener, as it is here, use a heavy-bottomed pan and medium heat, stirring frequently to keep it from scorching.

# Pork Chops with Apple Chutney

PORK CHOPS AND APPLESAUCE IS A CLASSIC, BUT PREDICTABLE, COMBINATION. THIS recipe offers a different take without much more effort. A touch of vinegar gives the chutney a hint of savoriness, and the sweet glaze balances the fattiness of the pork and gives it special-occasion flair. Feel free to make the chutney ahead—it keeps for a week or two, so you can have it on hand whenever you want to serve pork chops, pork loin, roast chicken, or sandwiches.

**FOR THE MARINADE**

½ cup vegetable oil

3 cloves garlic, chopped

¼ cup orange juice

1 teaspoon kosher salt

4 (1-inch-thick) center-cut pork chops

**FOR THE CHUTNEY**

4 Granny Smith apples, peeled, cored, and diced (about 4 cups; Love Note 2, page 56, Butternut Squash and Apple Soup)

3 tablespoons golden raisins

¼ cup cider vinegar

¼ cup granulated sugar

¼ cup packed light brown sugar

¼ teaspoon ground nutmeg

¼ teaspoon ground cinnamon

2 whole cloves

½ teaspoon kosher salt

**FOR THE GLAZE**

1 cup apple juice

2 tablespoons honey

1 teaspoon cracked (or coarsely ground) black pepper

Grated zest of ¼ orange (¼ teaspoon)

**TO MAKE THE MARINADE**

In a medium mixing bowl, combine the oil, garlic, orange juice, and salt. Place the pork in a bowl or zip-top bag. Pour the mixture over the pork and marinate in the refrigerator for at least 4 hours or overnight.

*continued*

**TO MAKE THE CHUTNEY**

In a medium (4- to 6-quart) saucepan, combine the apples, raisins, vinegar, granulated sugar, brown sugar, nutmeg, cinnamon, cloves, and salt. Bring to a boil over high heat, then reduce the heat to a simmer and cook until the apples are soft and the liquid has evaporated, about 20 minutes, stirring frequently to prevent scorching. Remove from the heat, take out and discard the cloves, and cool to room temperature.

**TO MAKE THE GLAZE**

Combine the apple juice, honey, pepper, and orange zest in a saucepan set over medium-high heat. Simmer, stirring occasionally, until reduced by half (about ½ cup), 10 to 12 minutes. Remove from the heat and keep warm.

**TO COOK AND SERVE**

1. Heat the grill to medium-high (you should be able to hold your hand just above the grate for 2 to 3 seconds). Oil the grill (either pull the grate off and spray it with nonstick cooking spray, or put oil on a paper towel and rub it on the grate while using tongs to hold the towel). Place the pork chops diagonally on the grill as if facing 10 o'clock. After a few minutes, when they start to turn opaque on the grill side, use a spatula to lift the chops and turn them clockwise a quarter turn so they now face 1 o'clock. (This will give a nice crosshatch pattern.) Baste with the glaze once or twice. Flip the chops over and cook, basting once or twice, until they're done to your liking. (I like cooking pork to 145°F, which is a little underdone. Then I let the pork rest for 5 to 10 minutes before serving to reabsorb its juices. During this time the meat will continue cooking, and the temperature will rise another 10 to 15°F.)

2. Divide the pork chops among the plates with the crosshatch pattern on top and serve topped with the apple chutney (warmed or at room temperature), and mashed potatoes, sweet potatoes, or Creamed Corn Pudding (page 207) on the side.

# Pan-Seared Pork Loin Medallions

PORK LOIN, LIKE CHICKEN BREASTS, IS ENDLESSLY VERSATILE AND EASY TO COOK. Sweet caramelized onions are a delicious accompaniment, although they take a little patience—about 20 minutes of frequent stirring. You can make big batches of caramelized onions ahead of time (as we do at Mother's) and refrigerate them for up to 3 days or freeze them, so you can get dishes like this on the table in no time.

This has been on the menu at Mother's Bistro & Bar since we opened and remains one of our more popular dishes. Mother's Smashers (page 212) are a perfect partner.

1½ pounds boneless pork loin, trimmed and cut into about 10 (¼-inch-thick) medallions (Love Note 1)

2 teaspoons kosher salt

1 teaspoon freshly ground black pepper

¼ cup all-purpose flour

2 tablespoons vegetable oil

4 medium yellow onions (about 1 pound), thinly sliced, or 1 cup Carmelized Onions (page 118)

1 cup pilsner beer (like Budweiser or Pilsner Urquell, Love Note 2)

1 cup Brown Veal Stock (page 89) or canned low-sodium beef broth

1.  Arrange the pork medallions on a rimmed baking sheet or large plate in a single layer. Sprinkle evenly with the salt (use less if using canned broth) and pepper. Place the flour in a shallow dish. Dredge each medallion in flour on both sides, shaking off the excess.

2.  Place a large (12- to 14-inch) sauté pan over high heat for several minutes. When hot, add the oil and heat until shimmering. Add the floured pork medallions in a single layer (do not crowd the pan) and sauté until golden on the first side (you may have to brown them in batches), 1 to 2 minutes. Use tongs or a fork to turn the medallions over and brown the other side until golden, 1 to 2 minutes more. Transfer the pork back to the baking sheet as they finish browning (it's OK to use the baking sheet that had the raw meat because the pork will finish cooking later).

3. When the medallions are cooked and set aside, reduce the heat to medium-high and add the onions to the pan. Sauté until they start to color around the edges, about 5 minutes. Lower the heat to medium, and continue to cook until they are very soft, caramelized, and brown, about 15 minutes. If using already Caramelized Onions, add them instead and proceed with step 4.

4. Increase the heat to high and add the beer and veal stock to deglaze the pan, stirring with a rubber spatula or spoon to scrape up any browned bits. Simmer for about 2 minutes. Reduce the heat to medium-high and return the browned pork to the pan. Cook until the liquid is thickened and the pork is cooked through, about 3 minutes. Serve immediately.

*continued*

## LOVE NOTES

**1  Pork loin,** also called pork loin roast, is a lean and tender cut. It's where pork chops and baby back ribs come from. For this recipe, you want a piece of the loin without bones. Pork loin is not the same as pork tenderloin, which is long and narrow and often sold in packages of two.

Try to buy pork from natural meat processors—it tastes better and more like pork than factory-farmed pork, which is often "enhanced" with broth or salt water brine (and sometimes chemicals to help the meat retain water and keep it from spoiling). This process is meant to make the lean meat juicier but instead gives it the spongy texture and salty flavor of cold cuts.

**2  Pilsner is the best beer** for this recipe. It's not bitter or cloying and adds a brightness to the flavor of this dish.

## CARAMELIZED ONIONS

I LOVE THE SWEET-SAVORY FLAVOR THAT CARAMELIZED ONIONS ADD TO A RECIPE. We always cook ours in big batches, and I strongly urge you to do so as well.

About 5 cups of sliced onions equals 1 cup caramelized, so you'll need to cook *a lot* of onions to get a decent amount of caramelized onions. It doesn't sound like much return for all the effort, but the onions are concentrated in flavor, so a little goes a long way. You'll need to stick around while the onions cook, but don't have to be too vigilant.

¾ cup vegetable oil (divided)

5 pounds large yellow onions, sliced very thinly (18 cups, divided)

4 teaspoons kosher salt (divided)

2 teaspoons freshly ground black pepper (divided)

1. Heat a large (12- to 14-inch) sauté pan over high heat for several minutes. Add 3 tablespoons oil and 4½ cups onions. Season with 1 teaspoon salt and ½ teaspoon pepper, and stir well to combine. (You want only enough onions to tightly cover the bottom of the pan without being piled too high, and the amount depends on the size of your pan. The same goes for the oil and seasoning. If your pan is only 12 inches, then add only 2 tablespoons oil, about 3 cups onions, ½ teaspoon salt, and ¼ teaspoon pepper per batch.)

2. Sauté over high heat until the onions start to get a little color around the edges, about 5 minutes. Lower the heat to medium-high, stirring now and then. Cook the onions for about 20 minutes, or until they are mocha-colored and very soft. Remove from the pan onto a baking sheet to cool. Repeat until all onions have been caramelized and cooled.

3. Store the cooled onions in the refrigerator in a tightly sealed container for up to 1 week. Freeze in ½- to 1-cup portions for future use.

# Chicken Cacciatore

THERE ARE COUNTLESS RECIPES FOR CHICKEN CACCIATORE, SOME MADE WITH RED wine, some with white; some call for mushrooms, others don't. But most have at least a few core ingredients—onions, tomatoes, and a little garlic—that define this "hunter's style" dish. My version strives for a balance of fresh, bright flavors. If you prefer a deeper flavor, you can substitute red wine for the white and add 1 teaspoon of dry oregano.

This is quintessential comfort food and we had a few Mothers of the Month who considered Chicken Cacciatore their specialty (none of whom were actually Italian, by the way). I like my version best, so here it is.

1 (3½-pound) chicken, cut into eighths, or 3 pounds chicken legs and thighs (see Cutting Up a Whole Chicken, page 123)

2½ to 3½ teaspoons kosher salt (divided)

1⅛ teaspoons freshly ground black pepper (divided)

⅓ cup all-purpose flour

¼ cup plus 3 tablespoons extra-virgin olive oil (divided)

½ pound button or cremini mushrooms, cut into ¼-inch-thick slices (2 cups)

1 large yellow onion, cut into ¼-inch-thick slices (about 1½ cups)

1 large carrot, peeled and cut into ¼-inch-thick slices (about ¾ cups)

1 large green bell pepper, seeded and cut into ¼-inch-thick slices (about 1½ cups)

1 large clove garlic, finely chopped (about 1 tablespoon)

1½ cups dry white wine, such as Chardonnay, Pinot Grigio, or Sauvignon Blanc (Love Note 1)

1 (28-ounce) can whole tomatoes, with the juice (Love Note 2)

1. Heat the oven to 350°F. Arrange the chicken in a single layer on a rimmed baking sheet or plate. Season with 2 teaspoons of the salt and 1 teaspoon of the pepper. (I like to massage the seasoning into the chicken to ensure it's evenly distributed.) Place the flour in a shallow dish. Dip the chicken in the flour, making sure to coat it on all sides, then return it to the sheet.

*continued*

2. Place a large (12- to 14-inch), straight-sided sauté pan or a Dutch oven over high heat for several minutes. When hot, add ¼ cup of the oil and heat until shimmering. Add the chicken, skin side down (that way the fat "melts" as it cooks and gives you a bit more sizzle in the pan), in a single layer and sauté over high heat without moving it for about 4 minutes, or until browned on the first side. (If the pieces stick, that means they haven't browned long enough. Let them cook a bit longer. If sticking continues to be a problem, use a sharp-edged spatula to loosen the skin from the pan.) Turn the chicken over and repeat, lowering the heat to medium-high if it gets too dark too quickly. Transfer the browned chicken to a clean baking sheet, trying to leave as much oil as possible in the pan.

3. Let the pan heat up for a minute over high heat. Add the mushrooms, season with the remaining ½ teaspoon salt and ⅛ teaspoon black pepper, and let them sauté, without stirring, for about 2 minutes. Stir and let the mushrooms sauté undisturbed for another 2 minutes. Stir again and repeat, if necessary, until they're almost all seared and golden. Remove the mushrooms to the baking sheet with the chicken, leaving as much fat in the pan as possible.

4. Reduce the heat to medium-high. Add the remaining 3 tablespoons olive oil and then the onions, carrots, and peppers. Sauté until the onions are very soft, 10 to 15 minutes. Add the garlic and cook for 1 minute more, until fragrant.

5. Deglaze the pan with the wine, stirring to scrape up the browned bits. Add the tomatoes, squeezing them (with clean hands) as you add them to the pan to help them break down faster. Return the chicken and mushrooms to the pan and bring to a simmer. Cover the pan tightly with foil or a lid and place in the oven. Cook for about 40 minutes, or until the chicken is very tender (Love Note 3).

*continued*

6. The sauce should be the perfect consistency (like a rich soup rather than pasta sauce), but if it seems at all watery, transfer the chicken to a plate and tent with foil to keep warm. Simmer the sauce, uncovered, over medium-high heat until thickened, about 5 minutes. (How long this takes depends on how thin the sauce is and the dimensions of your pan. Just keep an eye on it so you don't over-reduce it). Taste and add 1 more teaspoon salt if needed. Serve with rice, pasta, or crusty bread.

## LOVE NOTES

**1** **Dry wines** have little residual sugar, so they add acidity and flavor without sweetness. White wines don't add unwanted color or tannins, which could make a delicate dish taste bitter. Good choices for dry whites are Sauvignon Blanc, Chardonnay (preferably unoaked), Pinot Grigio, and Chenin Blanc.

Don't spend a fortune on wine for cooking, but make sure it's something tasty enough to drink. If you don't think you'll drink the leftovers, pour into ice cube trays or small containers and freeze.

If you don't like cooking with alcohol, use lemon juice mixed with water or stock, about ¼ cup lemon juice to every 1 cup of water or stock.

**2** I use **whole canned tomatoes** and crush them, rather than buying already crushed tomatoes, because the whole tomatoes taste better and are better quality. Crushing them yourself is a snap.

**3** I cook **braised dishes in the oven** because the heat is distributed more evenly than on a stovetop, so I don't have to worry about scorching or burning. To cook this on the stovetop, in Step 5, cover the pot tightly with a lid or foil and simmer on low heat for about 40 minutes, or until the chicken is very tender.

## Cutting Up
## a Whole Chicken

It's cheaper to buy a whole chicken and cut it up yourself than to buy parts. Place the chicken, breast side up, on a work surface, pull the leg away from the body, and slice through the skin and meat between the thigh and the body using a sharp knife. You should now see the joint. Pull the leg away from the body to help pop the joint. Lodge your knife in the joint and press to cut through it. Do the same for the other leg. Now find the joint where the drumsticks meet the thighs (again, you can pull them apart with your hands to help pop the joint) and cut through that to separate.

If you're cutting a chicken into eighths for braising, you will want to cut each of the two breasts in half, so that two of the quarters have a wing attached. To do this, turn the chicken over, breast side down, and cut along both sides of the backbone (you will be cutting through the ribs), from neck to tail. Remove the backbone. You should now be able to see the breastbone that holds the two halves together. Place your knife tip in the center and press down to crack the bone. Bend the halves back and forth to help finish breaking the bone. Now turn the chicken breast side up and slice through the skin and meat to fully separate the halves. Cut each one in half crosswise (I like to do it at a diagonal) so you end up with four pieces of breast—two with wings attached. You can cut off the wing tips and save them, with the back, for making stock.

If you want the chicken wings separate from the breast, cut them off before cutting the breasts free from the carcass: Use your fingers to help you find the joint where the wing meets the body. Cut through the skin and flesh there to expose the joint. Bend the wings back to help pop the joint. Wedge the knife into the middle of the joint and press to cut through it.

# Coq au Vin

COQ AU VIN IS A FAVORITE FROM THE BURGUNDY REGION OF FRANCE, AND IT WAS created as a way to cook tough old roosters in the wine from that region. It's not easy to find rooster these days, but a good free-range bird works fine. Marinating the chicken in the wine and vegetables ensures that the flavors penetrate the chicken and that the acidity has a chance to tenderize the meat. And using the marinade as the cooking liquid is not only economical but also another way to add complexity to this dish.

If you don't plan ahead and want to make this at the last minute, you can forgo the marinating altogether. The final result won't be drastically different. Just leave out all the marinade ingredients except for the wine, and add the entire bottle after the chicken is returned to the pot.

1 (3½-pound) roasting chicken or 3 pounds legs and thighs (Love Note 1, and Cutting Up a Whole Chicken, page 123)

**FOR THE MARINADE**

1 large onion, thinly sliced (about 1½ cups)

1 large carrot, thinly sliced (about ¾ cup)

3 whole black peppercorns

½ bottle (1½ cups) dry red wine (preferably Burgundy or Pinot Noir)

1 bouquet garni (1 bay leaf, 2 sprigs fresh thyme, 3 sprigs Italian parsley)

**FOR THE STEW**

2½ teaspoons plus a pinch kosher salt (divided)

1¼ teaspoons plus a pinch freshly ground black pepper (divided)

¼ pound bacon or sliced salt pork, sliced crosswise into ¼-inch pieces (chill for 10 minutes in the freezer to make it easier to cut; Love Note 2, page 107, Boeuf Bourguignonne)

small yellow onion, finely chopped (½ cup)

½ carrot, peeled and finely chopped (¼ cup)

5 tablespoons unsalted butter (divided)

2 tablespoons brandy

½ bottle (1½ cups) dry red wine (preferably Burgundy or Pinot Noir)

2 cloves garlic, peeled and left whole

1 bouquet garni (1 bay leaf, 2 sprigs fresh thyme, 3 sprigs Italian parsley)

½ pound button or cremini mushrooms, sliced (2 cups)

10 to 12 ounces pearl onions, peeled (about 1½ cups; Love Note 3, page 107, Boeuf Bourguignonne)

3 tablespoons Chicken Stock (page 87), Brown Veal Stock (page 89), or canned low-sodium broth

**FOR THE BEURRE MANIÉ**

2 tablespoons all-purpose flour

2 tablespoons unsalted butter, softened

**IF USING A WHOLE CHICKEN**

Cut the chicken into two leg-and-thigh pieces and two wing-and-breast pieces with a sharp chef's knife or poultry shears. (Throw the back in a zip-top bag and put it in the freezer for making stock another day.) If using legs and thighs, skip to the next step.

**TO MAKE THE MARINADE**

In a large, nonreactive mixing bowl (Love Note 2), combine the onions, carrots, peppercorns, wine, and bouquet garni (don't bother tying the herbs together because they'll get strained out later). Add the chicken pieces, making sure they are covered with the marinade. Cover the bowl and let the chicken marinate overnight in the refrigerator.

**TO MAKE THE STEW**

1. Remove the chicken from the marinade and pat dry with paper towels; arrange in a single layer on a rimmed baking sheet or large plate.

2. Pour the marinade (including the vegetables and herbs) into a medium nonreactive saucepan. Bring to a boil, reduce the heat to medium, and simmer uncovered for 30 minutes. Remove from the heat and strain into a bowl; set aside. Discard the vegetables and herbs.

*continued*

3. Heat the oven to 350°F. Season the chicken with 2 teaspoons salt (use less if using canned broth) and 1¼ teaspoons pepper.

4. Place a large (12- to 14-inch) sauté pan or a Dutch oven over medium-high heat for several minutes. When hot, add the bacon or salt pork, and cook until the fat is rendered and the meat is cooked. Remove the pan from the heat and use a slotted spoon or slotted spatula to remove the bacon to a paper towel–lined plate, leaving behind as much of the rendered fat as possible.

5. Place the sauté pan over high heat. When hot, add the seasoned chicken pieces in one layer, skin side down (that way the fat "melts" as it cooks and gives you a bit more sizzle in the pan). Cook, without moving, for 4 to 5 minutes, or until golden brown on the first side. (If the pieces stick, that means they haven't browned long enough. Let them cook a bit longer. If sticking continues to be a problem, use a sharp-edged spatula to loosen the skin from the pan.) Turn the pieces, lower the heat, and brown for another 4 minutes. Transfer the chicken to a plate.

6. Add the onions and carrots to the hot pan. Lower the heat to medium and sauté until the vegetables are soft, about 10 minutes, scraping the fond to release the browned bits and adding 1 tablespoon butter if the mixture looks dry (the vegetables should sizzle in the pan).

7. Return the chicken to the pan and pour in the brandy. Flambé by holding a long match or barbecue lighter just above the surface of the liquid to ignite the fumes and burn off the alcohol (Love Note 4, page 107, Boeuf Bourguignonne). Try to keep the flames going as long as possible to burn off the alcohol.

8. Once the flames die down (sometimes they never ignite—don't worry about it, just proceed with the rest of the recipe), add the strained marinade and the red wine so the chicken is barely covered with liquid. Return the bacon to the pan with the chicken and add the garlic. Bring to a boil, cover, and transfer to the center rack of

the oven. Cook for about 45 minutes, or until the chicken is tender when pierced with a two-pronged fork. (The oven provides even heat so you won't end up with burned spots. You can also cook this dish over low heat on the stove, but keep your eye on the pot and make sure you stir it now and then, so nothing gets scorched. It should cook at a gentle simmer.)

9. While the chicken is cooking, heat a medium (8- to 10-inch) sauté pan over high heat. When very hot, add 2 tablespoons of the butter and the mushrooms in a single layer. (Use high heat and do not crowd the pan or the mushrooms will steam instead of sear. Cook the mushrooms in batches if necessary.) Sauté until the mushrooms are seared and golden. Season with the remaining $\frac{1}{2}$ teaspoon salt and $\frac{1}{8}$ teaspoon pepper. Remove the mushrooms from the pan and set aside.

10. Place the pan over medium-high heat. Add the remaining 2 tablespoons butter, swirl the pan to coat, and add the pearl onions. Season with a pinch of salt and pepper. Sauté until they begin to brown, about 5 minutes, shaking the pan every now and then to make sure they brown all over. Reduce the heat and add the stock or broth.

11. Cover and either place the pan in the oven with the chicken or continue to cook over low heat until the onions are fork-tender, about 10 minutes. If there is still liquid in the pan when the onions are done, remove the cover, turn up the heat, and cook, stirring, until the liquid has evaporated and the onions are glazed. Set aside.

**TO MAKE THE BEURRE MANIÉ AND FINISH THE STEW**

1. Place the flour in a small bowl. Using your fingertips, mix in the softened butter until it looks like dough.

2. When the chicken is done, remove the pot from the oven. Transfer the chicken to a plate and tent with foil to keep warm. Taste the sauce and adjust with more salt and

*continued*

pepper, if necessary. Whisk the flour mixture into the sauce and simmer over medium-high heat while whisking to make sure there are no lumps. Continue to cook until the mixture has thickened and coats the back of the spoon, about 5 minutes (your finger should leave a distinct trace when you run it across the back). Continue to simmer for a few minutes to cook the flour taste away.

3. Add the chicken, mushrooms, and onions to the pot, and stir gently to combine. Serve with Mother's Smashers (page 212), rice pilaf, or steamed new potatoes.

## LOVE NOTES

**1** I'm a big advocate of **cutting up your own chicken** because whole chickens are cheaper than parts, and you'll get to save the backs and wing tips for making stock. Whenever you need some chicken for a recipe, buy a few whole ones and cut them up, and then freeze what you don't need. Use breasts for quick-cooking dishes like cutlets (breasts can dry out when cooked for a long time) and save the legs and thigh meat for braised dishes like this.

**2** **Nonreactive bowls and pans** are *not* made of aluminum, which reacts with acidic things and infuses them with a distinctly metallic taste. Unless you want your dish to taste like metal (and believe me, it will), don't use aluminum pots, pans, and bowls with acidic ingredients like wine, tomatoes, lemon juice, and vinegar.

# Chicken and Dumplings

THIS DISH IS ALMOST AS POPULAR AS OUR POT ROAST (PAGE 95), PROBABLY BECAUSE so many people grew up eating their mother's or grandmother's version. Traditionally, chicken and dumplings is like a thick, creamy chicken soup with a layer of doughy dumplings that steam right on top while the soup simmers. Some make the dumplings "slippery," with just flour and water for a denser, chewier texture. But ours are layered with butter and leavened with baking powder, making them more like biscuits.

Back in the day, a lot of moms turned to biscuit mix to save time, so not many people remember dumplings as tender and delicious as these. Making the biscuits from scratch takes just a few more minutes than using a mix, and the results are far superior.

**FOR THE CHICKEN GRAVY**

8 tablespoons (1 stick) unsalted butter, cut into pieces

1 cup all-purpose flour

7 cups chicken broth from Belle's Chicken Soup (page 61; also Love Note 1)

2 teaspoons kosher salt

½ teaspoon freshly ground black pepper

2 large carrots, peeled and diced (1½ cups)

5 ribs celery, diced (2½ cups)

**FOR THE DUMPLINGS**

2 cups all-purpose flour

1½ teaspoons baking powder

1 scant teaspoon kosher salt

1 tablespoon finely chopped fresh Italian (flat-leaf) parsley

3 tablespoons cold unsalted butter, cut into ½-inch pieces

⅔ cup whole milk

**FOR SERVING**

5 cups cooked chicken (you can use the cooked chicken from making Belle's Chicken Soup; remove the skin and pick the meat off the bones, keeping the meat in large chunks; or cook a 3-pound chicken)

2 tablespoons finely chopped fresh Italian (flat-leaf) parsley, for garnish

*continued*

**TO MAKE THE GRAVY**

1. In a large (8- to 10-quart), heavy-bottomed soup pot or Dutch oven, melt the butter over medium heat. Add the flour and mix well to make a roux. Cook, stirring frequently, until the mixture is pale yellow and resembles fine, wet sand, about 3 minutes.

2. Whisk the broth into the roux a little at a time, allowing the roux to absorb the liquid before adding more (this will help prevent lumps). Add the salt, pepper, carrots, and celery. Bring the mixture to a boil over high heat, stirring occasionally, and then lower the heat and gently simmer for 15 to 20 minutes. Keep stirring occasionally and skim off any scum (Love Note 2) that rises to the surface.

**TO MAKE THE DUMPLINGS**

1. Whisk the flour, baking powder, salt, and parsley together in a large bowl, and then cut in the butter using a pastry blender, two knives, or a whisk until it's in small pieces. (Alternatively, you can use a food processor: Place the flour, baking powder, and salt in the bowl of a food processor. Pulse several times to combine. Add the parsley and pulse once or twice to incorporate. Add the butter and pulse until it is in small pieces.)

2. Add the milk and stir or pulse once or twice to moisten the flour mixture. (Do not overmix or you will develop the gluten in the flour and the dumplings will be chewy.) Gather the dough into a ball.

3. Using a large spoon or your hands, scoop out ¼-cup chunks of dough, lightly roll them between your palms to round them out, and then drop into the simmering gravy (it's OK if they sink), spacing them apart. Cover the pot and simmer until the dumplings are done (a knife inserted in the center should come out clean), about 20 minutes. (Avoid lifting the lid while the dumplings are cooking because it slows down the cooking process, and "if you're lookin' you're not cookin'!")

*continued*

Gently stir the cooked chicken into the pot with the dumplings, return the liquid to a simmer, cover, and cook for 5 more minutes to heat the chicken through. Using a serving spoon or tongs, divide the chicken and dumplings among soup bowls. Ladle the gravy over the dumplings and chicken, sprinkle with the parsley, and serve.

## LOVE NOTES

**1** This recipe is delicious with the **broth from Belle's Chicken Soup** (you need just the broth, with no other ingredients or additions). In a pinch you can use canned low-sodium chicken broth and a rotisserie chicken and still have a good meal. When you add the chicken, feel free to stir in any leftover vegetables you have lurking in the fridge, such as steamed broccoli or green beans or braised greens.

**2** When **simmering gravies or sauces** that include flour, be sure you skim off any scum that rises to the surface with a large serving spoon or ladle. This scum contains proteins and fibers from the flour that can make a sauce gummy.

##  Butter and Fat in Recipes

Among the credos in cooking school were "more fat, more flavor" and "mo' butter, mo' better." Unfortunately, this is true in many ways, and fried chicken, French fries, and baked potatoes slathered in butter are all proof of it. But in other recipes the butter and fat aren't necessarily so obvious. Many upscale restaurants use butter to thicken a sauce just before serving. At one of the restaurants I worked in, we'd take already concentrated veal and chicken reductions and *monter au beurre* (add a couple of tablespoons butter while whisking) just before spooning the sauce onto the plate.

When you cook at home, you are in control and know exactly what you're getting. And while there's a fair amount of butter and fat in some of the recipes in this cookbook, it is still a lot less fat than in most dishes you'd be getting if you ate out. Besides, for most of the recipes in this book, you can substitute low-fat versions of things like half-and-half and sour cream.

# Chicken Paprikas

THIS RECIPE COMES FROM THERESE DIERINGER, ONE OF OUR HUNGARIAN MOTHERS of the Month. Chicken Paprikas and goulash are undoubtedly the two most popular dishes from Hungarian mothers, and each mother has her own way of doing things. When we have a M.O.M., I always watch her make the dish her way, and I only make changes that I think might improve the dish. Therese really knows her stuff, so there was nothing for us to do with this recipe but make it her way.

1 (3½-pound) chicken, cut into eighths (Cutting Up a Whole Chicken, page 123), or 3 pounds chicken legs and thighs

2 teaspoons kosher salt

1 teaspoon freshly ground black pepper

2 tablespoons vegetable oil

3 large yellow onions, finely chopped (4½ cups)

2 tablespoons sweet Hungarian paprika (Love Note)

1½ cups Chicken Stock (page 87) or canned low-sodium chicken broth

2 tablespoons all-purpose flour

½ cup sour cream

1 pound egg noodles, cooked, or 4 cups Spaetzle (page 222), for serving

1.  Arrange the chicken on a rimmed baking sheet and season well with the salt and pepper. (I rub the seasoning into the chicken, something I learned from a former M.O.M., Beatriz de Proaño.)

2.  Place a large (8- to 10-quart) Dutch oven or heavy stockpot over high heat for several minutes. (The pan needs to be very hot so the chicken browns and sears instead of steams.) When hot, add the oil (heating the pan first keeps the oil from getting smoky while the pan heats), swirl the pan to coat, add the chicken in a single layer (skin side down first—that way the fat "melts" as it cooks and gives you a bit more sizzle in the pan), and brown on both sides (about 4 minutes per side), using tongs to turn the pieces. Transfer the chicken to a clean baking sheet or plate as the pieces finish browning and add more as room allows.

3. When all the chicken is cooked and removed from the pot, reduce the heat to medium-high and add the onions. Sauté, stirring frequently, until soft and golden, 15 to 20 minutes. Add the paprika and stir well to combine.

4. Return the chicken to pot, pour the stock over it, and bring to a boil. Cover, lower the heat to a simmer, and cook until the chicken is tender, 30 to 40 minutes.

5. Remove the chicken to a plate and tent with foil to keep warm. Whisk together the flour and sour cream in a small bowl, and then stir into the pot. Mix well with a whisk or wooden spoon to incorporate the flour mixture. (It will look a little lumpy, so continue to stir as it simmers; the lumps should cook away.) Cook for about 5 minutes, or until the sauce is thickened.

6. Return the chicken to the pot, turn to coat in the sauce, and simmer for about 1 minute, until heated through.

7. To serve, place noodles or spaetzle in serving dishes, ladle sauce over them, and arrange a couple of pieces of chicken on top.

*continued*

**LOVE NOTE**

**Paprika is made** from ground, dried red peppers. Depending on the variety of peppers used, paprika can be mild (aka sweet) or hot. Hungarian dishes are traditionally made with sweet Hungarian paprika or a combination of sweet and hot. Don't confuse either of these with smoked Spanish paprika (called pimentón de la vera), which is made with ground, smoked peppers and has a taste reminiscent of bacon. While delicious in many other dishes, smoked paprika is not a traditional choice for Hungarian food.

## Therese Dieringer
### { CHICKEN PAPRIKAS }

Therese Dieringer (formerly Kolbert) was born in Pecs, Hungary, in 1937. When she was seven years old, Therese and her parents fled Hungary to Dresden, Germany, to escape the Russian Communists. When Dresden was destroyed by firebombing, Therese's family joined a caravan and walked west until they reached Bavaria, Germany. They lived there for seven years, but because they were a displaced people, neither German nor Russian, Therese's family decided to move to America in 1952. The family ended up in Los Angeles thanks to a Hungarian priest who eagerly helped Hungarian immigrants get settled in his community.

Therese married in 1955, and in 1962 bought a farm in Scotts Mills, Oregon. She had never been a farmer, but she quickly learned how to milk cows and make butter and cheese. Therese did most of the farm work—tending to their herd of 60 cattle and growing the food for her family to eat, canning more than 800 quarts of vegetables, fruits, and broths each summer. Money was always tight, so Therese eventually got a job outside the farm as a cook for an abbey retreat kitchen. Because she was needed mainly on weekends, she eventually had to give up that job so that she could raise her three children. Later she took a job as a cook for a local school, treating the kids to made-from-scratch soups and other good foods, but she retired when the school insisted on using premade food with artificial ingredients.

Therese's favorite food memory is how her mother would bribe her to eat potato soup, which she made every Friday (she was a devout Catholic). Therese hated the soup but loved the palancsintas (crêpes) that her mom also made on Fridays. Her mother would promise her all the crêpes she could eat as long as she ate three spoonfuls of potato soup. She still doesn't like potato soup, but she still smiles when she thinks of the palancsintas!

# CHAPTER 8

# Moroccan Couscous

IF THERE'S A NATIONAL DISH OF MOROCCO, THIS IS IT. MANY PEOPLE DON'T REALIZE that couscous is actually the name of a stew as well as the name of the tiny grain-like pasta on top of which it's served. In Morocco, the pasta is rarely eaten without the stew, although couscous desserts are rather common.

There are many different kinds of couscous (the stew), and every family has its own version. I learned how to make this dish from my ex-in-laws, who frequently served it Moroccan-style, sitting on the floor wearing traditional djellaba robes and encouraging everyone to eat with their fingers. I didn't realize how much they taught me about Moroccan cuisine until I went to Morocco, thinking I'd get to experience it first-hand. That's when I realized I had it in my hand all along!

**FOR THE STEW**

3 tablespoons vegetable oil

1 medium yellow onion, finely diced (about 1 cup)

1 (14-ounce) can whole tomatoes, with the juice

2 lamb shanks (about 1½ pounds)

1 (3½-pound) roasting chicken, left whole (it will fall apart on its own, so you don't have to cut it up)

1 cup dried garbanzo beans, rinsed, soaked overnight (preferably), and drained, or 2 (15-ounce) cans garbanzo beans (Love Note 1)

4 to 6 quarts (1 to 1½ gallons) Chicken Stock (page 87) or water (or a mix of the two)

2 tablespoons kosher salt (divided)

2 teaspoons freshly ground black pepper (divided)

1 small head green cabbage, cut into 2-inch wedges or eighths, with ⅛-inch core left on to hold it together (Love Note 2)

2 large carrots, peeled and cut in half widthwise, then quartered if large

1 turnip, peeled and quartered

2 leeks (white and light green parts), cut in half lengthwise with a tiny amount of root left on to help them hold together

2 zucchinis, partially peeled (so it looks striped) and cut in half widthwise

2 yellow summer squash, partially peeled (so it looks striped) and cut in half widthwise

*continued*

**FOR THE COUSCOUS**

6 cups couscous cooking liquid

2 cups Vegetable Stock (page 84), Chicken Stock (page 87), or canned low-sodium chicken broth

1 tablespoon kosher salt

½ teaspoon freshly ground black pepper

6 cups couscous (not pearl or Israeli couscous)

Harissa (page 142; optional; Love Note 3)

**TO MAKE THE STEW**

1. Place a large (8- to 10-quart) soup pot over medium-high heat for several minutes. When hot, add the oil and the onions. Lower the heat to medium-high and sauté until very soft, but do not let them color (lower the heat if necessary), about 10 minutes. Add the tomatoes, squishing them with (clean) hands as they are added, and simmer until slightly thickened, about 10 minutes.

2. Add the lamb, chicken, and garbanzo beans (if using canned, add them later with the zucchini and yellow squash). Add just enough of the chicken stock or water to barely cover the chicken, and bring to a boil over high heat. (If your pot requires more than 1½ gallons liquid, it's too big for the job. Look for something smaller.) Lower the heat to a simmer, add 1 tablespoon salt and 1 teaspoon pepper, and stir to incorporate. Simmer, partially covered, for 1 hour, skimming scum off as it rises to the top.

3. Add the cabbage, carrots, turnips, and leeks, tucking the vegetables under and between the lamb and chicken to make sure they're submerged. Season with the remaining 1 tablespoon salt and 1 teaspoon pepper and stir a bit to combine. Turn up the heat and return to a boil. Lower the heat, partially cover, and simmer for about 30 minutes.

4. Using two spatulas, lift out the chicken, trying to keep it together (it makes getting it out easier) and the leeks, keeping them separate.

*continued*

5. Add the zucchini and yellow squash to the stew (and the garbanzos if using canned instead of dried), and continue to simmer, uncovered, for about 30 minutes more, or until the lamb offers no resistance when pierced with a fork.

6. Remove the zucchini, squash, and lamb from the stew and set aside until ready to serve.

## LOVE NOTES

**1** For this recipe I prefer **dry garbanzos** because they do have more flavor than canned. In addition, the stew has to cook for a long time anyway, so you might as well be cooking the dried garbanzo beans, which are much cheaper than canned, while you're at it. Before soaking, check the beans for pebbles and debris and rinse well. Place in a large bowl or pot, cover with an inch of water, and soak overnight. (If you forget to soak them overnight, see Black Bean Soup, page 70, for the quick-soak method.)

**2** The best way to **cut the cabbage** without it falling apart in the stew is to cut it in half lengthwise, and then cut each half in half to make quarters. Cut each quarter in half to make eighths.

Trim out most of the core, leaving 1/8 inch, which is just enough to hold each piece of cabbage together during cooking.

**3** **Harissa is a spicy Moroccan sauce** made with hot chiles, garlic, cumin, and coriander. With increasing interest in Moroccan cuisine, you can now find it at well-stocked grocery stores or gourmet shops, but the canned stuff is nothing like the fresh version found in the open-air markets in north Africa. I highly recommend making your own (recipe follows). It keeps indefinitely in the freezer and for up to 1 month in the refrigerator. Harissa is never served straight with couscous. A spoonful of it is mixed with a cup of the couscous stew liquid and passed at the table as a condiment.

**TO MAKE THE COUSCOUS**

1. Ladle out 6 cups of stew broth into a medium (4- to 6-quart) saucepan. (Use a 1-cup ladle so you won't have to dirty a measuring cup.) Add 2 cups Vegetable Stock, Chicken Stock, or canned broth (so you have 8 cups of liquid in the saucepan) and bring to a boil over medium-high heat.

2. Add the salt, pepper, and couscous and quickly stir to combine and remove all lumps. Turn off the heat, cover tightly, and let stand for 10 minutes until the liquid is absorbed. (Do not remove the lid before 10 minutes, or the precious steam needed to cook the couscous will escape.) Fluff with a fork before serving.

**TO SERVE**

1. Divide the couscous among plates and top each with a piece of zucchini, yellow squash, cabbage, carrot, leek; a chunk of chicken; a chunk of lamb; and a ladle of cooking liquid with garbanzo beans. Or pass a platter of the meat and vegetables (I like to have separate platters for each), a serving bowl of couscous topped with a ladle or two of the stew cooking liquid, and a bowl of the cooking liquid with the chickpeas and let diners serve themselves.

2. Mix some of the stew's cooking liquid with Harissa (1 tablespoon Harissa for every cup of cooking liquid) in a small bowl and pass around with the platter of meat and vegetables.

*continued*

## HARISSA

2 ounces (1 cup) small dry hot red chiles (such as chiles de árbol or guajillo peppers)

1½ teaspoons caraway seeds

1 teaspoon cumin seeds or ground cumin

1 teaspoon coriander seeds

8 cloves garlic minced

1 teaspoon kosher salt

¼ teaspoon freshly ground black pepper

¾ cup extra-virgin olive oil

1. In a small (2- to 3-quart) saucepan, bring water to a boil. Remove from the heat. Stir in the chile peppers, cover, and let sit for 1 hour.

2. While the peppers are soaking, toast the spices. Heat a small sauté pan over medium heat. Add the caraway seeds and toast, stirring occasionally (and watching vigilantly so they don't burn) until fragrant and lightly browned, a minute or two. Remove and repeat with the cumin seeds and coriander seeds. Grind the toasted spices in a spice grinder (or a blade coffee grinder) until very fine.

3. Drain the peppers, reserving the soaking liquid. Remove and discard the stems from the peppers and place the peppers, spices, garlic, salt, and pepper in the bowl of a food processor fitted with a metal blade. Purée the peppers. This can take a bit of time, and you will need to alternately pulse and leave the machine running (for as long as 1 to 2 minutes); be sure to scrape down the sides of the bowl. Use some of the soaking liquid, if necessary, to get things started.

4. With the processor running, slowly drizzle the olive oil through the feed tube.

5. Pour into a glass jar or other container and refrigerate for up to 2 weeks. You can also freeze it in small portions either in an ice cube tray or in small blobs on a parchment-lined baking sheet (once frozen, remove to a zip-top freezer bag).

# Nana's Chicken Fried Chicken

WE ALL KNOW THE BEST PART OF CHICKEN FRIED STEAK IS THE CRISPY BREADING, so there's no reason you can't use chicken instead of beef and bring the cholesterol down at least a little. This recipe is delicious topped with a ribbon of strained Country Sausage Gravy (page 282). Garnish the dish with fresh parsley (it's not just for looks but for flavor, too) and serve Mother's Smashers (page 212) on the side.

4 boneless, skinless chicken breasts (about 2 pounds)

1¼ cups all-purpose flour

¼ teaspoon poultry seasoning (Love Note 1)

½ teaspoon freshly ground black pepper

1 tablespoon garlic salt

Pinch cayenne pepper

⅔ cup milk

2 large eggs

½ cup vegetable oil

¼ cup clarified butter (Love Note 2)

1½ cups strained Country Sausage Gravy (page 282; Love Note 3)

1. Spread a 12-inch piece of plastic wrap on the counter. Place a chicken breast on top and lay another 12-inch sheet of plastic on top. Using a meat mallet or large, heavy skillet, pound the breast to a ¼-inch thickness. Repeat with the remaining breasts.

2. In a shallow mixing bowl, mix together the flour, poultry seasoning, black pepper, garlic salt, and cayenne. Use a 2-cup liquid measuring cup to measure the milk. Add the eggs to it and whisk to combine. Pour the mixture onto a separate shallow, rimmed plate or into a shallow bowl. Have another dish ready to hold the breaded cutlets.

3. With your dominant, or working, hand, dredge one cutlet in the flour on both sides, shaking off the excess. Transfer it to your other hand and dip both sides in the egg mixture (keeping one hand dedicated to the egg step will keep your dominant hand from getting gummy), allow the excess to drip off, and then drop it

*continued*

back in the plate of flour. Use your dominant hand to scoop flour on top, pick it up, and shake off the excess. Set on the empty plate and repeat with the remaining cutlets. If you have time, place the breaded cutlets in the refrigerator for about an hour to dry out the coating and help it adhere.

4.   Place a large (12- to 14-inch) sauté pan over high heat for several minutes. When hot, add the oil and clarified butter and heat until shimmering. Add the cutlets (redip them in the seasoned flour if they feel gummy) and sauté for 3 to 4 minutes on each side, until golden brown and cooked through. Drain on a paper towel–lined plate. (You may have to cook the chicken in batches. Keep the cooked pieces warm in a 200°F oven while you finish.)

5.   Serve topped with the Country Sausage Gravy (page 282).

# LOVE NOTES

**1** **Poultry seasoning** is a blend of spices that you can find in the spice aisle at any grocery store. It's just as easy to make your own: Combine 2 tablespoons sage, 1 tablespoon thyme, 1 tablespoon marjoram or oregano, 1 teaspoon black pepper, and ¼ teaspoon nutmeg or cloves.

**2** When you look at **melted butter** you see two things: bright yellow oil and creamy white milk solids floating around. Those milk solids burn easily, and that's why whole butter isn't good for frying (the milk solids burn before the butter can get hot enough to fry). But if you remove these solids in a process called clarifying, you'll end up with pure butterfat—all the butter flavor and a much higher smoke point—which is great for frying.

It's a good idea to clarify a lot of butter at a time because it will keep in your refrigerator indefinitely or on your counter in an airtight jar for at least a couple of weeks—as long as you get all the milk solids out. (It becomes hard and solidified when cold, so you'll need to rewarm it to spoon it.)

To clarify butter, gently heat the butter in a small saucepan over medium-low heat until it has completely melted and the foamy solids have floated to the top. Using a ladle, skim the creamy foam from the top and continue to cook over very low heat until all the remaining milk solids fall to the bottom of the pot and start to get slightly golden. The butter should be completely clear and not at all cloudy (as one of my teachers at the Culinary Institute used to say, "so clear that if you dropped a penny in it heads up, you could see Lincoln's whiskers").

Remove the butter from the heat and pour through a cheesecloth-lined strainer (or very fine-mesh strainer) set over a heatproof container (like a stainless-steel bowl). When the butter is cool but still pourable or scoopable, transfer it to an airtight container.

**3** This dish is already very rich and flavorful, so **leaving the sausage** in the gravy would be overwhelming. Strain it out and use it to make extra-hearty biscuits and gravy for breakfast.

# Parisian Chicken

BEFORE I WAS COOKING FOR A LIVING, THIS WAS MY FAVORITE DISH TO MAKE FOR dinner parties. It's elegant and tastes rich and delicious but is really not that hard to make. I've perfected it over the years and love it with rice pilaf and either green beans or asparagus.

4 boneless, skinless chicken breasts (about 1½ pounds)

1¼ teaspoons kosher salt (divided)

¾ teaspoon freshly ground black pepper (divided)

2 tablespoons whole milk

2 large eggs

¼ cup all-purpose flour

2 tablespoons clarified butter (Love Note 2, page 145, Nana's Chicken Fried Chicken) or vegetable oil

½ cup dry white vermouth

2 tablespoons lemon juice (about 1 lemon)

4 tablespoons (½ stick) unsalted butter, cut into small pieces

1 tablespoon chopped fresh Italian (flat-leaf) parsley

1.  If the breasts are very thick, you may slice them in half horizontally to get 2 cutlets per half. Spread a 12-inch piece of plastic wrap on the counter. Place a chicken breast on it, then lay another 12-inch sheet of plastic on top. Using a flat meat mallet or large, heavy skillet, pound the breast to a ¼-inch thickness. Repeat with the remaining breasts.

2.  Lay the cutlets on a rimmed baking sheet and season each on one side with ¼ teaspoon salt and a pinch black pepper.

3.  In a shallow bowl, whisk together the milk and eggs. Place the flour in a plate or shallow dish. Set these near the stove.

4.  Place a large (12- to 14-inch) sauté pan over medium-high heat. When hot, add the clarified butter. Use one hand to dip one cutlet in the flour, dredging it on both sides, and then in the egg mixture. Use the other hand to immediately add it to the pan. Repeat until you have a single layer of chicken. (The cutlets will shrink after a minute, so they might all fit in one pan. If not, you'll have to cook them in batches, adding more butter if necessary.) Cook until lightly golden on the first side, 2 to 3 minutes. Turn over, lower the heat to medium, and continue to cook until the other side is golden and the chicken is cooked through, 2 to 3 minutes.

5.  Transfer the cutlets to a serving plate and tent with foil to keep warm. Return the pan to high heat. Add the vermouth and lemon juice to the sauté pan (to deglaze), stirring to scrape up any browned bits. Season with ¼ teaspoon salt and ¼ teaspoon black pepper. Reduce by half, remove from the heat, and whisk in the butter pieces. Add the parsley. To serve, place the chicken on individual serving plates and pour the sauce over the chicken.

# Chicken Souvlakia

CHICKEN SOUVLAKIA IS AS POPULAR WITH GREEK MOTHERS AS PAPRIKAS IS WITH Hungarian mothers. It's almost always made with lemon and garlic, but the amounts vary from mother to mother. You can easily substitute beef or lamb for the chicken, adding 1 cup dry red wine to the marinade mixture. The recipe for Tzatziki that should accompany this dish came from Sophia Damiani (read her story on page 154), who was introduced to us by Cheryl Hale, a devoted regular who's now like family. (That's what happens when I go into the dining room and say hello to my guests—we see so much of each other, we become family!)

This is a great summer party dish because you can marinate the meat and assemble the skewers ahead of time, and then pop them on the grill for something quick and different.

**FOR THE MARINADE**

¾ cup olive oil

2 tablespoons lemon juice (about 1 lemon)

2 teaspoons chopped fresh Italian (flat-leaf) parsley

¼ teaspoon chopped fresh oregano, or ½ teaspoon dried oregano

1 bay leaf, crumbled

½ medium yellow onion, thinly sliced (½ cup)

**FOR THE SKEWERS**

2 pounds boneless, skinless chicken breasts or thigh meat, cut into 1½-inch cubes

1 large red onion

½ pound whole button mushrooms

2 small bell peppers (try a combination of red, green, yellow, or orange)

½ pint cherry tomatoes

1 tablespoon kosher salt

½ tablespoon freshly ground black pepper

Tzatziki (page 152)

*continued*

**TO MAKE THE MARINADE**

Combine all ingredients in a medium bowl or zip-top bag.

**TO MAKE THE SKEWERS**

1.  Add the chicken cubes to the marinade and marinate in the refrigerator for at least 6 hours, or overnight.

2.  When ready to cook, peel the onion, cut it in half widthwise, and then cut each half into thirds or quarters, depending on how big it is (you want big onion squares); set aside.

3.  Slice the ends off the mushroom stems; set aside.

4.  Cut around the stems of the bell peppers and remove. Cut the peppers in half lengthwise and remove the ribs and seeds. Cut into 1-inch squares; set aside.

5.  Heat the grill to medium-high (you should be able to hold your hand just above the cooking grate for 3 seconds before it gets too uncomfortable). Brush the grill with vegetable oil or spray with nonstick cooking spray (if using spray, take the grate off the fire so you don't end up spraying oil at the flames).

## LOVE NOTE

It's important to **soak wooden skewers** for about ½ hour before using them on the grill so that they don't catch fire. Sometimes foods on a skewer will twirl around on the stick, which makes it hard to cook them properly. An easy trick: Use two skewers instead of one.

6. Remove the chicken from the marinade and place on a plate. Thread the chicken and vegetables on metal skewers or (10-inch) wooden skewers that have been soaked for at least 30 minutes in cold water (Love Note). Alternate the ingredients, adding a piece of chicken after every two or three pieces of vegetable (my preferred arrangement is pepper, chicken, onion, chicken, pepper, mushroom, onion, chicken, pepper, chicken, onion, chicken, pepper, cherry tomato—that way there's an aromatic vegetable next to each piece of chicken for flavor). You should have 8 to 10 skewers (how many skewers you end up with depends on how big you cut the chicken and vegetables). Arrange the skewers in an even layer on a baking sheet and sprinkle generously on all sides with the salt and pepper.

7. Grill for 4 to 5 minutes on each side, or until the vegetables soften and the chicken is no longer pink in the middle (which you can see where the skewer pierces the chicken). Serve with Tzatziki sauce for dipping and rice pilaf.

*continued*

## TZATZIKI

THIS REFRESHING GREEK SAUCE MADE WITH DRAINED YOGURT CAN BE USED AS A condiment for grilled meats and veggies or as a dip with pita or crudités.

½ cucumber (preferably English) peeled, seeded, and diced (about 1 cup; Love Note 1)

1 teaspoon kosher salt

1 clove garlic, finely chopped

2 teaspoons olive oil

1 teaspoon lemon juice (about ¼ lemon)

Pinch freshly ground black pepper

1 teaspoon chopped fresh Italian (flat-leaf) parsley

8 ounces (1 cup) plain Greek whole-milk yogurt (Love Note 2)

1. Place the diced cucumbers in a colander set over a bowl, sprinkle with the salt, and toss (Love Note 3). Refrigerate for 3 hours to drain.

2. Grabbing a handful of cucumbers at a time, squeeze out the liquid and place them in the bowl of a food processor fitted with a metal blade. Pulse a few times to chop up the cucumber, but don't let it turn to mush. Add the garlic, olive oil, lemon juice, pepper, and parsley and pulse once or twice. Pour the yogurt into the bowl and pulse a few times. (Alternatively, chop the squeezed cucumbers a little smaller by hand and place in a medium bowl; add the rest of the ingredients and whisk well to combine.)

3. Serve immediately, or refrigerate for a few hours to let the flavors develop. Tzatziki can be served cold or at room temperature.

*continued*

## LOVE NOTES

**1** **English cucumbers** are long and thin and have very few seeds, which is why they're perfect in this recipe. They're often wrapped in cellophane in the produce section of the supermarket.

**2** **Greek yogurt** is very thick and strained already, which saves you the step of having to strain the yogurt yourself. If you can't find it, you can use plain whole-milk yogurt, but you must drain it overnight (to remove the excess liquid, which would make your sauce watery). Make sure the yogurt doesn't have gelatin or other thickeners, which will keep it from draining properly.

To drain: Set a strainer in a bowl and line it with several layers of cheesecloth or a lint-free kitchen towel. Scoop the yogurt into the cloth and fold the ends

over it. Set in the refrigerator overnight (make sure the strainer sits above the bottom of the bowl, or the yogurt won't drain properly).

**3** **Salting cucumber** accomplishes several things at once: It pulls out excess liquid so the cucumbers won't make the sauce watery, it helps them preserve their crunchy texture after being added to the sauce, and (as long as you don't use too much) the residual salt on the cucumbers seasons the sauce. Kosher or sea salt is best for salting vegetables because the crystals are coarse and have a larger surface area, making them more efficient than table salt at extracting water so that you don't need as much salt.

## Sophia Damiani
{ TZATZIKI }

Anthony Damiani went to Greece in the early 1960s to marry a woman with whom he had corresponded for years. When he finally met the woman, he realized they weren't a good match. But he decided to spend one more day in Greece to see some sights and hired a taxi to take him around. He told his story to the driver, who thought Anthony would be a perfect match for his cousin, Sophia, and took him to her house (this was a Thursday). Anthony spoke no Greek and Sophia spoke no English, but it was love at first sight, and they were married three days later, on Sunday. Anthony headed home to America on Wednesday, and Sophia followed him three months later.

Sophia's grandmother was sad when her granddaughter left for America, but she knew it was destiny. She had promised Sophia's mother, who died shortly after giving birth to Sophia, that her new baby would be OK. She promised her that her daughter would end up in America—a land of promise and plenty—and she did.

# Grilled Salmon with Sesame Noodles

THE RICH, NUTTY, SPICY NOODLES PROVIDE A WONDERFUL BACKDROP FOR THE garlicky, gingery salmon. In fact, the noodles are so good that you can serve them alone as part of a buffet spread (that's why the recipe makes a lot). And if salmon is not available, feel free to substitute firm tofu or boneless, skinless chicken breasts.

**FOR THE SALMON**

¼ cup soy sauce

2 tablespoons seasoned rice vinegar

1 tablespoon vegetable oil

2 tablespoons honey or packed light brown sugar

1 teaspoon grated fresh ginger

2 cloves garlic, minced

1 tablespoon sesame oil

6 (6-ounce) salmon fillets

½ teaspoon freshly ground black pepper

**FOR THE NOODLES**

1 clove garlic

½ cup peanut butter (any kind will do, but natural is best)

¼ cup tahini (or Chinese sesame paste; Love Note 1)

2 tablespoons soy sauce

2 tablespoons seasoned rice vinegar

1 tablespoon honey

2 tablespoons toasted sesame oil (Love Note 2)

1 teaspoon sambal oelek chile paste (Love Note 2, Hummus, page 12)

½ cup brewed and cooled Chinese or English breakfast black tea made with 1 bag

½ teaspoon kosher salt, plus more to cook the pasta

1 pound linguine or lo mein noodles

1 cup blanched peas (optional)

¾ cup thinly sliced scallions, for garnish

1 cup shredded carrots, for garnish

2 tablespoons sesame seeds, toasted (Love Note 3), for garnish

*continued*

**TO PREPARE THE SALMON**

In a bowl or baking dish, whisk together the soy sauce, vinegar, oil, honey or brown sugar, ginger, garlic, and sesame oil. Add the salmon, turn to coat, and set aside to marinate for at least 30 minutes and up to 2 hours in the refrigerator.

**TO MAKE THE NOODLES**

1. Place the garlic in the bowl of a food processor fitted with a metal blade and process until chopped. Add the peanut butter, tahini, soy sauce, vinegar, honey, sesame oil, chile paste, tea, and salt. Process until smooth. Taste and adjust the seasoning, if necessary.

2. Bring a large stockpot of water to a boil. Season generously with salt (it should taste like the sea) and add the linguine or lo mein. Cook, according to the package instructions. Drain and run under cold water until cold. (You can cook the noodles up to 1 day ahead, but be sure not to overcook them because they'll get mushy the longer they sit. Toss the noodles in a little sesame oil after draining to keep them from sticking. Don't combine them with the sauce until just before serving.)

3. Combine the sauce, noodles, and blanched peas (if using) in a large bowl, mixing well with tongs or clean hands. Refrigerate until ready to serve.

**TO COOK AND SERVE**

1.  Heat the grill (Love Note 4) to medium heat (you should be able to hold your hand just above the grate for only 3 seconds) and brush with vegetable oil or spray with nonstick cooking spray (if using spray, take the grate off the fire so you don't end up spraying oil at the flames). Season the salmon with the pepper (it shouldn't need salt because of the soy sauce in the marinade) and place it diagonally on the grill, skin side up, as if it's facing 10 o'clock. After a few minutes, when it starts to look opaque, use a spatula to lift the salmon and turn it clockwise a quarter-turn so that it faces 1 o'clock. This will impart a nice crosshatch pattern on the fish. Cook for another 3 minutes and flip the salmon over, continuing to grill until it is almost opaque throughout and flakes easily, about 8 minutes total (or until it registers 140°F on an instant-read thermometer). Use a spatula to remove it from the heat (leaving the skin behind if you like; Love Note 5).

2.  To serve, pile the noodles high in the center of each plate. Lean the grilled salmon against the pile of noodles. Top each serving with 1 tablespoon scallions and 2 tablespoons carrots, and sprinkle each with a scant teaspoon of toasted sesame seeds.

*continued*

# Wild Salmon vs. Farmed

Pacific Northwesterners worship wild salmon. The fish is part of our economy, identity, and culture. In fact, Native American tribes of the Pacific Northwest still catch salmon in the protected fishing grounds they have used for centuries (though hardly as much as they used to, given the ever-reduced supply). It's no surprise, then, that most of us wouldn't think about cooking with farmed salmon. They aren't locally raised (most come from the East Coast) and there are also serious ecological disadvantages to farmed salmon. Besides, the flavor of wild salmon can't be beat—it's fattier and firmer, and the dark rose color comes naturally, not from dyes. Wild salmon is more expensive, but if you can afford it, it's truly worth buying.

There are a number of problems with farmed salmon. They're fed antibiotics to stave off the diseases that are a constant threat in the overcrowded fish pens. They're also fed red dye so that their color mimics that of wild salmon. But the biggest threat of all comes from the open-net pens, placed in the waters where wild salmon swim. Many farmed salmon escape the pens, spreading disease and parasites to wild species, competing with them for food, and disrupting their efforts to spawn.

In British Columbia, sea lice from infested fish farms have already depressed the wild salmon population in the area—so much so that experts say one species of wild salmon in that area will be extinct by 2010. Until salmon can be farmed sustainably, I highly recommend wild or nothing at all.

# LOVE NOTES

**1** **Chinese sesame paste** is made from roasted unshelled sesame seeds, so it has a stronger flavor than tahini, which is made from raw or lightly toasted shelled sesame seeds. Chinese sesame paste can be hard to find and is more expensive, so feel free to use tahini for this recipe even though it's typically a Middle Eastern ingredient.

**2** **Toasted sesame oil** is brown and has a much stronger, nuttier flavor than untoasted oil. Because it's so flavorful, it should be used sparingly and more like a condiment—drizzled or stirred into finished dishes and sauces.

**3** **To toast sesame seeds,** place in a dry skillet over low heat. Stir occasionally until the seeds become fragrant and turn golden brown. (Watch carefully, because they go from toasted to burnt in seconds.) If your oven is already on for another purpose (but not hotter than 375°F), you can place the seeds on a baking sheet and bake until golden (the time varies according to the temperature of your oven, but 7 minutes at 350°F works well).

**4** **To cook the salmon on the stove,** place a sauté pan over medium-high heat

for several minutes. When hot, add 2 tablespoons of oil and heat until shimmering. Add the salmon skin side up, fleshside down first and cook for about 4 minutes per side (the rule is 10 minutes per inch of thickness at the thickest part of the fillet), until the fish is almost opaque and flakes easily.

**5** To prevent fish from **sticking to the grill,** first make sure the grate is clean by using a wire brush to scrape off any stuck-on food while the grate is hot. Next, oil the grate using a paper towel or clean rag doused in vegetable oil. Grasp the towel with tongs so you don't burn yourself while rubbing it on the surface of the grate. Or spray the grate with nonstick cooking spray, but remove the grate first so that you're not spraying the oil at the flames. Coat the fish with oil, and once it's on the grill, don't move it until it has seared.

If the fish still sticks when it's cooking on the skin side, you can use the skin to your advantage (this is also a handy way to remove the skin): Slip a spatula between the skin and the flesh, leaving the skin behind, and turn the fish. When the grill is cool, scrub the cooking rack to remove any leftover skin.

# Macadamia Nut–Crusted Red Snapper with Mango Salsa & Coconut Rice

IT'S AMAZING HOW THE BRIGHTNESS OF MANGO AND THE HEAT OF CHILES, COMBINED with the natural richness of coconut milk and macadamia nuts, can transform something as simple as red snapper fillets into a showstopping warm-weather dinner.

**FOR THE MANGO SALSA**

1 large mango, peeled, seeded, and cut into ¼-inch dice (about 1 cup)

½ small red onion, finely chopped (about ½ cup)

¼ red bell pepper, ribs and seeds removed, finely chopped (¼ cup)

2 tablespoons finely chopped fresh basil (about 2 sprigs)

½ jalapeño pepper, minced (1 tablespoon, or to taste; remove the ribs and seeds for less heat)

¼ teaspoon kosher salt

⅛ teaspoon freshly ground black pepper

1 tablespoon lime juice (about ½ lime)

1 tablespoon orange juice

**FOR THE MACADAMIA NUT CRUST**

¼ cup all-purpose flour

2 large eggs

¾ cup macadamia nuts, coarsely chopped

¾ cup panko (Japanese bread crumbs; Love Note 2, page 177, $15,000 Crab Cakes with Creole Mustard Sauce)

4 (6-ounce) red snapper or tilapia fillets, bones removed (about 1½ pounds)

1 teaspoon kosher salt (divided)

½ teaspoon freshly ground black pepper (divided)

⅓ cup vegetable oil

Coconut Rice (page 217)

Chive Oil (page 163; optional)

**TO MAKE THE SALSA**

In a medium bowl, combine all ingredients. Set aside or refrigerate for up to 24 hours.

**TO MAKE THE CRUST**

1. Place the flour on a shallow plate. Beat the eggs in a wide, shallow bowl. In another wide, shallow bowl, combine the macadamia nuts and panko. *continued*

Place an empty plate for the breaded fillets next to the bowl with the nut and panko mixture.

2. Season one side of each fillet with ¼ teaspoon salt and a pinch of pepper. With your dominant, or working, hand, dredge a fillet in the flour on both sides, shaking off the excess. Transfer it to your other hand and dip both sides in the egg mixture (keeping one hand dedicated to the egg step will keep your dominant hand from getting gummy), allow the excess to drip off, and then drop it into the nut-panko mixture. Use your dominant hand to scoop the mixture on the top and sides, gently pressing to help it adhere, and then pick it up and shake off the excess. Set on the empty plate and repeat with the remaining fillets. If you have time, place the breaded fillets in the refrigerator for 30 to 60 minutes to dry out the coating and help it adhere.

3. Place a large (12- to 14-inch) sauté pan over medium-high heat for several minutes. When hot, add the oil and heat until shimmering. Add the fish and cook until golden, 3 to 4 minutes. (You may have to sauté the fillets in batches, adding more oil as needed.) Lower the heat and use a spatula (preferably a fish spatula, Love Note 2, page 166, Pan-Seared Cod Puttanesca) to turn the fish over and continue cooking until the other side is golden brown and the fish is cooked through, 6 to 7 minutes more. (Don't try to flip the fish before one side is golden or it will stick

## LOVE NOTE

Fish and meats coated in breadcrumbs are usually dipped in flour and egg first because the flour helps the egg adhere, and the egg helps the breadcrumbs adhere—and an even coating of crispy breadcrumbs is the goal. If you have the time, it's a good idea to let anything breaded sit in the fridge for 30 to 60 minutes to help the coating adhere even more.

to the pan and possibly break up. If there is any difficulty at all, the fish is not ready to be turned. Wait a few more minutes and try again.)

4. Remove the fish from the pan and place on paper towels to drain.

**TO SERVE**
Place a mound of Coconut Rice on the upper third of the plate, lean a piece of fish on the rice, and top the center of the fish with Mango Salsa. Drizzle the plate with a ribbon of Chive Oil for color (either use a squeeze bottle or let it drip off the end of a spoon). Serve hot.

## CHIVE OIL                                          MAKES ABOUT ½ CUP

ALTHOUGH THIS MAKES A BIT MORE THAN YOU NEED FOR THE SNAPPER RECIPE, IT will keep in the refrigerator and can be used on mashed potatoes, in marinades, or as a salad dressing.

| | |
|---|---|
| 1 large bunch fresh chives or cilantro | ¼ teaspoon kosher salt |
| ½ cup olive oil | ⅛ teaspoon freshly ground black pepper |

Place the chives or cilantro in a blender, pushing the leaves down into the blade. (Make sure the blender jar is removed from the base, just in case you accidentally turn it on!) Place the blender jar on the base, and then turn the blender on and drizzle the olive oil in a slow, steady stream through the small hole in the lid. If necessary, add a little more oil to help the herbs become fully puréed. Season with the salt and pepper, place in a squeeze bottle, and keep at room temperature if using within 2 hours. Otherwise, store, covered, in an airtight container in the refrigerator for up to 5 days. Because the olive oil congeals, bring it to room temperature before using.

# Pan-Seared Cod Puttanesca

PUTTANESCA SAUCES ARE BOLD, BRASH, AND IRRESISTIBLE. PERHAPS THAT'S WHERE the sauce got its name, which is derived from the Italian word for—ahem—ladies of pleasure. Another theory: It's named after these ladies because they'd often have to put dinner together quickly from what was in their kitchen cabinets.

The quality of the sauce is best with fresh, seasonal tomatoes and elegant olives such as Niçoise, oil-cured Moroccan, or Kalamata, but it's almost as good with any kind of tomato and California black olives. You can also add red pepper flakes and anchovies for an even more robust flavor.

4 (6-ounce) red snapper or cod fillets (about 1½ pounds)

1½ teaspoons kosher salt (divided)

¼ teaspoon freshly ground black pepper (divided)

¼ cup all-purpose flour

3 tablespoons olive oil

6 cloves garlic, finely chopped (about 3 tablespoons)

2 medium tomatoes, diced (1½ cups), or 1 (15-ounce) can whole tomatoes, diced

⅓ cup pitted black olives, preferably Niçoise

2 tablespoons capers, rinsed and drained

¼ cup dry white wine, such as Chardonnay or Pinot Grigio (Love Note 1, page 122, Chicken Cacciatore)

1 tablespoon chopped fresh Italian (flat-leaf) parsley

2 tablespoons unsalted butter, cut into pieces

Cooked orzo, for serving

Sautéed spinach, for serving

1. Heat the oven to 200°F. Place the fish on a baking sheet and season the top of each fillet with ¼ teaspoon salt and a pinch of pepper.

2. Place the flour in a shallow bowl or plate. Dip the fish in the flour on both sides and return it to the baking sheet until ready to cook.

*continued*

3. Meanwhile, place a large (12- to 14-inch) sauté pan over medium-high heat for several minutes. When hot, add the oil and heat until shimmering. Add the fish, presentation side down (Love Note 1). Cook until golden on one side, about 3 minutes. (You may have to cook the fish in two batches, adding more oil if necessary.) Flip the fillets over (Love Note 2) and continue to cook until golden, another 3 to 4 minutes. Place the fish on a heatproof serving platter and keep warm in the oven.

4. Return the pan to medium-high heat. Add the garlic and sauté until fragrant, stirring once or twice (about 1 minute). Add the tomatoes, season with the remaining $^1/_2$ teaspoon salt and $^1/_8$ teaspoon black pepper, and cook for 2 minutes, stirring occasionally. Add the olives, capers, white wine, and parsley. Increase the heat to high and simmer the sauce until slightly reduced, about 5 minutes.

5. Remove the pan from the heat and whisk in the butter. Remove the fish from oven, pour the tomato mixture on top, and serve with buttered orzo and sautéed spinach.

## LOVE NOTES

**1. All fish have a prettier side,** which should be served facing up. Fish should be cooked on the presentation side first, then turned skin side down to finish things off. Then, when you're ready to serve, you don't have to flip the fish again; simply transfer it to a plate.

**2. A fish spatula is long, thin, and very flexible,** making it perfect for maneuvering delicate fish fillets in a pan without damaging them.

# Mama's Cioppino

WHEN PLANNING THE MENU FOR MAMA MIA TRATTORIA, I WANTED TO INCLUDE a seafood dish that was something a mother might typically make. This easy, tomato-based seafood stew, bubbling with so many vibrant flavors, was just the ticket.

Although its origins are hazy, cioppino is usually credited to San Francisco fishermen at the turn of the century. They'd each throw a bit of their day's catch into a communal pot. The result was so good that it wasn't long before cioppino found its way into mama's soup pot—and, now, onto restaurant menus.

There's no hard and fast rule about what kinds of fish and seafood you can put in it—just include what you and your family enjoy. If you like calamari, add some. Don't like shrimp? Leave them out. If you have kids, make sure you add at least a few clams in their shells. Kids love to scoop out the clams and use the shells as castanets.

¼ cup olive oil

2 medium cloves garlic, chopped (2 teaspoons)

1 teaspoon crushed red pepper flakes

4 cups (1 quart) Mama Mia Trattoria's Pomodoro Sauce (page 170) or store-bought tomato-basil pasta sauce

1½ cups Fish Stock (page 86) or bottled clam juice

2 tablespoons finely chopped fresh Italian (flat-leaf) parsley

¼ teaspoon dried thyme

¼ teaspoon dried basil

16 littleneck or other clams, soaked (about 1½ pounds; Love Note 1, page 76, Manhattan Clam Chowder)

16 mussels, scrubbed clean and debearded (about 10 ounces; Love Note)

12 large (size 21–30) shrimp, peeled and deveined (Love Note 3, page 26, Spicy Shrimp Rémoulade)

1 pound non-oily fish fillets (such as cod, red snapper, or flounder), cut into finger-size strips or chunks

½ cup dry white wine, such as Chardonnay, Pinot Grigio, or Sauvignon Blanc (Love Note 1, page 122, Chicken Cacciatore)

*continued*

| 1 teaspoon kosher salt (divided) | 3 cups washed spinach leaves (about 4 ounces) |
| ½ teaspoon freshly ground black pepper (divided) | Crostini, (page 172) for garnish |

1. Place a large (12- to 14-inch) skillet over medium-high heat for several minutes. When hot, add the olive oil, garlic, and crushed red pepper flakes and cook just until the garlic softens slightly, 1 minute, but do not let it brown (or it will be bitter).

2. Stir in the pomodoro sauce, stock, parsley, thyme, and basil. Bring to a boil over high heat, reduce to medium-high, and add the clams and mussels. Cover and cook until the shells open, 5 to 7 minutes. (Try not to lift the cover until a few minutes have passed or you'll let all the precious steam out, which is what cooks the shellfish.) Discard any shellfish that have not opened after 7 minutes; they could be spoiled.

3. Add the shrimp, fish, wine, and ½ teaspoon of the salt and ¼ teaspoon of the pepper. Cover and simmer for 5 to 6 minutes more, or just until all the seafood is cooked through. (The shrimp and fish will be opaque rather than translucent.) Stir in the spinach and season with the remaining ½ teaspoon salt and ¼ teaspoon pepper.

4. Ladle the fish and broth into wide, flat soup bowls. Place 2 crostini, crossed, on one side of each bowl, and serve.

*continued*

**Mussels** are primarily farm-raised and so don't need to be soaked, but they do need to be scrubbed of any barnacles or other bits of marine life and debearded.

After rinsing, look for those with a "beard" protruding from the shell. (This is the bristly byssus threads the mussels use to cling to rocks.) Just grab it and pull it out, but only do this a few minutes before cooking or they will die and spoil. Don't worry if your mussels don't seem to have a beard. Some fishmongers clip these threads but don't remove them entirely. The mussels stay alive, and you don't have to do any prep work.

However, it's common to find at least one dead mussel in the bunch. Don't use any mussels that are open and don't close when you tap the shell.

## MAMA MIA TRATTORIA'S POMODORO SAUCE       MAKES ABOUT 4 QUARTS

THIS IS IT . . . OUR SECRET TOMATO SAUCE WE SERVE WITH MANY DISHES AT MAMA Mia Trattoria. It's bright, naturally slightly sweet, and perfect with a bowlful of pasta or as an ingredient in other dishes. Take the time to sauté the onions and garlic slowly so they get soft and flavorful, but not brown, and use the best tomatoes you can afford. Keep some sauce in the freezer to have on hand for a quick meal in a pinch.

¼ cup olive oil

2 medium yellow onions, finely chopped (about 2¼ cups)

4 large cloves garlic, minced (about 2 tablespoons)

5 (28-ounce) cans whole tomatoes in purée

½ bunch fresh basil (6 to 8 sprigs), stems removed and leaves coarsely chopped

1 tablespoon kosher salt

2 teaspoons freshly ground black pepper

1. Heat a large (6- to 8-quart) saucepan over medium-high heat. When hot, add the olive oil and the onions at the same time. Sauté until very soft, about 12 minutes.

2. Add the garlic and sauté until fragrant, 1 to 2 minutes, but do not let it brown (turn down the heat if you see browning).

3. Add the tomatoes and bring to a boil over high heat, stirring occasionally. Lower the heat to a simmer and cook, uncovered, for 20 minutes. Add the basil and cook for 5 minutes more.

4. Remove the pan from the heat and season with the salt and pepper. Using an immersion blender, food processor, or regular blender, purée until mostly smooth but still chunky. (If you use a blender or food processor, steam pressure can cause the sauce to spray out of the appliance. So purée the sauce in small batches, crack the lid on blenders to let some steam escape, make sure to cover the lid with a kitchen towel, and hold your hand on it to keep it down.)

*continued*

## CROSTINI

THESE LITTLE TOASTS ARE A WONDERFUL GARNISH IN SOUPS AND STEWS AS WELL as a sturdy vehicle for all sorts of toppings. I prefer brushing the slices of baguette with olive oil *before* toasting instead of after because it prevents the bread from drying out too much while they crisp in the oven. A sprinkle of salt ensures every bite will be delicious, but you can also rub the slices with garlic like you would for bruschetta. Cut a garlic clove in half and rub the cut side on the bread. Just two or three swipes will do.

½ baguette, cut into ¼-inch-thick slices (Love Note)

2 tablespoons olive oil

1½ teaspoons kosher salt

1. Heat the oven to 375°F. Arrange the bread slices ½ inch apart in a single layer on a rimmed baking sheet. (You want the hot air to circulate around each piece of bread, otherwise you may have some areas that don't crisp up.) Brush the top of each slice with olive oil and sprinkle lightly with salt.

2. Bake the crostini for 7 to 8 minutes, or until they feel crisped on top and the edges are beginning to brown. (You may want to rotate the sheet from front to back halfway through to ensure even crisping.) Let cool. Crostini can be made 1 day ahead and stored in an airtight container.

## LOVE NOTE

**Cut the slices a little thicker** if you want to serve a chunky, hearty topping on the crostini. Cook them at 450°F for 5 minutes to ensure the thicker slices crisp up quickly before the edges become too hard to bite.

# $15,000 Crab Cakes with Creole Mustard Sauce

OUT OF THE HUNDREDS OF RECIPES CHEFS SHARED WITH ME WHILE I WAS A student at the Culinary Institute of America, I use only two—and this is one of them. Since I paid $30,000 for my tuition (compared to today's cost, that's a bargain!), I figure this recipe cost me about $15,000, hence the name.

Crisp on the outside, and moist and rich on the inside, these crab cakes are exceptional—especially with the tart mustard sauce. We serve these with coleslaw and matchstick potatoes because the flavors work great together. If you can't find Dungeness crab, use whatever crab is available in your neck of the woods.

½ pound cod fillets (Love Note 1)

¼ teaspoon kosher salt

⅛ teaspoon freshly ground black pepper

2 teaspoons unsalted butter

2 tablespoons finely chopped celery

¼ pound bacon, finely diced (about 6 strips; chill for 10 minutes in the freezer to make it easier to cut)

¼ pound Ritz® crackers (35 crackers, 1 sleeve)

1 pound Dungeness or blue crab meat

2 scallions, (white and green parts), finely chopped (about ¼ cup)

¾ cup mayonnaise

½ tablespoon Dijon mustard

½ tablespoon Worcestershire sauce

½ teaspoon Tabasco sauce

½ cup all-purpose flour

2 large eggs, beaten

1½ cups panko (Japanese breadcrumbs; Love Note 2)

½ cup vegetable oil, or more if needed (oil should come up to a third the height of the crab cakes in the pan)

Creole Mustard Sauce (page 176)

*continued*

1. Heat the oven to 350°F. Lightly oil a baking pan or spray with nonstick cooking spray. Place the cod on the pan and season with the salt and pepper. Bake until cooked through, 10 to 15 minutes. Remove from the oven and set aside to cool. When cool enough to handle, flake the fish into a large bowl and remove any bones. Set aside.

2. Place a small sauté pan over medium-high heat for several minutes. When hot, add the butter and celery. Sauté the celery until soft, about 5 minutes, lowering the heat if necessary to prevent any browning. Transfer to a plate and let cool, and then place in the bowl with the cod.

3. Return the sauté pan to medium-high heat, add the bacon, and cook until crispy and the fat has rendered, reducing the heat slightly if the bacon starts to burn, about 8 minutes. Transfer the bacon to a paper towel–lined plate; set aside.

4. Place the crackers in a food processor fitted with a metal blade and pulse to grind into fine crumbs (or place them in a zip-top bag and crush with a meat mallet or rolling pin). Transfer to the bowl with the cod. Pick through the crab to remove any bits of shell or cartilage and then add half of it to the cod (try to reserve any big chunks for folding in at the end). Add the scallions, cooked bacon, mayonnaise, mustard, Worcestershire, and Tabasco. Mix gently but thoroughly with your hands (make sure they're clean!). Fold in the remaining crab.

5. Using a medium (2-ounce) ice cream scoop or a ¼-cup dry measuring cup, scoop out the crab mixture, shape into a ball, and then flatten into a patty. Place the patty on a large plate or baking sheet and repeat with the remaining mixture.

6. Place the flour on a large plate. Beat the eggs in a shallow bowl. Place the panko on another large plate. Set the dishes on the counter in a row in that order.

*continued*

7. With your dominant, or working, hand, dredge a patty in the flour on both sides, shaking off the excess. Transfer the patty to your other hand and dip both sides in the eggs (keeping one hand dedicated to the egg step will keep your working hand from getting gummy), allow the excess to drip off, and then drop it in the plate of panko. Use your dominant hand to scoop crumbs on top and around, pat them to help them adhere, pick up the patty, and shake off the excess. Set the patty back on the baking sheet and repeat with the remaining patties. If you have time, place the breaded crab cakes in the refrigerator for about an hour to dry out the coating and help it adhere.

8. Heat the vegetable oil in a large (12- to 14-inch) sauté pan (Love Note 3). Place a paper towel–lined plate and a cooling rack next to the stove. When the oil is sizzling hot (375°F on a deep-fry thermometer, or if you don't have one, drop a small piece of bread in and see if it immediately starts sizzling), add the crab cakes in a single layer and fry on each side until golden brown, 3 to 4 minutes per side. Remove from the pan as they finish cooking, blot dry on the paper towels, and then transfer to the rack so the crust doesn't get soggy.

9. Serve with Creole Mustard Sauce drizzled on top.

### CREOLE MUSTARD SAUCE

MAKES ABOUT ¾ CUP

½ cup mayonnaise

¼ cup Dijon mustard

2 tablespoons plus 2 teaspoons
coarse-grain mustard

1 teaspoon granulated sugar

1½ teaspoons cider vinegar

Place all ingredients in a mixing bowl, whisk together, and set aside until ready to serve. This can be put in a squeeze bottle for drizzling on crab cakes. Leftovers can be used on sandwiches. Place in an airtight container and refrigerate for several weeks.

# LOVE NOTES

**1** **Crab is expensive,** so adding cod allows you to use less crab and save some money. Cod is much cheaper and has a nice flavor.

**2** **Panko** are Japanese-style breadcrumbs that are flakier and lighter than traditional breadcrumbs, making them ideal for breading when you want a crispy crust.

**3** You can **reuse frying oil,** but follow these rules: Let it cool completely before handling and strain it through a fine-mesh strainer lined with cheesecloth (or a coffee filter if the oil is particularly dirty) to remove any bits of food. (Oil used to fry seafood or fish will retain a slightly fishy flavor, so save it for another fish fry.) Store it in an air-tight container in a cool, dark place (like the refrigerator, if there's room). It will keep for several months.

Although oil is safe to reuse several times, it will start to break down at some point. If it smells rancid, starts to smoke before it reaches frying temperature (375°F), or looks dark and thicker than normal, it's time to throw it away and start fresh.

When it's time to toss it, either throw it in the trash (never pour it down the drain—it can clog your pipes and also causes problems for septic systems and water treatment plants) or find a recycling center. With the popularity of biodiesel, there are more places accepting cooking oil from households (not just restaurants) to turn into fuel.

# Stuffed Cabbage

THERE MUST BE A HUNDRED VERSIONS OF STUFFED CABBAGE, AND WE'VE OFFERED many of them over the years at Mother's. They're a bit fussy to make—you have to blanch the leaves, make the stuffing, and then roll each one up—but the final dish is the epitome of Mother Food. Put some of the cabbage rolls in the freezer and reheat them for lunch or dinner (Love Note).

This version is from Laurie Rogoway, who was featured as a Mother of the Month. I like her stuffed cabbage because the onions, ketchup, and sugar add a little sweetness, while the lemon juice provides a tart note. It all makes the final dish a bit more complex and flavorful.

1 large head green cabbage

**FOR THE FILLING**

½ cup white rice

1 cup water

2½ teaspoons kosher salt (divided)

¼ cup vegetable oil

2 large yellow onions, finely chopped (3 cups)

2 large eggs

2 pounds 80 percent lean ground beef

½ teaspoon freshly ground black pepper

**FOR THE SAUCE**

1 (11.5-ounce) can tomato juice

1 (10.75-ounce) can condensed tomato soup

10 ounces water (just fill up the tomato soup can to measure)

1¾ cups ketchup

1 cup packed light brown sugar

⅓ cup lemon juice (about 2 lemons)

1 teaspoon kosher salt

½ teaspoon freshly ground black pepper

**TO PREPARE THE CABBAGE**

Bring a large pot of water to a boil. Salt it generously (it should taste like the sea). Meanwhile, remove any damaged leaves from the cabbage and set aside. Turn the head upside down and use a sharp knife to cut around the core and remove it. Place the whole head in the boiling water until the outer leaves begin to wilt and come off, about 1 minute. Use tongs or a spider to remove the head from the water and carefully pull off the wilted leaves. (Try not to rip or damage them, because they'll be used as wrappers. If a leaf gets stuck to the core, use a paring knife to loosen it.) Set the leaves on a baking sheet lined with clean kitchen towels or paper towels. Return the cabbage head to the hot water and repeat the process until you have 20 leaves (this should take 15 minutes in all). Set the rest of the cabbage aside.

**TO MAKE THE FILLING**

1. Place the rice, water, and ½ teaspoon of the salt in a medium saucepan. Cover, bring to a boil over high heat (watch carefully so you can turn the heat down immediately when it starts to boil, otherwise it'll boil over), give a quick stir, cover, and immediately reduce the heat to medium-low. Simmer, covered (don't peek!), until the water is absorbed, 12 to 15 minutes. Remove from the heat and let stand, covered, for 5 minutes (this ensures the grains end up evenly cooked). Then fluff with a fork (to gently separate the grains and keep them from sticking together when scooped) and set aside to cool.

2. Meanwhile, place a large (12- to 14-inch) sauté pan over medium-high heat for several minutes. When hot, add the oil and onions at the same time. Cook, stirring occasionally, until soft and lightly browned, about 12 minutes. Set aside and let cool.

3. Crack the eggs into a large mixing bowl and beat lightly with a fork. Add the rice, cooled onions, ground beef, the remaining 2 teaspoons salt, and the pepper. Gently stir the mixture until well combined.

**TO FORM THE ROLLS**

1. Heat the oven to 350°F. Using a knife, finely shred some of the cabbage that hasn't been used to form the rolls and arrange on the bottom of an 11x17-inch roasting pan (this helps to keep the rolls from burning during cooking). *continued*

2. Place a blanched leaf on the work surface. Add ¼ cup of the filling in the center of the leaf nearest the stem end. Fold the sides of the leaf over, then roll up like a jellyroll. Repeat until all the filling is used. (If some of the leaves have tough middle veins, be sure to cut them out and place the filling a little higher on the leaf, because the veins don't get soft enough during cooking.)

3. Place the cabbage rolls, seam side down, in rows on top of the shredded cabbage (they should fit snugly, in a single layer, but not be wedged in too tight or they won't cook evenly and the sauce won't be able to get in between them).

**TO MAKE THE SAUCE**

In a medium (4- to 6-quart) saucepan, whisk together all of the ingredients. Heat over medium-high heat until simmering.

**TO BAKE THE ROLLS**

1. Pour the hot sauce over the rolls, making sure there is enough liquid to almost cover them (you may need to add more water or tomato juice). Cover the pan with

**LOVE NOTE**

**Cabbage rolls freeze** and reheat very well. You can freeze a pan of them before baking. Or bake them first, but cut down on the cooking time by about 15 minutes so the cabbage doesn't overcook and fall apart when reheated. Allow the pan to defrost in the refrigerator overnight, and skip the step where the sauce is heated on the stove. Just pop the covered pan into a 400°F oven and cook until the already baked rolls are heated through, at least 1 hour. Unbaked rolls will need 2 hours to cook.

foil and place in the oven for $1\frac{1}{2}$ hours. Remove the foil and bake for an additional 30 minutes, or until cabbage is soft and the meat is cooked through.

2. Cool slightly in the pan before handling. Lift the rolls out with tongs and serve alone or with Mother's Smashers (page 212). The cabbage rolls can be served hot or at room temperature.

## VARIATION: Stuffed Peppers

You can use the filling and sauce to make stuffed peppers instead of stuffed cabbage (but you'll only need half as much sauce, so cut that part of the recipe in half). Peppers have a bit more presence on the plate, and they're easier to stuff, too. Since you can pack more filling into a pepper, the recipe makes enough for 6 peppers.

1. Cut off the top $\frac{1}{2}$ inch of 6 medium to large red, green, yellow, or orange bell peppers (just cut enough to take off the stem and rounded shoulders), scoop out the seeds and membranes with a metal spoon, and rinse.

2. Fill each pepper with the meat and rice mixture. Stand them up in a small oven-proof Dutch oven just big enough to fit all the peppers (you want them to be a little snug so they help prop each other up—a 12-inch pan with 4-inch sides works great). Add sauce to the pot and bring to a boil over medium-high heat. Cover, lower the heat to a simmer, and cook for 20 minutes.

3. Meanwhile, heat the oven to 350°F. After simmering, stir the sauce, cover, place the pot in the oven, and bake for 1 to $1\frac{1}{2}$ hours, or until the peppers are very soft and the filling is cooked through.

*continued*

## Laurie Rogoway
### { STUFFED CABBAGE }

Laurie Rogoway was born in a small town (population 3,000) in the center of Canada in 1944. While her father was Canadian, most of her other family members had emigrated from Russia. Her childhood home was always filled with guests and people coming to eat her mother's cooking. Due to their remote location, her mother made everything from scratch, and she loved doing it. There was always a crowd around the family table, particularly on Friday nights.

Laurie was a quick learner—she skipped two grades and was then sent to school in Winnipeg so that she could be more intellectually challenged. She began college at only 16, and when she finished, she went to Portland, Oregon, to visit some relatives. Two weeks later she was engaged to Bert, and they are still married after 39 years. They raised three children and now have four grandchildren.

Laurie loves to cook and entertain and fondly remembers when her grandfather showed her how to make gefilte fish. The hardest part was trying to figure out how much a "handful" and a "pinch" equaled, and she would follow him around so she could empty the contents of his hands and pinched fingers into measuring devices so she'd have an actual recipe by the time the lesson was through.

# Jan's Stuffed Eggplant

JAN BOCUZZI IS ONE OF MY FAVORITE FORMER MOTHERS OF THE MONTH. SHE'S an excellent cook and a great friend. Her recipe for eggplants stuffed with garlic, Parmesan, and breadcrumbs makes a perfect vegetarian supper when paired with a crisp green salad. It's also a great way to use up stale bread. I like to serve this with pasta tossed with pomodoro sauce.

4 large eggplants (about 1 pound each)

2 tablespoons kosher salt (divided)

1 (8-ounce) baguette

1 cup vegetable oil

4 large cloves garlic, chopped (2 tablespoons, divided)

5 large eggs, lightly beaten

1½ cups grated Parmesan cheese

1 tablespoon chopped fresh Italian (flat-leaf) parsley

2 cups shredded mozzarella cheese (divided)

½ teaspoon freshly ground black pepper

3 cups Mama Mia Trattoria's Pomodoro Sauce (page 170; divided)

1. Heat the oven to 350°F. Cut off the stem and bottom of the eggplants, and then cut them in half widthwise. Cut each half in half again from top to bottom so you have quarters (they will be almost square-shaped). Using a paring knife, cut as much flesh out of the skins as possible while still leaving the skins intact. (Make sure you don't cut the skin and make sure to leave a tiny bit of eggplant still on, about ⅛ inch.)

2. Place the eggplant skins on a baking sheet. Sprinkle the skins with 2 teaspoons salt and set aside for 20 minutes (the salt helps get out the bitterness and excess moisture).

*continued*

3. Dice the eggplant flesh into ¼-inch cubes, and place in a colander or sieve set over a bowl. Sprinkle with 1 tablespoon salt, mix together, and set aside for 20 minutes.

4. Break up the French bread into 2- to 3-inch chunks, place in a large bowl, and cover with cold water. Let soak for a few minutes to soften. Remove and discard as much crust as possible. Grab a handful of bread, squeeze out as much water as you can, and place it in another large bowl. Repeat with the remaining bread. Break up the soaked bread into smaller pieces (no bigger than ½ inch) and set aside.

5. Place a large (12- to 14-inch) sauté pan over high heat for several minutes. When hot, add the oil and heat until shimmering. Add the eggplant skins and sauté over high heat, turning now and then until just limp and pliable, about 3 minutes (you may have to do this in batches). Transfer to a paper towel–lined plate to drain.

6. Grab handfuls of the diced eggplant and squeeze out as much moisture as possible (and therefore any bitterness and extra salt), and transfer to another bowl.

7. Drain half the oil out of the sauté pan, reserving the drained oil. Place the pan over medium-high heat. When the remaining oil is hot, add half the squeezed eggplant and sauté until golden, about 5 minutes, stirring now and then. Add half the garlic and cook for another 2 to 3 minutes. Remove to a baking sheet to cool, and repeat with the other half of the eggplant and garlic, adding 3 tablespoons of the oil used to cook the skins before adding more eggplant.

8. Once cooled, add the sautéed eggplant to the bread pieces in the mixing bowl.

9. Add the beaten eggs, Parmesan, parsley, and 1 cup of the mozzarella to the bowl with the eggplant and bread. Mix well. Season with the remaining 1 teaspoon salt and the pepper.

*continued*

10. Cover the bottom of a 9x13x2-inch baking dish with ½ cup of pomodoro sauce. Cup one of the eggplant skins in one hand and fill it with about ⅓ cup of the stuffing. (The amount depends on the size of the eggplant, but it should be enough filling so they're three-quarters full and look like a stuffed pasta shell. Try to pack in the filling so it doesn't come out.) Repeat with the remaining skins, placing them side by side in the pan after they are filled (they should prop each other up but shouldn't be crammed together).

11. Pour the remaining pomodoro sauce over the stuffed eggplants, cover the pan with foil, and bake for 30 minutes. Remove the foil, sprinkle the eggplants with the rest of the mozzarella, and continue to bake until the sauce is bubbly, the mozzarella is lightly browned, and the interior of the eggplant is hot, 15 to 20 minutes.

## Jan Bocuzzi

{ JAN'S STUFFED EGGPLANT }

Crescenza (we all know her as "Jan") is from a family of eight; she was born in the small town of Conversano outside Bari, Italy, in 1945. Jan met her husband, Tony, when she was 15, and they were married when she was 20.

While life was good in the old country, Tony and Jan had four daughters and were concerned at the prospect of marrying them all off. (In some regions of Italy, parents of daughters must not only pay for the wedding, but they also traditionally buy the bride and groom their bedroom furniture and pay for many of the new couple's expenses.) So when Jan's brother, who had moved to Portland, Oregon, suggested they move there, Jan and Tony decided to give it a try. This was no easy decision—they had no money, spoke not a word of English, and their youngest daughter was only a year old. But in 1977, they borrowed money from their family and arrived in America with nothing but a few bags and their four children.

It was a struggle at first, and it took them four months to get a job where English wasn't a necessity. Jan's brother helped them find jobs at an upholstery house, where she and Tony worked together for the next 20 years. Now Jan and Tony have their own upholstery business (T. J. Upholstery) and are responsible for the lovely cushions and pillows at Mother's Bistro.

Everybody loves to eat at Jan and Tony's house. They make their own ricotta and other cheeses, and relatives come from far and wide when it's a cheese-making weekend. Family and friends gather around the kitchen table almost nightly, and everyone swears that nobody cooks like Jan.

# Grandma Mary's Meatballs and Sunday Gravy

MY SIGNIFICANT OTHER, ROB, LIVED MOST OF HIS CHILDHOOD NOT ONLY WITH HIS parents and siblings, but also with his Italian grandmother Mary and grandfather George. Grandma was an excellent cook from Sicily and cooked for the whole family most of the time.

Every Sunday she would make this sauce, and its alluring aroma tormented everyone throughout the day. They'd walk by the pot on the stove, dip in a piece of bread, and pop it in their mouths before anyone might catch them. "Roberto! Whaddya doin'? Wait for the dinna!" Grandma Mary would shout. To this day, Rob and his siblings drool every time they even think of their grandma's meatballs simmering in the sauce on the stove.

When I first opened Mama Mia Trattoria, Rob's sisters, Gigi and Carol, would come downtown twice a week and make their grandmother Mary's meatballs for the restaurant. The seasoned kitchen crew would chuckle as the two 60-plus-year-old sisters tied aprons on so they wouldn't get dirty, and kibitzed and amused themselves the entire time they were rolling the meatballs and frying them in the pan. Eventually they grew tired of schlepping downtown, so we took on the meatball-making ourselves.

**FOR THE MEATBALLS (MAKES 18)**

4 large eggs

2 pounds 80 percent lean ground beef (Love Note 1)

4 large cloves garlic, chopped (2 tablespoons)

¼ cup coarsely chopped fresh Italian (flat-leaf) parsley

⅓ heaping cup dry breadcrumbs

⅔ cup grated locatelli or pecorino romano cheese

2 teaspoons kosher salt

1 teaspoon freshly ground black pepper

¾ cup water (Love Note 2)

¼ cup olive oil

**FOR THE GRAVY**

1 pound 3-inch-long mild Italian sausages (or cut them so they are close to that size)

2½ pounds boneless pork shoulder (Boston butt), cut into large (5- by 3-inch) pieces

3 teaspoons kosher salt (divided)

3 teaspoons freshly ground black pepper (divided)

6 medium yellow onions, chopped (6 cups)

¼ cup olive oil

12 large cloves garlic, finely chopped (6 tablespoons)

8 cups (2 quarts) water

2 (28-ounce) cans tomato purée, preferably San Marzano (Love Note 3)

5 (6-ounce) cans tomato paste

2 ribs celery, broken in half

2 bay leaves

4 whole cloves

1 cinnamon stick

2 teaspoons granulated sugar

¼ cup chopped fresh Italian (flat-leaf) parsley

### FOR SERVING

2 pounds pasta (preferably De Cecco® or Barilla®), cooked according to package directions (Love Note 4)

**TO MAKE THE MEATBALLS**

1. In a large mixing bowl, beat the eggs. Add the ground beef, garlic, parsley, breadcrumbs, cheese, salt, and pepper. Mix well with your hands to combine.

2. Continue working the mixture with your hands while gradually adding the water.

3. Scoop out the meat in ¼-cup portions (an ice cream scoop works great for this) and drop onto a baking sheet. When all the meat has been scooped, fill a small bowl with cold water. Dip your hands in the water and roll one of the mounds of meat in the palms of your hands to create a smooth ball (the water keeps the meat from sticking). Repeat the process until all the meatballs have been shaped.

4. Heat a large (12- to 14-inch) sauté pan over high heat. When hot, add the oil and heat until shimmering. Arrange the meatballs in a single layer in the pan (you might need to cook in batches) and brown on all sides, turning with tongs or a

*continued*

spatula. (If they stick to the pan, leave them alone and let them cook for another minute. They'll let you know when they're ready to be turned–they'll be easy to move.) Remove the meatballs to a clean baking sheet as they finish browning. Repeat with the remaining meatballs. Cover and refrigerate until ready to use or freeze.

**TO MAKE THE GRAVY**

1.  Scrape any browned bits from the bottom of the meatball frying pan and strain the oil from the pan through a sieve into a bowl. Place the browned bits in a Dutch oven. Pour the strained oil from the bowl back into the large sauté pan. Turn the heat to medium high and let the pan heat for a few minutes. Add the sausage and cook, turning occasionally, until browned on all sides. Remove from the heat and transfer to a plate using tongs or a slotted spoon, leaving behind as much fat in the pan as possible. Cover and refrigerate until ready to use.

2.  Meanwhile, season the pork with 1 teaspoon salt and 1 teaspoon black pepper sprinkled evenly over the pieces. (I like to massage the salt and pepper into the meat so that I know it's evenly seasoned.) Place the pork in the sauté pan and brown the pieces on all sides (use tongs to turn the pieces), removing them to the Dutch oven as they are evenly browned.

3.  Add the onions to the pan and up to $\frac{1}{4}$ cup olive oil if necessary for the onions to sizzle as they sauté. Cook the onions until very soft, lowering the heat if necessary to keep them from browning, about 15 minutes. Add the garlic and sauté until fragrant, about 3 minutes more. Transfer to the Dutch oven. Deglaze the pan with some of the water, stirring to scrape up any browned bits. Add this and the remaining water to the Dutch oven.

4. Add the tomato purée, tomato paste, celery, bay leaf, cloves, cinnamon, sugar, and 2 teaspoons salt and remaining 2 teaspoons pepper to the Dutch oven. Stir well to combine.

5. Bring the sauce to a boil over medium-high heat, lower the heat to a simmer, and cook partially covered for 2 hours, stirring occasionally to prevent scorching. (It can also cook in the oven: Heat the oven to 325°F. Bring the sauce to a simmer, cover, and bake for 2 hours.)

6. Add the sausage to the pot and cook partially covered for 1 hour more (cover if cooking in the oven).

7. Add the meatballs and cook partially covered for 1 hour more (cover if cooking in the oven).

8. Check the pork for tenderness—it should offer no resistance when pierced with a fork. If not fork-tender, continue to cook until it is, checking every 30 minutes.

9. When the pork is tender, add the parsley; cook for another 15 minutes. Taste and add more salt and pepper if necessary.

10. If serving immediately, remove the celery and cinnamon. Ladle some of the sauce (without the meat) over cooked pasta and mix. Divide the pasta into individual serving bowls, top with a piece of sausage, a meatball, a piece of pork, and another ladle of sauce (Love Note 5). Serve immediately.

*continued*

# Mary Grillo

### { GRANDMA MARY'S MEATBALLS AND SUNDAY GRAVY }

Mary Grillo was born in Pennsylvania in the late 1800s. After a disgruntled nephew murdered her parents, she was sent to Sicily and raised by her aunt and uncle. She eventually moved back to Pennsylvania, married, and had four children, one of whom was Tony, father of Rob Sample, who is co-owner of Mother's. (Sample is a simplified form of Zampaglione, Rob's grandfather's name.)

Grandma Mary lived near her son and grandchildren for quite some time and did most of the cooking. Rob fondly remembers her pounding and rolling the meat for the braciole and shaping the meatballs for the sauce. He recounts stories of how he and his siblings fought over leftover meatballs and stovepipes (rigatoni), resorting to guerilla tactics when necessary to get their fair share.

We honored Grandma Mary as our first Mother of the Month. She was loved for many reasons and will forever be remembered for her cooking.

# LOVE NOTES

**1** Many people like a **combination of ground meats** in their meatballs, but we use only ground beef at Mama Mia Trattoria because a number of people don't eat pork or veal. Feel free to substitute some of the beef with veal and/or pork, if desired.

**2** **Water is extremely important** to the meatballs and should not be omitted, as it makes them light in texture.

**3** **San Marzano tomatoes** are a special variety of Roma tomato that has more flesh and fewer seeds than other Romas, making it the best for sauces. They're also sweeter and less acidic. Although you can get canned San Marzanos that have been grown in parts of Italy or even the United States, "real" San Marzanos are grown in a small region of rich volcanic soil near Naples and are given DOP (Protected Designation of Origin) status. As for the tomato paste, you'll have half a can left over after making this recipe. Just freeze it in 1-tablespoon portions on a cookie sheet

or in ice cube trays, then transfer to zip-top freezer bags.

**4** You can **serve the meatballs** and gravy with any pasta you like. Rob's family always ate Grandma's gravy with rigatoni (they called them stovepipes), probably because the shape stands up to the thick sauce. If you want noodles, linguine is a little more robust than regular spaghetti. If you're not serving 10 people and are planning on freezing the leftover gravy for later, just cook the amount of pasta you need. A good rule of thumb is ¼ pound of pasta per person.

**5** **This recipe yields** a large amount. That's because the meatballs and sauce taste even better reheated, and they freeze very well. To freeze, use a slotted spoon or spider to lift out the meatballs, being careful not to break them, onto a clean baking sheet. Lift out the sausage and pork and place on another baking sheet. Cool the sauce and meats before freezing separately.

sides

OLD FRENCH MARKET

D H HOLMES

When it comes to dinner, it's easy to focus on the main dish
and forget about the sides. But a hunk of meat on a plate is not a well-
balanced meal. Besides, it can look a little lonely without something colorful
to cozy up to or something starchy to soak up all its juices. And now that the
Department of Agriculture has modified the food pyramid so that meat takes
a back seat to starches and vegetables, it's even less the center of attention.

In the restaurant business, sometimes it's the side dish that sells the main
course. Guests are enticed to order a fish dish when they know the fish is
going to perch on top of tiny homemade dumplings (Spaetzle, page 222), or
they might go for the prime rib when accompanied by Potatoes au Gratin
(page 209). Luckily, a nutritious and delicious side dish can be as easy as
wilting spinach with a little garlic and olive oil or roasting a baking sheet of
red potatoes. Even smashed potatoes and rice pilaf—essential partners to
saucy entrées like Perfect Pot Roast (page 95) and Chicken Souvlakia (page
148)—are quick to put together.

Admittedly, some dishes in this chapter, like braised collard greens or corn
pudding, require a little more planning and a trip to the grocery store, but
that's not a big deal if you plan your weekly menus in advance—a practice
I highly recommend if you want to get out of the "It's 5 o'clock and I don't
know what to make for dinner" rut.

So forget the boring bags of frozen peas, and don't even think about a
box of instant spuds! Stock up on some veggies and pantry staples, turn the
page, and I'll show you some tasty—and fresh—ways to serve them.

# Sautéed Shredded Vegetables

LONG, VIBRANT STRANDS OF SUMMER SQUASH AND CARROTS LOOK SO ELEGANT that they can dress up any plate. It's amazing how much more exciting a dish can seem when the ingredients are simply cut in an unexpected way. Colorful yet subtle in flavor, this makes a great accompaniment to almost any dish, particularly mild fish such as halibut and cod.

Feel free to experiment with herbs and spices to create a dish with flavors that marry well to your entrée. Any fresh herbs would be wonderful in this side dish, as would a little garlic or shallot.

2 large carrots, peeled and trimmed

1 large zucchini, trimmed

1 large yellow squash, trimmed

2 tablespoons unsalted butter

1 teaspoon kosher salt

¼ teaspoon freshly ground black pepper

1. Using the fine julienne cutter on a mandoline (Love Note 3, page 210, Potatoes au Gratin) or food processor, or the coarse holes of a box grater, shred the vegetables lengthwise. Try to keep the pieces as long as possible, turning the vegetables a quarter-turn every other stroke. (Don't use the middle, seeded part of the squash.) You should end up with about 6 cups of vegetables.

2. Place a large (12- to 14-inch) sauté pan or heavy skillet over medium-high heat for a couple of minutes. When hot, add the butter (don't wait for it to melt) and vegetables at the same time. Season with the salt and pepper and cook over high heat, stirring now and then, until the vegetables just start to become soft and floppy, 2 to 3 minutes.

3. Remove from the heat and serve immediately (they get mushy if they sit).

# Creamed Spinach

THIS IS A GREAT WAY TO SERVE SPINACH—ESPECIALLY TO KIDS—AND ALTHOUGH it's a steakhouse staple, it's just as delicious with meatloaf or roast chicken. We also serve it in an omelet filled with Asiago cheese.

4 bunches fresh spinach (or one 1-pound bag spinach leaves; Love Note 1)

3 tablespoons unsalted butter (divided)

¼ cup minced shallots (about 2)

1 teaspoon kosher salt (divided)

½ teaspoon freshly ground black pepper (divided)

3 tablespoons all-purpose flour

1½ cups whole milk

1. If using bunched spinach, remove the stems from the spinach leaves by pinching them where the stem connects with the leaf and tearing up toward the top of the leaf. (This helps tear off the stringy parts.) Place the leaves in a large bowl set in the sink, and fill with water. Swish the leaves around in the water to remove dirt and debris. Lift them out (so the sand stays behind) and place in a colander set in the sink. Rinse out the bowl, fill with water, and repeat the process until the water in the bowl ends up clean. Leave the spinach in the colander to drain.

2. Place a large (12- to 14-inch) straight-sided sauté pan or wide Dutch oven over medium-high heat for a couple minutes. When hot, add 1 tablespoon of the butter and the shallots at the same time. Sauté until the shallots start to soften, about 1 minute. Increase the heat to high and add the spinach, a handful at a time, stirring until it wilts. (Let the first handful wilt before adding the next handful, and stir after each addition). Season with ½ teaspoon salt and ¼ teaspoon pepper. Transfer to a colander to let excess moisture drain off, pressing down with the back of a spoon to squeeze out as much liquid as possible.

3. Melt the remaining 2 tablespoons butter in a medium (4- to 6-quart), heavy-bottomed saucepan over medium heat. Add the flour and mix well with a wooden spoon to make a roux. Cook, stirring frequently, until the mixture is pale yellow and resembles fine sand, 3 to 5 minutes. Whisk the milk into the roux a little at a time, allowing the roux to absorb the liquid before adding more. This will help prevent lumps. Return the mixture to a boil, and then lower the heat and simmer, stirring occasionally, for about 15 minutes to cook off any flour taste. (This sauce is called béchamel; Love Note 2.) Season with the remaining $\frac{1}{2}$ teaspoon salt and $\frac{1}{4}$ teaspoon pepper.

4. Stir the spinach and shallots into the cream sauce. Cook for 1 minute to meld the flavors, and serve.

## LOVE NOTES

**1** **Bagged spinach** has usually been washed and had the tough stems removed (check the label), so you can skip step 1 in the instructions (a real time-saver). But it's a good idea to wash bagged spinach if you plan to eat it raw.

**2** **Béchamel is one of the French "mother sauces,"** so called because it's used as the base in other sauces. It's incredibly easy to make and extremely versatile. Stir in shredded cheese and you have a quick, kid-friendly cheese sauce that you can slather on everything from broccoli to pasta.

# Fashoulakia (Green Bean Stew)

THIS RECIPE COMES FROM SOPHIA DAMIANI, A FORMER GREEK MOTHER OF THE Month (her story is on page 154). In this country, we've grown fond of veggies cooked just until tender-crisp, but here's an example where green beans taste wonderful when slow cooked until soft with garlic and tomatoes. Serve warm or at room temperature for a lovely addition to a barbecue buffet or with Chicken (or lamb) Souvlakia (page 148).

⅓ cup olive oil

1 medium yellow onion, finely chopped (1 cup)

2 cloves garlic, finely chopped

⅓ cup finely chopped fresh Italian (flat-leaf) parsley

1 tablespoon finely chopped fresh mint

1 tablespoon finely chopped fresh dill

2 pounds fresh green beans, trimmed

2 (14.5-ounce) cans stewed tomatoes

¼ cup water

1 teaspoon kosher salt

⅛ teaspoon freshly ground black pepper

1. Place a large (6- to 8-quart) saucepan or Dutch oven over medium-high heat for a couple of minutes. When hot, add the oil and onions. Sauté until the onions begin to soften, about 4 minutes.

2. Reduce the heat to medium and add the garlic, parsley, mint, and dill; stir well and cook until the onions start to turn golden, about 5 minutes more.

3. Add the green beans, stewed tomatoes, water, salt, and pepper. Cover and cook until the beans are soft, 30 to 40 minutes. Serve either warm or at room temperature.

# Braised Red Cabbage

CABBAGE IS A COLD-CLIMATE VEGETABLE THAT'S CHEAP AND KEEPS WELL THROUGH the winter months. Here, shredded apples and onions, plus spices, vinegar, and red wine, transform a head of cabbage into a sweet-tart accompaniment to all kinds of pork and beef dishes. This recipe makes a lot because it keeps and reheats well.

4 large Granny Smith apples

3 pounds red cabbage (1 head)

¼ cup vegetable oil

1 large yellow onion, thinly sliced

½ cup red-wine vinegar

½ cup dry red wine

⅓ cup granulated sugar

1½ teaspoons kosher salt

2 whole cloves

10 whole black peppercorns

1 bay leaf

1. Peel the apples, and grate them on the large holes of a box grater, rotating the apple as you reach the core. Remove any damaged outer leaves from the cabbage. Cut the head in quarters, cut out the tough core, and then slice the cabbage across the grain into shreds. (A mandoline is great for this.)

2. Heat the oil in a large (8- to 10-quart) Dutch oven or stockpot over medium-high heat for a couple of minutes. Add the onions and sauté until slightly softened, about 5 minutes. Add the apples and sauté for another 3 minutes, or until a little soft.

3. Add the vinegar, red wine, and sugar, stirring to scrape up any browned bits. Stir in the cabbage and toss to coat. Put the cloves, peppercorns, and bay leaf in a piece of cheesecloth, tie it closed with kitchen string, and add to the pot. (If you don't have a piece of cheesecloth, you can tie them up in a square cut from a clean white T-shirt.)

4. Bring to a boil over high heat, then reduce the heat to low, cover, and simmer for about 30 minutes, or until the cabbage is tender. Remove from the heat and serve.

## Nada Chunta Orlik
{ BRAISED RED CABBAGE }

Nada Chunta Orlik was born in Karlovy Vary (Carlsbaad), Czechoslovakia, in 1948, on a large farm with cows, sheep, horses, and goats. Four years later, the Communists took everything her parents had—their land, their home, and most of their possessions. Her family moved to Vsetin, in Moravia, and Nada's parents started life anew, working in a factory. No matter how difficult their life was, her father was always happy and played the mandolin at family get-togethers. Both of Nada's parents did the cooking (which is how she learned to cook), and they always ate dinner together. One of Nada's shining culinary moments was when she was 13 and made her first soup. Her father proclaimed it to be the best soup he had ever had and told her how happy and proud of her he was.

Nada studied electronics in school, and she played handball in a league for 16 years. She got married when she was 20 and had the first of her three children a year later. In 1969, her brother escaped Czechoslovakia while on vacation in Yugoslavia. Because of this, Nada and her family weren't allowed to leave the country for 12 years. In 1980, when their children were 7, 9, and 11, they requested and received permission to leave the country for vacation. To ensure their return, her husband's boss wrote on his paperwork that he could not take his children. Thankfully, they forgot to write the same exclusion on Nada's. They left the country in their car and landed in an Austrian refugee camp with no money and only their suitcases. Six months later, when the sponsorship paperwork from her brother came through, they moved to Cleveland, Ohio. They weren't happy in Cleveland ("it was too flat"), and had heard that Portland, Oregon, resembled the "old country," so they moved there in 1984.

Both Nada and her husband always worked, yet Nada managed to have dinner on the table for the family every night by 6 P.M., just like her parents did when she was growing up. Sunday dinners were even bigger and provided an opportunity for the whole family to catch up with each other. All of her children rave over her cooking to this day, and thanks to the efforts of her daughter Dagmar we got to serve Nada's delicious food. *Dobrou Chut!*

# Collard, Mustard, or Turnip Greens

DARK, LEAFY GREENS ARE A POWERHOUSE OF NUTRIENTS, BUT FEW OF US EAT enough of them. We'd be wise to take a lesson from the South, where greens braised with a ham hock are a beloved—and flavorful—staple (Love Note). This recipe from Carolyn Putnam makes a generous amount (about 7 cups), because if you're going to spend the time cooking these greens, you might as well make it worth your while. They reheat well (and freeze well, too), so you can serve them again later in the week or use them in something different like frittatas, bean soups, or pasta.

4 bunches collard, mustard, or turnip greens

¼ pound bacon (3 to 4 strips; chill for 10 minutes in the freezer to make it easier to cut)

1 small yellow onion, diced (½ cup)

2 teaspoons chopped garlic (about 2 cloves)

¼ teaspoon crushed red pepper flakes

1 cup water or Chicken Stock (page 87)

2 teaspoons kosher salt

½ teaspoon freshly ground black pepper

Tabasco sauce (optional)

Cider vinegar (optional)

1. Cut the stems off the greens, and discard any discolored leaves. Remove the thick middle vein from the rest of the leaves: Fold the leaves in half lengthwise with the outside facing you and slice off the vein with a sharp knife. Cut the greens into dollar-size pieces (or leave them whole, if desired).

2. Place the leaves in a large bowl set in the sink and fill with cold water. Swish the leaves around in the water to remove dirt and debris. Lift them out (so the dirt stays behind) and place in a colander set in the sink. Rinse out the bowl, fill with water, and repeat the process until the water in the bowl ends up clean. Leave the greens in the colander to drain (it's fine to leave a little water on the leaves).

3. Stack the bacon strips and cut in half. Cut in half again lengthwise. Cut the strips across into ¼-inch dice.

4. Place a large (8- to 10-quart) stockpot or Dutch oven over medium-high heat for a couple of minutes. When hot, add the bacon and fry until it is almost crispy and has rendered its oil, about 4 minutes.

5. Leave the bacon in the pan and add the onions. Sauté until very soft and translucent, about 5 minutes. (Do not let them color. Reduce the heat if necessary.)

6. Add the garlic and red pepper flakes; sauté until fragrant, about 1 minute more. Add the greens a handful at a time and toss with the bacon and onions. Cook for another minute or two. Add the water or stock, cover, and cook over medium heat until the greens are tender, at least 45 minutes (there's no harm in cooking them longer). Season with the salt and pepper. Add Tabasco to taste, if desired, or a splash of cider vinegar for a truly southern dish.

*continued*

## LOVE NOTE

**Tough braising greens like kale,** collards, mustard greens, and turnip greens (the tops of turnips) are nutritious, plentiful, and cheap year-round, particularly in the winter, when other vegetables may be scarce. After slowly braising, the greens end up meltingly soft and infused with flavor. Feel free to mix and match, using a little of this green and a little of that green.

# M.O.M.

Carolyn is special because she is the mother of our pastry chef, Debbie. Carolyn was born in Magnolia, Arkansas, in 1929, and spent most of her adult life in Texas. Although she moved to Portland, Oregon, in 1995, we deemed Carolyn our Texas mother. She was a working mother of four before there were convenience foods, take-out services, and deliveries, so most of Carolyn's cooking revolved around easy-to-make dinners for her family. And because she was a southern mother, fried chicken, catfish, and hushpuppies made it to the table at least a few times a month.

Carolyn told us that when she was young, every week a man with live chickens in the back of a horse-drawn cart would pull up in front of her house and ask her mother, "Miss Hester, how many chickens will you be needin' today?" Her mother would always take three, and the children would watch as he snapped their necks, then plucked and cleaned them—all within 15 minutes. Hester would pay him 30 cents per chicken, take them to the kitchen, and immediately proceed to fry them up for the family.

# Creamed Corn Pudding

IN THE HEIGHT OF SUMMER, WHEN FRESH, SWEET CORN ON THE COB IS BOTH plentiful and cheap, I always buy way more than my fridge can handle. When I tire of eating it on the cob, I slice the kernels off to make this decadent corn pudding. It comes together pretty quickly and is great with pecan-crusted catfish, pork chops, steak, and just about anything off the grill. It also freezes well (Love Note 1).

| | |
|---|---|
| 10 ears fresh corn on the cob (or about 5 cups kernels; Love Note 2) | 3 tablespoons maple syrup (any grade) |
| 5 large eggs | 1¼ teaspoons kosher salt |
| 1¼ cups heavy cream | ½ teaspoon freshly ground black pepper |

1. Heat the oven to 425°F. Butter a 13x9x2-inch baking dish or spray with non-stick cooking spray.

2. Shuck the corn, removing the fine strands of cornsilk in the process. Break the corn in half (Love Note 3). Stand the flat end of the corn on a rimmed baking sheet (to catch the kernels), and use a sharp knife to cut down the length of the cob to remove the kernels, being careful not to cut too far into the cob, which will give you hard bits. Rotate the corn as you work.

3. Measure the kernels (you should have about 5 cups) and place half (2½ cups) of them in a food processor. Process the kernels until puréed.

4. In a mixing bowl, beat the eggs, cream, and maple syrup together. Add the corn purée and the remaining 2½ cups whole corn kernels, and season with the salt and pepper. Mix well, then pour into the prepared dish (make sure to evenly distribute the whole corn kernels).

*continued*

5. Cover with foil and bake for 50 to 60 minutes, or until a toothpick inserted into the center comes out clean.

## LOVE NOTES

**1** **Freeze any leftovers** in an oven-safe dish and thaw in the refrigerator overnight. Bake, covered with foil, at 350°F until heated through, then uncover for the last 5 minutes of baking.

**2** **Fresh corn** makes this pudding sublime, but in a pinch you can substitute 28 ounces thawed frozen corn.

**3** It's easier to **break the corn in half with your hands** than to cut it with a knife, and that gives you a flat base to rest the corn on as you work. Also, it means the kernels will fall a shorter distance and won't bounce as much, so they're more likely to stay on the baking sheet and not end up on your floor.

# Potatoes au Gratin

MADE WITH LAYERS OF THINLY SLICED POTATOES NESTLED IN A BATH OF CREAM AND topped with Cheddar cheese, this dish is perfect with roast beef or chicken. Using a food processor to slice the potatoes makes it a snap to make, but if you don't have one, a sharp knife and a little elbow grease works great, too—plus, you'll get to perfect your knife skills. Feel free to be creative with this. Change up the cheese for an entirely different dish. You can add broccoli, bacon, or spinach for even more variety. This recipe makes a lot, but if you're not cooking for company, wrap individual servings of leftovers tightly in plastic and freeze. Reheat in the microwave.

If you want to get ahead, you can peel the potatoes and cover them in water (raw potatoes discolor when exposed to air), but leave them whole. Don't slice them until you're ready to cook; otherwise, you'll rinse away the natural potato starch, which is what helps thicken the cream and hold everything together.

| | |
|---|---|
| 3 pounds russet potatoes (about 4 medium; Love Note 1) | ¾ teaspoon freshly ground black pepper |
| 1½ teaspoons minced garlic (about 2 cloves) | 3 cups half-and-half or heavy cream |
| 1 tablespoon unsalted butter, softened, or nonstick cooking spray | 3 cups packed grated sharp Cheddar cheese (Love Note 2) |
| 2 teaspoons kosher salt | |

1. Heat the oven to 350°F. Peel the potatoes and cut into ¼-inch-thick slices (if you have a food processor use it—it makes this dish a breeze! Love Note 3).

2. Smear the garlic on the inside of a 13x9x2-inch baking dish (to give it the essence of garlic). Alternatively, rub the inside of 8 to 12 individual 1- to 1½-cup oven-proof dishes with the garlic. Allow the garlic juices to dry, then coat the dish with the softened butter or nonstick cooking spray.

*continued*

3. Put the potatoes, salt, pepper, and half-and-half or cream into a 6- to 8-quart saucepan. Bring to a boil over medium-high heat, stirring occasionally. Lower to a simmer and cook, stirring occasionally (make sure no potatoes are sticking to the bottom and getting scorched), until the liquid thickens slightly, about 5 minutes.

4. Pour the potatoes and cream into the prepared baking dish (or dishes). Press down on the top layer with a rubber spatula to submerge the potatoes. Sprinkle the cheese evenly over the top and press down again.

5. Bake until the top is golden and the potatoes are tender, 45 to 60 minutes for a large baking dish, 30 to 45 minutes for small dishes. Let cool for about 10 minutes before serving.

## LOVE NOTES

**1** **Potatoes are categorized** into two camps: starchy (baking) and waxy (boiling). Starchy potatoes, like russets, have more starch and less moisture, so they absorb more liquid and have a fluffy texture when cooked. They're perfect for baked potatoes or dishes like this, where you want the potatoes to both absorb and thicken the cream. Waxy potatoes, like red boiling potatoes, contain more moisture, so they hold their shape better. They're perfect for things like Roasted Reds (page 215) or potato salad.

**2** **Use any flavorful cheese,** like Swiss, Gruyère, or smoked Cheddar. Mild cheese just adds fat and calories and not much else.

**3** **A food processor** fitted with the slicing disk creates even slices in no time. A mandoline (kind of like a manual version of a food processor) is a cheaper option. Ideal for the home kitchen, a mandoline features blades of three thicknesses as well as an adjustable slicing blade so you can vary the thickness.

# Mother's Smashers

ONE OF MY RESPONSIBILITIES WHILE WORKING AT LE CIRQUE WAS TO MAKE THE *purée de pommes de terre*, or mashed potatoes. After the potatoes were peeled, cooked, drained, and dried, I had to use a rubber spatula to push them through a *tamie*, a wood-framed screen that sits over a mixing bowl. This was an arduous task. Although the potatoes turned out silky smooth and delicious, I vowed to serve lumpy yet equally delicious "smashers" at my own restaurant. After all, whose mother didn't serve lumpy potatoes? I choose to leave the skin on not only because I like the added flavor but also because I don't want to have to peel 25 pounds of potatoes every night!

8 whole large red potatoes (about 3 pounds)

1¼ cups (2½ sticks) unsalted butter, at room temperature

1½ cups half-and-half, plus more if necessary (Love Note 1)

2 teaspoons kosher salt

1 teaspoon freshly ground black pepper

1. Heat the oven to 350°F. Scrub the potatoes clean with a vegetable brush under cold running water.

2. Place the whole potatoes in a large (8- to 10-quart) stockpot or Dutch oven and cover with cold water by about 1 inch (Love Note 2). Place the pot over high heat and bring to a boil (put the lid on the pot to make it come to a boil faster—just make sure you remove it when the water begins to boil or it could boil over). Lower the heat and simmer, uncovered, until the potatoes are fork-tender (a fork should be able to slide in and out very easily), about 30 minutes (better to slightly overcook than slightly undercook).

3. When the potatoes are tender, drain in a colander set in the sink. Put the potatoes in a single layer on a rimmed baking sheet (use tongs—they're hot!). Transfer to the oven and bake for about 8 minutes (to dry out excess moisture), but do not allow them to brown (Love Note 3).

4. While the potatoes are drying out, place the butter in a warm spot to soften and the half-and-half in a small saucepan over low heat (adding warm cream to the potatoes will help keep them piping hot).

5. Return the potatoes to the cooking pot and smash them with a heavy-duty wire whisk or a potato masher (don't worry if they're lumpy—that's what makes them smashers). Add the butter and warm half-and-half. Add additional half-and-half, if necessary, to achieve a creamy consistency. Season with the salt and pepper and serve.

*continued*

 ## Using Up Leftover Smashers

Leftover smashers are quite versatile. You can reheat them on the stove with some half-and-half and butter to smooth them out. You can also use them to top a casserole, like pot pies or shepherd's pies. Or make croquettes: Mix them with a little flour and egg (1 egg and 1 tablespoon of flour per 2 cups of smashers), add your favorite seasonings like shredded cheese or herbs, and shape into patties. You can pan-fry the croquettes in oil over high heat, or first dip them in a dish of beaten egg and then in a dish of breadcrumbs to create a crispier coating.

A fantastic way to use up these potatoes is in a stuffed potato soup: For every cup of smashed potatoes, add ½ cup milk, 2 tablespoons cooked crumbled bacon, and ¼ cup shredded sharp Cheddar cheese. Top with a dollop of sour cream and chopped chives or scallions.

# LOVE NOTES

**1** **The amount of half-and-half** needed depends on the potatoes, so you are going to have to use your best judgment on how much to add. Mother's Smashers are very creamy and look "wet." They are not stiff—they fall off a tilted spoon and do not fall in a big blob on the plate. Ideally, you should serve the smashers right away, since they tighten up as they sit (even for just a few minutes) and become a little less wonderful. If making them a little ahead of time, make sure they are even creamier, cover them very well with plastic wrap and then a layer of aluminum foil, and keep them warm by placing them in a 200°F oven until ready to serve.

**2** **Starting potatoes in cold** water helps them to cook more evenly because the whole potato has a chance to warm up as the water warms. If you drop potatoes into boiling water, the outsides will cook much faster than the insides. Don't be tempted to use hot tap water to speed up the process. No matter how old or new your plumbing is, most systems contain lead at some level, and hot water can leach the lead out of the pipes and into your cooking pot, where it doesn't boil away.

**3** Strange as it may seem, **the drier the potatoes,** the creamier your smashers will be. That's because the less water they have, the more half-and-half and butter they can absorb, making them extra rich and creamy. That's why the potatoes are cooked whole, so they absorb less water, and why I like to pop them in the oven to dry out the excess moisture.

# Roasted Reds

WHEN IT CAME TIME TO DECIDE WHAT POTATOES TO SERVE FOR BREAKFAST AT
Mother's Bistro & Bar, I had my work cut out for me. I didn't want to serve the same
roasted potatoes I served at Besaw's, where I was the chef for two years. I couldn't
serve hash browns because our kitchen wasn't big enough to sauté them and still cook
eggs and pancakes. I knew the potatoes had to be great, because most people judge
their breakfast based on the potatoes (I do, at least!). After much experimentation, I
came up with these flavorful, easy-to-make potatoes, which are great for dinner, too.

1½ pounds small red boiling pota-
toes (Love Note 1, page 216, and
Love Note 1, page 210, Potatoes au
Gratin)

½ teaspoon (generous) dried
thyme (Love Note 2), or
1½ teaspoons fresh thyme
leaves

¼ teaspoon kosher salt

½ teaspoon (scant) freshly ground
black pepper

½ teaspoon (generous) garlic salt
(Love Note 3)

¼ cup extra-virgin olive oil (or
¼ cup half olive oil and half canola
oil), plus more for the pan

1. Heat the oven to 450°F. Gently scrub the potatoes with a vegetable brush under
cold running water. Cut in half lengthwise (don't peel), and then cut in half
lengthwise again (Love Note 4) and place in a large mixing bowl. Add the thyme,
salt, pepper, garlic salt, and oil to the potatoes. Gently toss with your hands to
coat evenly.

2. Oil a rimmed baking sheet. Pour the potatoes onto the pan, spreading into a single
layer. Place in the oven and bake for 1 hour, or until golden brown and tender
when pierced with a fork. Be sure to stir the potatoes with a spatula and rotate the
pan every 20 minutes to help them cook evenly. The potatoes can be made a few
hours ahead (but undercooked slightly), kept at room temperature, and reheated in
a 350°F degree oven for about 15 minutes, or until heated through.

*continued*

# LOVE NOTES

**1** **Use potatoes about 6 inches** in diameter and cut them into quarters. If you buy potatoes smaller than that, you can roast them whole. Just make sure to choose potatoes that are the same size so they'll all cook in the same amount of time. Small new potatoes (new potatoes are very small immature boiling potatoes) or small fingerling potatoes are perfect for this.

**2** **We use dried thyme** at Mother's because we cook 200 pounds of potatoes every weekend, and we'd be plucking the leaves off fresh thyme stems all morning and still not have enough. When you're only making 1½ pounds of potatoes, though, I highly recommend using fresh. You'll need three times as

much fresh as dried, but the flavor will be fantastic.

**3** **Fresh garlic** tends to burn (which makes it taste bitter), particularly in a dish like this that's roasted at high heat for a long period of time. That's why I use dried garlic in the form of garlic salt instead. I'm partial to garlic salt because my mom used it, and I think it distributes the garlic flavor better than garlic powder or granulated garlic, which can be overpowering.

**4** **The potatoes can be cut** a day ahead and kept in cold water in the refrigerator (but drain well before using).

# CHAPTER 4

# Coconut Rice

TO FIGURE OUT THE BEST ACCOMPANIMENT FOR MY MACADAMIA NUT–CRUSTED Red Snapper with Mango Salsa (page 161), I used the same trick I use whenever I'm devising a new menu or recipe: Combine ingredients that come from the same part of the world. Since coconuts thrive in the same tropical climate as mangoes and macadamia nuts, I came up with this rice, which complements the fish and salsa perfectly.

1 cup unsweetened coconut milk, stirred (Love Note)

1¼ cups water

½ teaspoon kosher salt

2 thin slices peeled fresh ginger (optional)

1 cup jasmine rice or other long-grain white rice

2 tablespoons unsweetened shredded coconut, for garnish (optional)

1. Heat the oven to 400°F. Place the coconut milk, water, salt, and ginger, if using, in a medium (4- to 6-quart) oven-safe saucepan. Bring to a boil over high heat, and stir in the rice. Return to a boil (stir frequently to keep the rice from sticking), and then remove from the heat, cover, and bake for 20 minutes.

2. Meanwhile, if using the coconut, place a small sauté pan over medium heat. Add the shredded coconut and toast, stirring often to prevent burning, until most of the flakes are golden brown. Transfer to a plate to cool.

3. When the rice has absorbed the liquid and the grains are tender, remove from the oven and let stand for 10 minutes, covered (to finish steaming and ensure each grain is evenly cooked).

4. Fluff the rice with a fork (so you don't end up mashing the grains when you scoop out the rice) and put it in a serving dish. Sprinkle the toasted coconut on top of the rice as a garnish just before serving.

*continued*

## LOVE NOTE

**Coconut milk is extracted from the coconut** flesh itself; it's not the clearish liquid you see when you crack open a coconut. There are a lot of brands of canned coconut milk, and a lot of variation in quality, too (trusted brands include Mae Ploy®, Chao Koh®, and Thai Kitchen®). The milk is always diluted, but you want to look for a brand that doesn't go overboard in the process. You can tell the difference when you shake the can—it should be silent because the flavorful cream is congealed at the top. If the can makes a sloshing sound, put it back. Be sure to give the can a good shake before opening to loosen up the cream. Store unused coconut milk in the refrigerator for 2 to 3 days, or freeze it.

# Vegetable Couscous

THIS IS ESSENTIALLY A VEGETABLE PILAF MADE WITH COUSCOUS INSTEAD OF RICE. All the vegetables are sautéed and then added to the couscous for a colorful accompaniment to saucy dishes. By including the vegetables with the grain you get two food groups in one dish and don't need another side on the plate. Any leftover couscous can be reheated, covered, in a microwave.

| | |
|---|---|
| 2 tablespoons canola oil | 1¾ teaspoons kosher salt |
| 1 medium yellow onion, diced (¾ cup) | ¼ teaspoon freshly ground black pepper |
| 1 medium red bell pepper, diced (¾ cup) | 1 large carrot, peeled and diced (¾ cup; Love Note) |
| 2½ cups Chicken Stock (page 87), Vegetable Stock (page 84), or canned low-sodium broth | 1 medium zucchini, diced (¾ cup) |
| | 2 cups couscous |

1. Place a large (12- to 14-inch), straight-sided sauté pan or a Dutch oven over medium-high heat for a couple of minutes. When hot, add the oil, onions, and red bell peppers at the same time. Sauté until the vegetables start to soften, about 6 minutes (reduce the heat to medium if the vegetables seem to be burning or browning too fast).

2. Meanwhile, pour the stock into a medium (4- to 6-quart) saucepan and bring to a boil over high heat. Add the salt and pepper and stir to mix well. Add the carrots and cook until just softened, about 6 minutes. Remove the carrots with a slotted spoon and set aside. Reduce the heat to low, cover, and keep the stock hot.

3. Add the zucchini to the onions and peppers in the sauté pan. Sauté until it begins to soften, about 3 minutes. Add the cooked carrots and sauté for a few minutes more.

*continued*

4. When all the vegetables are tender and a little brown around the edges, spoon them into the saucepan with the hot stock. Turn off the heat, add the couscous, and stir well. Remove from the stove, cover with a tight-fitting lid, and let sit for about 10 minutes without removing the cover.

5. Fluff with a fork and serve.

## LOVE NOTE

**Peeling carrots** can seem like an unnecessary step, especially when you've taken the time to scrub them clean. But carrot peels taste bitter, so they should always be peeled before using. You might worry that you'll be removing much of the vegetable's nutrients, but that's not the case. Because the flesh of the carrot is the same color as the peel, they have essentially the same nutritive value. By peeling the carrot, you simply end up with a little less carrot. Potatoes, however, are a different story. The peel is very different from the flesh and is the source of most of the vegetable's fiber.

# Spaetzle

THESE TINY DUMPLINGS ARE A DELICIOUS CHANGE OF PACE FROM POTATOES AND rice. This makes a big batch because spaetzle freeze and reheat beautifully. Just crisp them up with a quick sauté in butter whenever the craving strikes. You can add parsley, horseradish, mustard, or even poppyseeds to the batter for flavor variations. Spaetzle can also be combined with sautéed onions, topped with cheese, and baked, rather than sautéed.

6 large eggs

1 cup milk

3 teaspoons kosher salt (divided), plus more for salting the water

¾ teaspoon freshly ground black pepper (divided)

3 cups all-purpose flour

Vegetable oil

9 tablespoons (1 stick plus 1 tablespoon) unsalted butter

1.  Combine the eggs, milk, 2 teaspoons salt, and ¼ teaspoon black pepper in a large mixing bowl. Gradually whisk in the flour until well combined (the mixture should look thick and smooth). Cover the bowl with plastic wrap and place it in the refrigerator to let the dough rest for 10 minutes.

2.  Meanwhile, bring a large (8- to 10-quart) stockpot of water to a boil. Salt generously (it should taste like the sea). Place a bowl of ice water and a spider (Love Note 1) near the stove.

3.  Place some of the dough in a spaetzle maker or slotted spoon (Love Note 2) and hold it over the boiling water. Push the dough through the holes into the water (you don't want to cook too much at once or they'll cool the water down too much, take too long to cook, and end up waterlogged and mushy).

4.  Simmer the spaetzle, stirring occasionally to keep them from sticking, until they float to the surface, 1 to 3 minutes. When they're all floating, cook a minute or two more.

5. Remove with a spider or slotted spoon and place in the ice water to cool. Once all the spaetzle are cooked, use the spider or spoon to remove ice floating in the water bath; discard. Pour the spaetzle into a colander to drain. Shake off excess water, and then toss them in a little vegetable oil (not olive oil because the flavor is too strong) to keep them from sticking. Refrigerate if not using immediately, or freeze in a single layer on a baking sheet until hard, then pack into zip-top bags.

**TO SERVE**

Place a medium (8- to 10-inch) sauté pan over medium-high heat for a couple of minutes. When hot, add 1 tablespoon butter, swirl the pan to coat, and then add 1 cup spaetzle. Season with a pinch of salt and a pinch of pepper and sauté, stirring, until warmed through, lightly browned, and crisp in places, 5 to 7 minutes. If serving a crowd, repeat until all the spaetzle have been sautéed. Otherwise store for later use.

## LOVE NOTES

**1** **A spider,** or wire skimmer, is best for lifting things out of a pot without bringing along any of the cooking liquid. It can be found in restaurant supply stores. Or look for a Chinese version that is sold near woks in most cookware stores.

**2** You can buy a **spaetzle maker,** or use what we do at Mother's—a perforated half hotel pan (available at kitchen supply stores). It measures about 12x 10x2 and has evenly spaced holes along the bottom and sides. (Get one with large, not small, holes.) Place the pan on top of the pot of water, add some of the dough to the pan, and use a rubber spatula to push the dough through the holes. A slotted spoon will also work. Fill it with dough, nest another spoon on top, and push it down to pass the dough through the holes.

# Savory Onion Pudding

I MET RICK BROWNE, MASTER BARBECUER AND COOKBOOK AUTHOR, AND HIS WIFE when they were dining at Mother's Bistro. Father's Day was approaching and I wanted to honor a father that month, so I asked Rick. His wife brought me his cookbooks and we put together a menu that included this dish. Ironically, it came from his mother.

Think of this dish as a blank slate. Consider the flavors of what you're planning to serve it with and add a little of that flavor to the mix, things like fresh thyme or rosemary; bacon crumbles or roasted garlic; goat cheese, Gruyère, Cheddar, or blue cheese.

4 tablespoons (½ stick) unsalted butter (divided), plus more for greasing the dish

2 tablespoons olive oil (divided)

4 large yellow onions, thinly sliced (8 cups)

2½ teaspoons kosher salt (divided)

½ teaspoon freshly ground black pepper (divided)

¼ cup dry vermouth

1 clove garlic, minced

4 heaping cups French bread cut into 2-inch squares (6 to 7 ounces), preferably a day or two old (Love Note)

3 large eggs

2 cups half-and-half

2 cups (about 8 ounces) shredded Swiss or Emmentaler cheese

1. Butter the inside of a 13x9x2-inch baking dish.

2. Heat a large (12- to 14-inch) sauté pan over medium-high heat for a couple of minutes. When hot, add 2 tablespoons of the butter, 1 tablespoon of the oil, and half of the onions at the same time. Season with ½ teaspoon salt and ⅛ teaspoon black pepper. Sauté over high heat until the onions start to color around the edges, about 5 minutes. Lower the heat to medium and sauté for 20 minutes, or until the onions are soft and lightly caramelized. Transfer the cooked onions to a baking sheet and cook the second half of the sliced onions like the first, making sure the pan is hot before adding the butter, oil, and onions and seasoning with salt and pepper.

3.  When the second batch of onions is caramelized, add the first batch back to the onions in the pan. Add the vermouth and deglaze the pan by stirring and scraping up any browned bits from the bottom. Simmer until all the liquid evaporates. Return all the onions to the baking sheet and let them cool to room temperature. This can be done up to two days ahead and refrigerated or frozen.

4.  In a large mixing bowl, combine the garlic, bread cubes, onions, and the remaining $1\frac{1}{2}$ teaspoons salt and $\frac{1}{4}$ teaspoon black pepper. Spread evenly in the prepared baking dish.

5.  In the same mixing bowl (so you don't have to dirty another one), beat together the eggs and half-and-half. Pour evenly over the bread, pressing down with a rubber spatula or your hands to make sure the bread soaks up the liquid.

6.  Place a sheet of plastic wrap over the top of the baking dish, then set another similar-size pan on top of the bread mixture to press the bread down into the liquid. Put the pans in the refrigerator and let rest for 1 hour (so the bread absorbs the egg mixture).

7.  Heat the oven to 350°F. Remove the baking dish from the refrigerator, remove the top pan and the plastic, and sprinkle cheese evenly over the top of the bread mixture. Bake for 40 to 50 minutes, until puffed and golden. Remove from the oven, cut into squares, and serve.

## LOVE NOTE

**Fresh bread works** great, too. Cut it up ahead of time and dry it out on baking sheets. Some people prefer the crusts cut off, but Rick likes the texture difference between the soft bread and the chewy crust.

# macaroni &
## cheese

**Ask any adult what dish he or she enjoyed most as a child and still likes now and you'll probably hear about macaroni and cheese.** Ask any mom what her kids willingly eat, and the same thing rises to the top of the list—yup, macaroni and cheese. Most kids are picky eaters, but it's the rare child who doesn't like noodles smothered in creamy cheese sauce.

Unlike hot dogs or peanut butter and jelly, macaroni and cheese is one of those tremendously kid-friendly meals that can easily be dressed up into something gourmet. And if you change the noodles or cheese or add something interesting like andouille sausage, you've got an entirely grown-up meal with minimal effort.

I knew I wanted to serve mac and cheese in my restaurant, but I couldn't settle on just one kind—how could I when I had ideas for so many? Since our main menu changes only slightly now and then, I decided I could keep things interesting by varying our macaroni and cheese every day.

I don't use elbow macaroni in any of my macaroni and cheese dishes. As long as the pasta complements the ingredients, different shapes are another way to keep things interesting. In these recipes, the shapes are merely suggestions. If you prefer a different shape or you want to use up something in your pantry, go right ahead.

The macaroni and cheese we make at Mother's uses a technique that's a little different than what your mom might have done, and it's a real time-saver. We like to call it "nouvelle" macaroni and cheese—"nouvelle" because it's a new way of doing a traditional dish. Instead of making a traditional white sauce thickened with a roux (see Love Note 3, page 112, Meatloaf Gravy), we use heavy cream, reduce it slightly in a wide sauté pan, and let the cheese do the thickening. This eliminates a few steps and means the sauce can be made in the time it takes to boil the pasta water.

### SAUCY, GOOEY, OR BAKED

My nouvelle mac and cheese might not be what you're used to. These dishes aren't gooey, baked mac and cheese casseroles. They're creamier and saucier, and more flavorful as a result. But if you're looking for something traditional, feel free to add more cheese and reduce the cream more by cooking the dish even longer than the recipe indicates. You'll have gooey in no time!

And if you like a topping of browned cheese, you can also bake most of these dishes (with the exception of the Smoked Salmon, Cream Cheese, and Dill Macaroni & Cheese and the Greek Macaroni & Cheese—both of which just don't lend themselves to a gooey version). After coating the pasta with the cheese sauce, pour it into a buttered 3-quart casserole dish, sprinkle with 1 more cup of shredded cheese (the same cheese added to the cream in the recipe), and bake at 400°F for 5 to 10 minutes, or until the cheese is melted and browned.

### COOKING PERFECT PASTA

When cooking pasta, it's important to use a very large pot with plenty of water to give the pasta space to move. It's important to stir pasta after adding it to boiling water to keep it from sticking together because the surface starches immediately swell up and get gluey. Pieces that are touching will end up fused together. Generously salt it with at least 2 tablespoons of salt *after* it comes to a boil, so the salt dissolves quickly and won't damage your pots. I know 2 tablespoons seems like a lot of salt, but the water should taste as salty as the ocean. This ensures that the pasta is properly seasoned—in fact, that it will even taste good on its own. Most of the salt drains off with the cooking water anyway, and you'll add that much less salt to the sauce.

One way we get ahead at Mother's is by precooking our noodles so that we can get the mac and cheese out of the kitchen and to the dinner table in a flash. If you like working ahead, precook your noodles in plenty of boiling salted water until they're almost done—5 minutes (no more!). Drain the noodles, toss with a tiny bit of vegetable oil to keep them from sticking (but don't use olive oil—the flavor's too strong and can overpower most macaroni and cheeses), and refrigerate them in an airtight container or zip-top bag (so they don't absorb the flavors of the refrigerator). When you're ready to eat, add the noodles to a pot of boiling water for 30 to 60 seconds to heat them through and finish the cooking.

Keep in mind that the pasta isn't the only thing you can prepare ahead. Chop your vegetables and shred your cheese the night before or in the morning, and you can have a meal in minutes come dinnertime.

### SIMPLE TOUCHES FOR GREAT MAC AND CHEESE

Because the sauce is so elemental—just cream and cheese—I give it a flavorful base with sautéed aromatic vegetables such as garlic, onions, or peppers. Be patient when sautéing these ingredients, and let them truly soften and caramelize for the best flavor. The sauce is also seasoned generously with salt and freshly ground black pepper, whose flavor and aroma is a world apart from pre-ground pepper.

Strong-flavored cheeses, like sharp Cheddar, Gruyère, or Parmesan are also essential to the dish—the better the cheese, the better the sauce. Do not use preshredded cheeses, which lack flavor and are typically coated with starches that will make the sauce clumpy.

Be adventurous and make up your own mac and cheese recipe by varying the meat, vegetables, and cheeses. Just make sure you don't go too far. Adding the entire contents of the fridge will only muddy the flavors. Think about what ingredients traditionally work well together in other dishes and cuisines and give them a try. With something this crowd-pleasing, it's hard to go wrong.

# Bacon and Cheddar Macaroni & Cheese

WHEN LOOKING FOR INSPIRATION FOR MY MACARONI AND CHEESES, I TURNED TO stuffed potatoes and omelets, believing that what works well with eggs and potatoes would be delicious with pasta, too. Boy, was I right! Bacon, Cheddar cheese, sour cream, and scallions are classic additions to stuffed potatoes, and with pasta they're perfection.

1 teaspoon kosher salt, plus more for salting the pasta water

1 pound fusilli (corkscrew) or other pasta, preferably De Cecco

¾ pound bacon, diced (about 1 cup cooked; Love Notes 1 and 2)

3 cups heavy cream

2 cups firmly packed shredded sharp Cheddar cheese (about ½ pound; Love Note 3)

¼ teaspoon freshly ground black pepper

½ cup sour cream, for garnish

½ cup thinly sliced scallions, (white and green parts), for garnish

1. Bring a medium (6- to 8-quart) pot of water to a boil. Salt it generously (it should taste like the sea). Stir in the pasta and cook according to the package directions. Drain (but don't rinse, or you'll rinse away starches that will help thicken the sauce) and return to the empty pot.

2. Meanwhile, place a large (12- to 14-inch) sauté pan over high heat for several minutes. When hot, add the bacon and sauté until browned and crispy (lower the heat to medium-high if necessary to prevent scorching), about 5 minutes. Remove the pan from the heat and, using a slotted spoon or spatula, remove the bacon from the pan and drain on paper towels.

3. Pour off the fat from the pan (into a metal can or heatproof cup, not down the drain or you'll potentially clog your pipes) and return the pan to medium-high heat. Add the heavy cream and bring to a boil, scraping up any browned bits from

*continued*

the bottom of the pan. Lower the heat to medium and continue to simmer until the cream is reduced slightly, about 3 minutes.

4. Add the Cheddar cheese and bacon. Stir well and cook over medium-high heat, stirring now and then, until the cheese has melted and the mixture thickens, about 3 minutes. Season with the salt and pepper.

5. Stir the sauce into the cooked and drained pasta in the pot. Place over medium heat and simmer for 1 to 2 minutes to thicken the sauce and allow the pasta to absorb the flavors, stirring now and then.

6. Serve in individual bowls topped with a dollop of sour cream and a sprinkle of sliced scallions.

## VARIATION: Lorraine Mac & Cheese

You can easily change up this recipe by using the classic flavors of a quiche Lorraine for inspiration. You just have to add caramelized onions and substitute Swiss cheese for the Cheddar.

Pour off all but 2 tablespoons grease from the cooked bacon. Add 2 cups of finely sliced yellow onions and sauté over medium heat until soft, brown, and caramelized, about 20 minutes. Pour in the 3 cups of cream and continue with the recipe (step 3), substituting firmly packed shredded Gruyère or Swiss cheese for the Cheddar.

If you have cooked, crumbled bacon and caramelized onions on hand, the recipe is even easier. When stirring the cheese into the reduced cream, just add 1 cup bacon crumbles and 1/2 cup caramelized onions, too. Then proceed with the recipe.

## LOVE NOTES

**1** At Mother's, we **prepare a lot of our components** in large batches ahead of time, like the bacon crumbles in this recipe. It's a real time-saver, and a good idea for home cooks, too. To make things easier, try fitting the work into a recipe you're already cooking, like this one. That way you're not getting pots and pans dirty just for the heck of it. For example, cook twice the amount of bacon and save the rest in the fridge or freezer for salads, scrambles, or sandwiches.

**2** **Dicing slippery, floppy bacon** is tough—unless you firm it up with a 10- to 15-minute stint in the freezer. Stack the strips to make the job go even faster.

**3** **Avoid preshredded cheese.** It may seem like a time-saver, but much of the cheese's flavor has dissipated, and the starchy coating on the outside will interfere with the sauce.

# Spinach, Ricotta, and Parmesan Macaroni & Cheese

THE INSPIRATION FOR THIS MACARONI AND CHEESE CAME FROM MARCELLA HAZAN'S *Essentials of Classic Italian Cooking,* but my version is a bit creamier and cheesier. Don't be tempted to add anything else like garlic or onions, but leftover grilled chicken would be great. And be sure to use Parmigiano Reggiano—real parmesan cheese from Parma, Italy. Though simple, this dish is perfect as it is and needs nothing more. It's like deconstructed ravioli.

1½ teaspoons kosher salt (divided), plus more for salting the pasta water

1 pound penne or fusilli pasta, preferably De Cecco

2 tablespoons unsalted butter

5 packed cups fresh spinach leaves (about 8 ounces or 2 bunches), washed and stems trimmed

¾ teaspoon freshly ground black pepper (divided)

3 cups heavy cream

1 cup whole-milk ricotta cheese (Love Note)

1½ cups grated Parmigiano-Reggiano cheese (divided)

1. Bring a medium (6- to 8-quart) pot of water to a boil. Salt it generously (it should taste like the sea). Stir in the pasta and cook according to package directions. Drain (but don't rinse, or you'll rinse away starches that will help thicken the sauce) and return to the empty pot.

2. Meanwhile, place a large (12- to 14-inch) sauté pan over medium-high heat for several minutes. When hot, add the butter and spinach and sauté, stirring, until wilted. Season with ½ teaspoon salt and ¼ teaspoon black pepper while the spinach is cooking.

3. Add the heavy cream and bring to a boil, stirring to scrape up any browned bits. Lower the heat to medium and simmer until thickened slightly, stirring now and then, about 3 minutes. Season with ½ teaspoon salt and ¼ teaspoon black pepper.

4.  Add the ricotta and 1¼ cups of the Parmigiano-Reggiano cheese. Stir well and continue to cook, stirring occasionally, until the cheese has melted and the mixture has thickened, about 3 minutes. Season with the remaining ½ teaspoon salt and ¼ teaspoon black pepper.

5.  Stir the sauce into the cooked and drained pasta in the pot. Place over medium heat and simmer for 1 to 2 minutes to thicken the sauce and allow the pasta to absorb the flavors, stirring now and then. Adjust the consistency with more cream if necessary.

6.  Serve in individual bowls topped with the remaining cheese.

**LOVE NOTE**

Tubs of **part-skim ricotta cheese** are everywhere, but I urge you to look a little harder to find whole-milk ricotta, which is (no surprise) much richer in texture and flavor. If you don't see it in the refrigerated case with the usual suspects like cream cheese and preshredded cheeses, look in the gourmet cheese area. You can also make it yourself in about an hour with milk and lemon juice or vinegar. You can find many recipes for it online.

# Broccoli and Smoked Cheddar Macaroni & Cheese

BROCCOLI AND CHEDDAR CHEESE IS A MARRIAGE MADE IN HEAVEN—SO MUCH SO that I've paired the two in everything from soup to macaroni and cheese to omelets. Even those not fond of broccoli will be won over by this dish—that's why it's perfect for kids. I like to use smoked Cheddar to add another layer of complexity.

1 teaspoon kosher salt, plus more for blanching the broccoli and salting the pasta water

1 head broccoli, cut into florets (about 4 cups; Love Note 1)

1 pound penne or fusilli pasta, preferably De Cecco

2 tablespoons unsalted butter

3 cups heavy cream

2 cups shredded smoked Cheddar cheese (about ½ pound; Love Note 2)

½ teaspoon freshly ground black pepper

¼ cup grated Parmesan cheese, for garnish

1. Bring a medium (6- to 8-quart) pot of water to a boil. Salt it generously (it should taste like the sea).

2. Have a bowl of ice water next to the stove. Add the broccoli florets to the boiling water and blanch for about 1 minute. Remove with a slotted spoon and immediately place in the ice water to stop the cooking. Drain and set aside.

3. Return the broccoli blanching water to a boil. Stir in the pasta and cook according to the package directions. Drain (but don't rinse, or you'll rinse away starches that will help thicken the sauce) and return to the empty pot.

4. Meanwhile, place a large (12- to 14-inch) sauté pan over medium-high heat for several minutes. When hot, add the butter and blanched broccoli florets. Sauté over medium-high heat, stirring occasionally, for 2 to 3 minutes to warm through.

5. Add the heavy cream, raise the heat to high, and bring to a boil. Lower the heat to medium and simmer until the cream is reduced slightly, about 3 minutes.

6. Add the Cheddar cheese and stir well. Cook over medium-high heat until the cheese has melted and the mixture has thickened, about 3 minutes. Season with the salt and pepper.

7. Stir the sauce into the cooked and drained pasta in the pot. Place over medium heat and simmer for 1 to 2 minutes to thicken the sauce and allow the pasta to absorb the flavors, stirring now and then. Adjust the consistency with more cream if necessary.

8. Serve in individual bowls topped with grated Parmesan cheese.

## LOVE NOTES

**1** To **cut the florets off a head of broccoli,** first cut off the main stem as close to the florets as possible. Turn the head on its side and use a sharp knife to slice off each floret where it joins the stem. If the florets are big, slice them in half or quarters to make them smaller and equal in size.

For this recipe, they should be bite size: about 1 inch in diameter.

**2** **Smoked Cheddar cheese** can be intense as well as expensive. You can get a more subtle smokiness by using half smoked and half sharp Cheddar cheese. Your pocketbook might be heavier, too!

# Smoked Salmon, Cream Cheese, and Dill Macaroni & Cheese

WHEN I WAS GROWING UP, MY FATHER MADE A MEMORABLE CREATION OF PASTA tossed with cream cheese. It was simple but yummy. Wanting to create an elegant macaroni and cheese for a weekend special at Mother's, I remembered his creation and added a trio of ingredients made for each other: smoked salmon, caramelized onions, and dill.

Fresh pasta can absorb more sauce than dry, so you may need to add a touch more cream (Love Note 1) to make the dish as saucy as it should be. If fresh fettuccine isn't available, use bow-tie pasta because the shape catches just the right amount of sauce.

1 teaspoon kosher salt, plus more for salting the pasta water

2 tablespoons unsalted butter

2 medium yellow onions, finely sliced (2 cups), or ½ cup Caramelized Onions (page 118)

2 (9-ounce packages) fresh fettuccine (Love Note 2) or 1 pound dried farfalle (bow-tie) pasta, preferably De Cecco brand

3½ cups heavy cream if using fresh fettuccine, 3 cups if using dried pasta

1 cup whipped cream cheese or 1 (8-ounce) package cream cheese, cut into small dice

¼ pound smoked salmon or lox, broken up into pieces or cut into ¼-inch strips (about ¾ cup)

½ teaspoon freshly ground black pepper

2 tablespoons capers, rinsed and drained, or more to taste

1 tablespoon chopped fresh dill, plus small sprigs for garnish

1.  Bring a medium (6- to 8-quart) pot of water to a boil. Salt it generously (it should taste like the sea).

2.  Meanwhile, place a large (12- to 14-inch) sauté pan over high heat for several minutes. When very hot, add the butter and onions (even before the butter has melted). Sauté until the onions start to color around the edges, about 2 minutes. Lower the heat to medium and continue to cook until the onions are very soft, caramelized, and evenly golden brown, about 15 minutes.

3. When the water comes to a boil, stir in the pasta and cook according to the package directions. Drain (but don't rinse, or you'll rinse away starches that will help thicken the sauce) and return to the empty pot.

4. When the onions are caramelized, add the cream to the pan and bring to a boil over high heat, stirring to scrape up any browned bits. Lower the heat to medium and simmer until the cream is reduced slightly, about 3 minutes.

5. Add the cream cheese and whisk until fully incorporated, at least 1 minute.

6. Add the salmon, and continue to simmer until warmed through, about 2 minutes, stirring now and then with a wooden spoon (so you don't break up the salmon too much). Season with the salt and pepper.

7. Stir the sauce into the cooked and drained pasta. Place over medium heat and add the capers and dill; simmer for 1 to 2 minutes to thicken the sauce and allow the pasta to absorb the flavors, stirring now and then. Add more cream if necessary.

8. Serve in individual bowls topped with dill sprigs.

## LOVE NOTES

1. **The fettuccine should swim** in the sauce. If it is too "tight" and the pasta sits in a lump in the pot, add more cream, ¼ cup at a time, to thin it, stirring and heating over low heat after each addition.

2. **Fresh pasta weighs more than dried,** so you need more than 1 pound of fresh fettuccine to equal the yield in 1 pound of dried.

# Greek Macaroni & Cheese

THIS IS ONE OF OUR LIGHTER VERSIONS OF MAC AND CHEESE (LIGHTER, NOT LOW calorie!) because it uses no cream. It does have a few more ingredients than some of the other recipes in this chapter, but if its popularity among our guests is any indication, your family will love it!

2 skinless, boneless chicken breasts (about ¾ pound), cut into 2 by ½-inch strips

1 teaspoon kosher salt (divided), plus more for salting the pasta water

½ teaspoon freshly ground black pepper (divided)

¼ cup all-purpose flour

2 tablespoons olive oil

1 tablespoon finely chopped garlic (about 2 large cloves)

3 medium tomatoes, diced (2 cups)

1 pound farfalle (bow-tie) pasta, preferably De Cecco

5 packed cups fresh spinach leaves (about 8 ounces or 2 bunches), washed and stems trimmed (Love Note 2, page 20, Three Cheese and Spinach–Stuffed Portabella Mushrooms)

1½ tablespoons chopped fresh oregano leaves, or 1 teaspoon dried oregano

2 cups dry white wine, such as Chardonnay

1½ cups crumbled feta cheese (about 7 ounces)

1 cup pitted Kalamata or other black olives (Love Note)

2 tablespoons unsalted butter

¼ cup grated Parmesan cheese, for garnish

1. Arrange the chicken strips in a single layer on a plate or baking sheet (this makes it easier to season and dredge them). Sprinkle evenly with ¼ teaspoon salt and ⅛ teaspoon black pepper. Place the flour in a shallow bowl, and dredge the chicken in flour on both sides.

*continued*

2. Place a large (12- to 14-inch) sauté pan over high heat for a couple of minutes. When hot, add the olive oil, swirl the pan to coat, and add the chicken strips in a single layer. Cook in batches if needed. Cook until slightly browned, about 1 minute. Turn the pieces or stir them so they brown evenly, about 1½ minutes more.

3. Reduce the heat to medium-high. Push the chicken strips to the side of the pan as they continue to cook, and add the garlic. Cook just until fragrant, about 1 minute, but do not let it brown or it will taste bitter.

4. Add the tomatoes, season with ¼ teaspoon salt and ⅛ teaspoon black pepper, and cook until they start to give off their juices, about 2 minutes.

5. Meanwhile, bring a medium (6- to 8-quart) pot of water to a boil. Salt it generously (it should taste like the sea). Stir in the pasta and cook according to the package directions. Drain (but don't rinse, or you'll rinse away starches that will help thicken the sauce) and return to the empty pot.

6. Add the spinach, oregano, remaining ½ teaspoon salt, and remaining ¼ teaspoon black pepper to the pan with the tomatoes. Stir until the spinach has wilted, about 5 minutes. Add the wine to the pan, stirring to scrape up any browned bits, and cook over medium-high heat until reduced slightly and the chicken is cooked through, about 10 minutes.

7. Add the feta and olives to the pan, stirring well to incorporate. Remove the pan from the heat and stir in the butter, a tablespoon at a time, until the sauce has thickened slightly. (Careful! Your pan can't be too hot or the butter and sauce will separate and look oily. If that happens, take the sauce off the heat and add more feta to help the sauce bind together.)

8. Stir the sauce into the cooked and drained pasta in the pot. Place over medium heat and simmer for 2 minutes to thicken the sauce and allow the pasta to absorb the flavors, stirring now and then.

9. Serve in individual bowls topped with Parmesan cheese.

**LOVE NOTE**

**Kalamata olives** are the quintessential Greek olive, with a salty and acidic flavor that does a great job of cutting through rich flavors. They're widely available either pitted or unpitted, but if their flavor is too sharp for you, try substituting milder Niçoise or other black olives.

# Southwestern Macaroni & Cheese

CHICKEN, MONTEREY JACK CHEESE, AND CHIPOTLE PEPPERS GIVE THIS DISH A Southwest kick. If you like the smoky-spicy flavor of the spices but want to avoid the extra fat in the sour cream garnish, just add a teaspoon of the sauce from canned chipotles in adobo to the macaroni and cheese itself and skip the garnish altogether.

1 teaspoon kosher salt, plus more for salting the pasta water

1 pound fusilli (corkscrew), rotini, or other pasta (Love Note 1), preferably De Cecco

2 tablespoons unsalted butter or canola oil

1 medium yellow onion, finely diced (1 cup)

1 cup finely diced bell peppers (preferably green and red)

¼ cup finely chopped fresh jalapeño peppers, stems and seeds removed

3 cups heavy cream

2 cups firmly packed shredded Monterey Jack or pepper Jack cheese (about ½ pound)

1 cup cooked shredded or diced chicken (about 1 chicken breast; Love Note 2)

½ teaspoon freshly ground black pepper

½ cup sour cream, for garnish

¼ teaspoon minced chipotle chile (from canned chipotles in adobo; Love Note 3), for garnish

½ cup thinly sliced scallions, (white and green parts), for garnish

1. Bring a medium (6- to 8-quart) pot of water to a boil. Salt it generously (it should taste like the sea). Stir in the pasta and cook according to the package directions. Drain (don't rinse, or you'll rinse away starches that will help thicken the sauce) and return to the empty pot.

2. Meanwhile, place a large (12- to 14-inch) sauté pan over medium-high heat for several minutes. When hot, add the butter or oil, onions, bell peppers, and jalapeños and sauté until they begin to soften, about 5 minutes.

3. Add the heavy cream. Bring to a boil, and then lower the heat to medium and simmer until the cream is reduced slightly, about 3 minutes.

4. Add the cheese and chicken. Stir well and cook over medium-high heat until the cheese has melted and the mixture thickens, about 3 minutes. Season with the salt and pepper.

5. Stir the sauce into the cooked and drained pasta in the pot. Place over medium heat and simmer for 1 to 2 minutes to thicken the sauce and allow the pasta to absorb the flavors, stirring now and then. If too thick, add a little more cream.

6. To make the garnish, in a small bowl, mix together the sour cream and minced chipotle. Serve the macaroni and cheese in individual bowls topped with a dollop of the chipotle sour cream and a sprinkle of sliced scallions.

## LOVE NOTES

1. I like **fusilli pasta** for this dish because the shredded chicken and peppers get caught in the curls, making every bite delicious.

2. Use **leftover chicken** or store-bought roast chicken, but avoid canned chicken, which is more like cold cuts.

3. **Chipotles are dried, smoked jalapeño** peppers that give a smoky, slightly sweet flavor to dishes. You can find cans of chipotles stewed in spicy adobo sauce in the Mexican foods aisle at the supermarket. Substitute chipotle chile powder, New Mexico chile powder, or regular chili powder to taste for canned chipotles.

Freeze any leftover canned chipotles in ice cube trays. Once frozen, move to a zip-top freezer bag.

# Roasted Garlic, Prosciutto, and Provolone Macaroni & Cheese

THIS IS ONE OF THE BEST MACARONI AND CHEESE COMBINATIONS ANYWHERE. Roasting makes the garlic mild and slightly sweet, and smoked provolone adds depth. The salty prosciutto gets a quick sauté to crisp it up and bring out its savory side. As great as these flavors are with pasta, they're also fantastic on pizza or scrambled into eggs, as in Mike's Special Scramble (page 259).

¼ teaspoon kosher salt, plus more for salting the pasta water

1 pound penne or other pasta, preferably De Cecco

1 tablespoon unsalted butter or canola oil

¼ pound thinly sliced prosciutto, cut into ¼-inch strips (¾ cup)

⅓ cup roasted garlic (about 2 heads; Love Note 1)

3 cups heavy cream

2 cups shredded smoked provolone cheese (about ½ pound; Love Note 2)

½ teaspoon freshly ground black pepper

¼ cup grated Parmesan cheese, for garnish

¼ cup chopped fresh Italian (flat-leaf) parsley, for garnish (optional)

1. Bring a medium (6- to 8-quart) pot of water to a boil. Salt it generously (it should taste like the sea). Stir in the pasta and cook according to the package directions. Drain (but don't rinse, or you'll rinse away starches that will help thicken the sauce) and return to the empty pot.

2. Meanwhile, place a large (12- to 14-inch) sauté pan over high heat for several minutes. When hot, add the butter or oil and prosciutto. Sauté until slightly brown around the edges and sizzling, about 2 minutes.

3. Reduce the heat to medium-high and add the roasted garlic and heavy cream. Bring to a boil, then lower the heat to medium and simmer, stirring occasionally, until the cream is reduced slightly, about 3 minutes.

4. Add the provolone. Stir well and cook over medium-high heat until the cheese has melted and the mixture has thickened, about 3 minutes. Season with the salt and pepper.

5. Stir the sauce into the cooked and drained pasta in the pot. Place over medium heat and simmer for 1 to 2 minutes to thicken the sauce and allow the pasta to absorb the flavors, stirring now and then.

6. Serve in individual bowls topped with Parmesan cheese and parsley.

## LOVE NOTES

**1 Roasted garlic is easy to make.** If you have the oven fired up to roast something, think about throwing a head of garlic in the oven, too. Cut the top quarter off the top of the head (the pointy side) to expose the cloves. Set the garlic on a double thickness of aluminum foil and drizzle with olive oil. Season with salt and pepper and toss to coat. Wrap tightly in foil and roast at 400°F for 30 to 40 minutes, until the cloves are squishy soft.

Remove from the oven and, when cool enough to handle, squeeze the head from the bottom so the cloves fall out. Pull off any remaining cloves that are full of garlic and squeeze the garlic out of the cloves one at a time or remove it with the tip of a knife.

Use right away, refrigerate for several days, or freeze in tablespoon-size dollops on a baking sheet until firm, then store in a zip-top freezer bag for several months.

**2 Top-of-the-line provolone** is aged for a long time and has a strong flavor that is too much for this dish. Just use mild provolone that has been smoked. If you don't find it in the cheese case, look at the deli counter.

# Macaroni & Cheese Cordon Bleu

HAM AND SWISS IS A PERFECT COMBINATION IN SO MANY DISHES—FROM SANDWICHES and scrambles to chicken Cordon Bleu—and I knew it would be a winner tossed with pasta and cream. This recipe is delicious with any dried pasta, but for a touch of elegance or when having guests over for dinner, use fresh fettuccine.

½ teaspoon kosher salt, plus more for salting the pasta water

1 pound cavatappi (spiral tube) or other dried pasta, preferably De Cecco, or 2 (9-ounce) packages fresh fettuccine (Love Note 2, page 239, Smoked Salmon, Cream Cheese, and Dill Macaroni & Cheese)

2 tablespoons unsalted butter

1½ cups thinly sliced button mushrooms (about 6 ounces) (Love Note 1)

½ teaspoon freshly ground black pepper

6 ounces cured deli ham, cut into 1-inch by ¼-inch strips (about 1 cup; Love Note 2)

3 cups heavy cream

2 cups firmly packed shredded Swiss cheese (about ½ pound)

¼ cup grated Parmesan cheese, for garnish

1 tablespoon chopped fresh Italian (flat-leaf) parsley, for garnish (optional)

1. Bring a medium (6- to 8-quart) pot of water to a boil. Salt it generously (it should taste like the sea). Stir in the pasta and cook according to the package directions. Drain (but don't rinse, or you'll rinse away starches that will help thicken the sauce) and return to the empty pot.

2. Meanwhile, place a large (12- to 14-inch) sauté pan over high heat for several minutes. When very hot, add the butter and mushrooms. Season with the salt and black pepper. Sauté over high heat until they begin to brown, about 5 minutes (lower the heat if necessary to keep the pan from scorching). Add the ham and sauté until it begins to turn golden around the edges, about 2 minutes.

3. Lower the heat to medium-high and add the heavy cream. Bring to a boil, stirring to scrape up any browned bits. Lower the heat to medium, and simmer until the cream is reduced slightly, about 3 minutes.

4. Add the Swiss cheese. Stir well and cook over medium-high heat, stirring occasionally, until the cheese has melted and the mixture thickens, about 3 minutes.

5. Stir the sauce into the cooked and drained pasta in the pot. Place over medium heat and simmer for 1 to 2 minutes to thicken the sauce and allow the pasta to absorb the flavors, stirring now and then.

6. Serve in individual bowls topped with Parmesan cheese and parsley.

## LOVE NOTES

**1. Button and cremini mushrooms** are cultivated rather than wild, and therefore they are not all that dirty. Plus, their smooth caps mean they're not usually caked with dirt and debris. Since they don't need a deep cleaning (and it's best not to waterlog them), just clean them with a damp paper towel or clean kitchen towel. Wipe the towel over the cap, and shake debris off the towel as you go.

**2. Cured hams are preserved** with a brine solution rather than smoked, so they have a sweet flavor that doesn't overwhelm the cheese. Any unsmoked ham from the deli counter will work for this dish.

# Cajun Macaroni & Cheese

SPICY ANDOUILLE SAUSAGE, ONIONS, AND GREEN PEPPERS ARE CLASSIC CAJUN
ingredients that go remarkably well with a very un-Creole combo of Cheddar cheese
and pasta. If you can take the heat, sprinkle a little hot sauce into the sauce along
with the salt and pepper.

1 teaspoon kosher salt, plus more
for salting the pasta water

1 pound fusilli (corkscrew), rotini
(spiral), or other pasta, preferably
De Cecco

2 tablespoons unsalted butter or
canola oil

¼ pound smoked andouille sausage, cut into half-moons (1 cup;
Love Note)

1 large yellow onion, finely diced
(1 cup)

1 cup finely diced bell peppers
(about 1 pepper; use ½ green and
½ red for color)

3 cups heavy cream

2 cups packed shredded sharp
Cheddar cheese (about ½ pound)

½ teaspoon freshly ground black
pepper

Tabasco or other hot sauce, to
taste (optional)

½ cup thinly sliced scallions,
(white and green parts), for
garnish

1.  Bring a medium (6- to 8-quart) pot of water to a boil. Salt it generously (it should
    taste like the sea). Stir in the pasta and cook according to the package directions.
    Drain (but don't rinse, or you'll rinse away starches that will help thicken the sauce)
    and return to the empty pot.

2.  Meanwhile, place a large (12- to 14-inch) sauté pan over medium-high heat for
    several minutes. When hot, add the butter or oil, andouille sausage, onions, and
    peppers. Sauté until the onions and peppers begin to soften and the andouille starts
    to brown, about 5 minutes. Lower the heat and continue to cook until the onions
    are golden and the sausage is evenly caramelized.

3. Add the heavy cream, increase the heat, and bring to a boil. Lower the heat to medium and simmer until the cream is reduced slightly, about 2 minutes.

4. Add the Cheddar cheese. Stir well and cook over medium-high heat, stirring now and then, until the cheese has melted and the mixture thickens, about 3 minutes. Season with the salt, pepper, and hot sauce, if using.

5. Stir the sauce into the cooked and drained pasta in the pot. Place over medium heat and simmer for 1 to 2 minutes to thicken the sauce and allow the pasta to absorb the flavors, stirring now and then.

6. Serve in individual bowls topped with sliced scallions.

## LOVE NOTE

**Andouille sausage** is a coarse, hard, smoked sausage with a spicy, robust flavor. Although it's European in origin (variations of the sausage are common in France and Germany), it's best known for being a staple in Cajun cooking. As you might expect, the Cajun version is the spiciest. I prefer buying smoked, precooked sausage, so when it comes time for breakfast, things take a little less time.

breakfast

**I know you don't need me to tell you that breakfast is the most important meal of the day.** But I am here to remind you that breakfast doesn't have to be as plain as a piece of buttered toast or as meager as a cup of coffee. It doesn't have to come from a box, a mix, or even a restaurant for that matter. Whether it's the weekend or a weekday, a holiday or a random Sunday in March, you can easily whip up flavorful meals that will get the whole family out of bed.

### GETTING GOOD FOOD ON THE TABLE

The recipes in this chapter might not be the fastest to prepare, but as with any other meal, the trick to getting breakfast on the table is planning ahead. It's how restaurants operate, and home kitchens should be no different. There are plenty of recipes in this chapter that can be prepared ahead so that you can have a delicious, nutritious breakfast in a jiffy.

For example, put a bag of unbaked scones in the freezer, and just pop one in the oven (frozen!) while you get ready for work. Get a head start by mixing the dry ingredients for pancakes on a weekend afternoon and keeping them in your pantry to combine with the wet ingredients on a weekday morning. Portion out the fruit for smoothies and keep it in plastic bags in the freezer. When it's time to whiz one up, just dump, pour, and blend.

The rewards for your efforts are huge. It's incredibly satisfying to gather everyone together before the day begins. You get to share a few moments of peace before the world steps in, and you'll know you're sending your family off to school, work, or weekend adventures well-nourished and energized, physically and emotionally.

This chapter will give you plenty of inventive ideas for breakfasts and brunches that are anything but ordinary (there's a reason why weekend brunches at Mother's have lines out the door). As exciting as these recipes are, they're not hard to duplicate at home if you have the right ingredients, tools, and techniques.

## BUTTER

At Mother's we use unsalted butter to cook all our breakfast entrées because it imparts such a delicious flavor. But we clarify it first so the milk solids don't burn and turn the omelets and scrambles brown before they're cooked through. It's just not visually appealing, and the dish may end up with a slightly burnt flavor.

While it does take time, you can clarify a few pounds of butter at a time and keep it in your refrigerator indefinitely. For the technique, see Love Note 2, page 145, Nana's Chicken Fried Chicken. But even if you don't use clarified butter, the dishes will still turn out delicious.

## EGGS

Eggs are an excellent, inexpensive source of 13 essential nutrients, including protein, iron, choline, folate, and zinc. Not long ago, eggs were condemned for being high in cholesterol, but studies have since found that, for healthy people, the cholesterol we eat doesn't really affect cholesterol levels in our blood. Saturated fat is what causes the most problems, but eggs are low in that regard.

These recipes call for large eggs, and make sure your eggs are fresh. If you have access to farm-fresh eggs from the farmers' market (or a backyard coop), so much the better. You can tell an egg is fresh by how thick the yolks and whites look when you crack them into the pan. An older egg has thin, watery whites, while the whites of a fresh egg are buoyant and perky. One other tip: If you have any doubts about the freshness of your eggs, drop one into a large glass of water. If it sits on the bottom, it's as fresh as it can be. The more it stands up, the less fresh it is, and if it floats, forget it!

## OMELETS

The right tool can mean the difference between success and heartache when making omelets. First and foremost, you need at least one nonstick pan. It should be 8 inches in diameter to make a perfectly sized single-serving omelet.

Personally, I think you should keep the nonstick pan for omelets only. That way it stays in tip-top condition (I'm not a big fan of using nonstick pans for much else). Protect the nonstick surface while storing by stacking nothing on top or by putting a paper towel in the pan to protect it from anything. Once that coating begins to wear off, you'll have trouble keeping the omelets from sticking. A heatproof rubber spatula will keep you from scratching the surface and is great for getting under the eggs. Remember, metal tools and dishwashers will ruin the nonstick finish on your pan.

As for the technique, I learned how to make perfect omelets when I was a line cook at Le Cirque. I'd start one on top of the stove, pouring the eggs into a nonstick pan, stirring them with a heatproof rubber spatula over medium-high heat until the eggs started to set. I'd stop stirring once I made sure the entire bottom was covered with cooked egg. Then I would remove the pan from the heat and put it under the broiler so that it cooked on top without further browning on the bottom. I still follow this technique today.

If you like your omelets on the soft side, put any cheese the recipe requires on top of the omelet before you put it under the broiler. That way it will melt as the egg finishes cooking.

If you like your eggs a bit more done, place the pan under the broiler until the top is mostly cooked. Remove from the broiler, sprinkle with the cheese, and return to the broiler until the cheese is melted. Top with the remaining filling ingredients and use a rubber spatula to flip one half of the egg over onto itself, and then slide onto a plate.

### FRITTATAS

Frittatas are another great way to cook eggs. A frittata is an open-face, unfolded omelet, but it's as forgiving and easy to make as a scramble. Everything cooks in one pan, starting with the flavoring ingredients, and then the eggs are added. It's cooked on top of the stove, stirred until the eggs set on the bottom, and then the pan is placed in the oven to finish cooking. When it comes out, it's puffy, fluffy, and basically looks like an egg pizza.

Frittatas can be served hot, cold, or at room temperature, making them great for serving crowds and adding to buffets. They're also at home in any meal. Serve them for breakfast with a side of potatoes or for lunch or dinner with a green salad.

If you're feeding several people at once, you'll have to decide how you want to serve it. Do you want everyone to have their own small, round frittata on their plate, or would wedges from a larger frittata work fine? If wedges suit you, then use a large (12- to 14-inch) nonstick sauté pan. After cooking, slide the frittata onto a cutting board (the rubber spatula can help) and cut into wedges like pizza. (You can even use the rubber spatula to do the cutting since the eggs are so tender.)

If you like the individual round frittatas (I do!), you can use an 8-inch nonstick pan and cook each one separately. To speed things up, you could have two pans going at the same time. Keep the cooked frittatas warm with tented foil while you make the rest (they will still be pretty good by the time you eat them, though not as magnificent as those right out of the oven). If you're really ambitious, get four sauté pans and make four at a time.

If you decide to make individual frittatas, a fun way to include the family is to have one person make all the filling and then have each family member mix a portion of it into his or her own eggs in the pan.

### SCRAMBLES

If you're intimidated by omelets, don't fear. Many omelet and frittata recipes (or bloopers thereof) can be turned into scrambles for an equally delicious dish. To make an omelet or frittata a scramble, just cook the filling as the recipe prescribes (without the cheese) in the pan first, then add the eggs, stirring with a wooden spoon or heatproof rubber spatula as they cook. When the eggs seem almost completely cooked but still look slightly wet, add the cheese and cook for just a few minutes more. Adding the cheese too early will melt it too much, making the eggs runny.

### PANCAKES AND OTHER SWEETS

When it comes to the sweeter side of breakfast, there is an almost endless array of ways you can dress up pancakes. You can add all manner of flavorings, from the spices in Pumpkin Pancakes (page 295) to the almond paste in the Almond Poppyseed Pancakes (page 287).

There are just two tricks to making perfect pancakes. First, don't stir the batter too much. After adding the wet ingredients to the dry, stir just until everything is moistened. There will still be lumps, but that's fine; they'll cook out. If you stir too much you'll end up with rubbery rather than fluffy pancakes. Second, when cooking pancakes, think of them as being *baked* on the griddle, not *fried*. You want moderate heat so they have a chance to cook evenly without the outside getting burnt before the inside is cooked; and don't use too much butter or you'll have lots of pockmarks rather than smooth pancakes.

Fruit compotes make delicious toppings for pancakes and are a festive departure from syrups. But when you do serve maple syrup, make sure it's the real thing. I like Grade B syrup, which is darker and fuller in flavor than Grade A. Slathering the pancakes with butter really enhances the flavor of the syrup. But cold butter is not easy to work with, so set your butter out on the counter the night before and it'll be nice and soft by morning. I leave my salted (salt acts as a preservative) butter out (covered, of course) on the counter, ready for a schmear anytime!

# Mike's Special Scramble

THIS IS MY FAVORITE DISH ON THE BREAKFAST MENU AT MOTHER'S BISTRO, IN PART because it's named after one of my favorite people, Michael Golub. One day I was hanging out with Mike, Rob (my significant other), and two other friends when we decided to order a pizza. We were debating what to get on it, and Mike took charge, ordering prosciutto, fresh tomato, basil, and roasted garlic. The combo was delicious and memorable. It inspired me to create an omelet with the same ingredients. It eventually became a scramble on our menu, and it bears Mike's name in his honor.

2 tablespoons unsalted butter, preferably clarified (Love Note 2, page 145, Nana's Chicken Fried Chicken)

3½ ounces (¾ cup prosciutto, cut into thin strips; Love Note)

2 medium tomatoes, diced (about 1 cup)

¼ teaspoon kosher salt

½ teaspoon freshly ground black pepper

¼ cup roasted garlic (about 2 heads; Love Note 1, page 247, Roasted Garlic, Prosciutto, and Provolone Macaroni & Cheese)

2 tablespoons chiffonade fresh basil (Love Note 2, page 44, Mama's Italian Chopped Salad)

12 large eggs, beaten

1 cup shredded provolone cheese (about ¼ pound)

¼ cup grated Parmesan cheese

1. Heat a large (12- to 14-inch), nonstick sauté pan over medium-high heat. When hot, add the butter and prosciutto and sauté until lightly golden around the edges, about 3 minutes. Add the tomatoes, salt, and pepper and sauté for another 2 minutes. Stir in the roasted garlic and basil.

2. Add the eggs and cook over medium-high heat, stirring occasionally with a heat-proof rubber spatula, until the eggs are mostly cooked but a little underdone (they should be in large fluffy curds and still look a little wet, though not liquidy). Add

*continued*

the provolone cheese and stir to melt and finish cooking the eggs. (Don't add the cheese until the eggs are almost cooked or the eggs will end up soupy and loose.)

3. Top with the Parmesan cheese and serve.

**LOVE NOTE**

**Prosciutto is an Italian ham** that's salt cured and air dried rather than smoked. The result is a deliciously savory, salty ham that's usually served in paper-thin slices. Although there are some U.S. producers making prosciutto, the best prosciutto is the real deal from the Parma area in Italy. If you're serving slices of prosciutto as an appetizer, you'll want the best; look for prosciutto di Parma or prosciutto di San Daniele on the label. But for this scramble, which has so many other ingredients, there's no need to pay top dollar for imported prosciutto.

# Tofu Scramble

WE HAVE A LOT OF VEGETARIANS IN PORTLAND, SO I CREATED AN EGG-FREE scramble that even an omnivore could enjoy. Tofu is a great source of inexpensive, lean protein, but I think most of us agree that it needs a little dressing up. I went a little crazy when I created this dish because I put everything in it but the kitchen sink. It's so yummy, though, that I can't bear to take anything out. It's an incredibly healthful way to start the day, and it makes a great vegan dish when sautéed in oil instead of butter. I think it's even tastier topped with cheese.

5 tablespoons unsalted butter, preferably clarified (Love Note 2, page 145, Nana's Chicken Fried Chicken), or 5 tablespoons vegetable oil

¾ pound tofu, drained and cut into ½-inch cubes (2 cups)

1½ cups thinly sliced mushrooms (about 6 ounces whole mushrooms)

1 teaspoon kosher salt (divided)

¼ teaspoon freshly ground black pepper (divided)

1 medium yellow onion, finely diced (1 cup)

½ green bell pepper, finely diced (½ cup)

½ red bell pepper, finely diced (½ cup)

1 teaspoon finely chopped garlic (about 1 clove)

3 cups diced Roasted Reds (page 215; also Love Note)

2 medium tomatoes, diced (1 cup)

2½ packed cups fresh spinach leaves (about 4 ounces)

2 cups shredded cheese, such as Cheddar, Monterey Jack, provolone, feta, or Swiss (optional)

1. If using cheese, heat the oven to 400°F. Place a large (12- to 14-inch), nonstick sauté pan over high heat for several minutes. When the pan is very hot, add the butter or oil and heat until shimmering. Add the tofu and cook over high heat until golden on one side (the tofu will spit and splatter, so cover the pan with a splatter screen

*continued*

if you have one and want to). Stir to cook the tofu on all sides (if it seems like the tofu is sticking, wait until it is golden before turning).

2. Add the mushrooms, season with ½ teaspoon salt and ⅛ teaspoon pepper, and sauté over high heat until the mushrooms are golden, 4 to 5 minutes.

3. Lower the heat to medium-high. Add the onions and peppers and sauté until soft, stirring now and then, 5 to 6 minutes. Add the garlic and sauté until fragrant, about 1 minute.

4. Add the potatoes and sauté until lightly golden in spots, stirring occasionally, about 5 minutes.

5. Add the tomatoes and spinach and season with the remaining ½ teaspoon salt and ⅛ teaspoon pepper. Stir well to distribute the ingredients and heat until the spinach is wilted and the tomatoes are warmed through (this takes only a minute or two).

6. If using cheese, sprinkle it on top and place the pan in the oven until the cheese is melted.

7. Divide the scramble among four plates or pile onto a platter, and serve.

When making a recipe that calls for **Mother's Roasted Reds,** don't substitute some other kind of potato. When I created these scrambles and hashes, I used my roasted red potatoes, so their seasoning (garlic salt, thyme, salt, pepper, and olive oil) is part of the flavor of these breakfast dishes.

Take note: The potatoes are dry and fluffy inside, which makes them a little tricky to dice cleanly, but that's OK. There's no need to agonize over perfect potato pieces. If you prefer clean slices, you can chill the roasted potatoes and cut them cold. If you want to get ahead, roast the potatoes the day before and refrigerate overnight.

# Migas (Scrambled Eggs with Corn Tortillas)

THE RECIPE FOR THIS TEX-MEX DISH CAME FROM ONE OF MY FORMER SOUS CHEFS, Edilberto (Edi) Rodriguez, Jr., who had an excellent way with food. He nominated his grandmother, Carmelina, as Mother of the Month, and then researched her recipes, helped put together a menu of Cuban specialties, including empanadas and tostones, and cooked it all for the entire month.

This recipe is Edi's adaptation of a dish created to use up stale corn tortillas. It's one of my favorites for a crowd. It holds up well, and guests can customize their breakfast with condiments like salsa, chipotle sour cream, green onions, and diced avocado.

4 tablespoons (½ stick) unsalted butter, preferably clarified (Love Note 2, page 145, Nana's Chicken Fried Chicken)

1 small to medium yellow onion, finely diced (¾ cup)

¾ cup finely diced bell peppers (preferably a mixture of green and red)

4 (6-inch) corn tortillas cut into long, narrow strips (1 cup)

½ teaspoon kosher salt

¼ teaspoon freshly ground black pepper

12 large eggs, beaten

1½ cups shredded Monterey Jack or pepper Jack cheese

½ cup Chipotle Sour Cream (optional; step 6, page 245, South-western Macaroni and Cheese)

½ cup Salsa (page 266), or store-bought salsa

½ cup thinly sliced scallions, (white and green parts; about 6)

1.  Place a large (12- to 14-inch), nonstick sauté pan over medium-high heat for several minutes. Add the butter, onions, and peppers, and sauté, stirring now and then, for about 2 minutes or until softened. Add the tortillas and continue to cook, stirring now and then, until they start to get slightly golden and the onions begin to cara-melize, 3 to 5 minutes more. Season with the salt and pepper.

*continued*

2. Pour the eggs into the onion-tortilla mixture and cook, stirring occasionally with a heatproof rubber spatula, until the eggs are almost fully cooked but still a little wet (though not liquidy).

3. Add the cheese and stir to combine and finish cooking the eggs (don't add the cheese too soon or it will make the eggs runny).

4. Divide the eggs among serving plates and top with a dollop of sour cream, a heaping tablespoon of salsa, and a sprinkle of scallions. Pass around extra salsa separately.

## SALSA

MAKES 5 CUPS

SURE, YOU COULD JUST BUY ONE OF THE MANY TUBS OR BOTTLES OF SALSA AT THE store, but the flavor of homemade salsa is so much fresher and brighter. Making it yourself also means you can control the texture—making it as chunky or smooth as you like. This makes more than you'll need for the migas, but it will keep for up to 4 days in the refrigerator and can be frozen in small containers and defrosted in the refrigerator. Just give it a good whisking before serving.

3 cloves garlic

2 serrano or jalapeño chiles, stems and seeds removed (Love Note)

½ red onion, cut into quarters

2 medium tomatoes, cut into quarters (1½ cups)

1 (28-ounce) can whole tomatoes, drained if you prefer a thicker salsa (if you're not sure, reserve the juice and add it back if desired)

1 tablespoon chopped fresh cilantro

½ teaspoon ground cumin

Juice of 1 lime (about 2 tablespoons)

½ teaspoon kosher salt

¼ teaspoon freshly ground black pepper

1. Place the garlic and chiles in a food processor fitted with a metal blade and pulse until finely chopped. Transfer to a medium bowl.

2. Place the onions in the processor and pulse until finely chopped. Transfer to the bowl with the garlic and peppers.

3. Place the fresh tomatoes in the processor and pulse until finely chopped. Transfer to the bowl. (If you like a chunkier salsa, dice the tomatoes by hand.)

4. Place the canned tomatoes, cilantro, and cumin in the processor. Pulse once or twice to combine. Transfer to the bowl.

5. Add the lime juice to the mixture in the bowl, season with the salt and pepper, and stir to combine. Taste and adjust the seasoning with more lime juice, salt, or pepper, if desired (but remember that you may be eating this with something salty, like corn chips.) Freeze extra salsa in pint containers for future use.

*continued*

## LOVE NOTE

**Hot peppers keep most of their heat** locked up in their seeds. The more seeds you remove, the milder the pepper—and the finished dish—will be. To seed the peppers, slice off the tops, then slice the peppers in half lengthwise and scrape out the seeds. Don't touch your eyes or nose—the capsaicin (which makes a pepper spicy) is potent and can really burn. If you're the sensitive type (I'm desensitized after years of hot pans), you should also consider wearing rubber gloves so that the oils don't burn your skin.

# M.O.M.

Carmelina Criada Rodriguez was born in Las Bolas, a small town in Cuba, in 1914. She was a country girl from a rural area and always wanted to stay that way. After completing second grade she began to train as a seamstress, which became a lifelong passion and career. She was 20 and still living with her mother when she met her husband, Abel, 17 years her senior. He was commuting back and forth to the United States., where he worked as a waiter, and promised Carmelina that she would never have to leave Cuba—until Castro came to power in 1956.

They moved to New York, where Carmelina worked in a textile factory for 32 years. During that time, she gave birth to three sons. When her husband died, Carmelina left New York for San Francisco to be near the rest of her family, including many grandchildren. Everyone gathered for family dinners at Abuela's (Spanish for Grandmother's), and she always did the cooking, with tamales, roast pork, and tostones being staples.

Carmelina would tell many stories of growing up in Cuba, including one she took very seriously: A man had two donkeys, one he fed and one he did not. Of course, the donkey the man did not feed eventually died. And so at Carmelina's table you never left hungry. *"Comer! Comer!"* ("Eat! Eat!") she would say.

# Italian Frittata

FRITTATAS ARE BIG IN ITALY; AFTER ALL, THAT'S WHERE THEY ORIGINATED. THEY'RE usually simple fare, with only a few ingredients, baked in a large pan and cut into wedges. Peppers and onions are common Italian frittata ingredients, but I wanted to make ours even more special, so I added sausage, cheese, and tomato sauce. A tasty and colorful addition to a brunch buffet, this frittata looks as good as it tastes. Frittatas taste delicious even cold, straight from the fridge, but room temperature is even better. For another layer of flavor, use smoked mozzarella instead of fresh.

1 tablespoon unsalted butter, preferably clarified (Love Note 2, page 15, Nana's Chicken Fried Chicken)

8 ounces mild Italian sausage, either bulk or sliced into rounds (Love Note)

1 medium yellow onion, finely diced (1 cup)

½ red bell pepper, finely diced (about ½ cup)

½ green bell pepper, finely diced (about ½ cup)

16 large eggs, beaten

2 cups shredded (fresh or smoked) mozzarella cheese

1 cup Mama Mia Trattoria's Pomodoro Sauce (page 170), for serving

½ cup grated Parmesan cheese, for serving

¼ cup finely chopped fresh Italian (flat-leaf) parsley, for serving

1. Heat the oven to 400°F. Place a large (12- to 14-inch), nonstick, oven-safe sauté pan over medium-high heat. Add the butter and sausage and sauté until it is mostly cooked through and golden around the edges, 2 to 3 minutes.

2. Add the onions and peppers and sauté until they are soft and starting to turn lightly golden, about 5 minutes. (The sausage should release some of its fat for sautéing the onions and peppers. If the vegetables aren't sizzling, add 1 more tablespoon butter.)

*continued*

3. Add the eggs and cook, stirring with a heatproof rubber spatula, until the ingredients are evenly distributed and the eggs start to set on the bottom. Continue stirring another minute longer until the eggs are halfway cooked but still very wet on top.

4. Remove from the heat and sprinkle the mozzarella cheese evenly over the top. Place the pan in the oven and bake until the eggs are puffy, the cheese has melted, and the frittata is cooked through, 7 to 9 minutes.

5. Remove the pan from the oven. Loosen the frittata from the pan with a rubber spatula. Using the rubber spatula to help, tip the pan up and slide the frittata out of the pan onto a cutting board. Cut the frittata into wedges using the rubber spatula or a sharp, straight-edged knife (a serrated knife will tear it apart) and divide among plates.

6. To serve, top each wedge with a spoonful of pomodoro sauce and a sprinkle of Parmesan cheese and parsley.

*continued*

## LOVE NOTE

**Italian sausage** usually comes either hot and spicy or mild. It comes in bulk, which is loose raw sausage, or squeezed into casings and formed into links. If you want the texture of the sausage to be crumbly like ground beef, buy bulk sausage or slice the casings open and scrape out the raw sausage. If you want the sausage to be in firmer pieces, buy links and slice them into rounds.

##  Mise en Place

A major difference between professional kitchens and home kitchens is the use of *mise en place*. It's a French term that means "everything in its place," and that's exactly what professional chefs do—they get everything ready and in its place before they begin cooking—and you should, too.

The recipes in this book are written with mise en place in mind. The prepping directions for the ingredients are stated in the ingredients list so that you can get those ingredients chopped, diced, minced, or mashed before you even turn on the heat. Only when your ingredients are prepped and waiting are you ready to cook.

Setting up your "mise" is the best way to ensure success with a recipe. It begins with "mental mise en place" (as my teachers in culinary school used to call it). Mental mise means you take the time to read through the recipe (at least once, but preferably twice) so that you're familiar with it before you even begin. With mental mise, you'll have a better idea of what to expect during the cooking process, and there will be no surprises like "marinate overnight before continuing."

Mental mise is also important when planning ahead. When you're chopping onions for today's black bean soup you can also be cutting onions for tomorrow's pot roast. With mental mise, you're always thinking ahead—when to go to the grocery store, what pots you'll need and where the lids are, what utensils and platters are needed for serving, and so forth.

An actual mise en place of prepped ingredients, utensils, and pots helps you make sure that you have everything you need so that won't have to stop cooking midway through to get something you've forgotten. So plan ahead, think ahead, and act ahead. Make sure everything on your ingredient list is measured, chopped, sliced, or peeled; your pots are clean and ready; you have a container of tools—from spatulas to spoons—near the stove; and you know what's in store from one step to the next.

# Corned Beef Hash

HAVING LEFTOVERS FOR CORNED BEEF HASH MAY BE THE BEST REASON TO COOK A corned beef on St. Patrick's Day. But you don't have to wait until the holiday to make this. Corned beef is a common staple at delis, where you can pick up just what you need without having to cook the whole roast.

Use the same recipe for pulled pork hash, which is a great way to use up leftovers (roast beef or turkey works great, too) and have a delicious breakfast at the same time.

3 tablespoons unsalted butter, preferably clarified (Love Note 2, page 145, Nana's Chicken Fried Chicken)

1 medium yellow onion, finely diced (1 cup)

2 cups diced or shredded corned beef (Love Note)

3 cups diced Roasted Reds (page 215; and Love Note, page 263, Tofu Scramble)

2½ packed cups fresh spinach leaves (about 4 ounces)

½ teaspoon kosher salt

½ teaspoon freshly ground black pepper

1½ cups Horseradish Cream (page 274)

1.  Place a large (12- to 14-inch), nonstick sauté pan over medium-high heat for several minutes. When hot, add the butter and onions; sauté until the onions are almost soft, stirring now and then, about 3 minutes. (Lower the heat to medium if you're getting a lot of color around the edges of the onions.)

2.  Add the corned beef, stir with a rubber spatula, and sauté over medium-high heat until golden around edges, another 3 minutes.

3.  Add the potatoes, stir, and sauté over high heat until slightly golden, about 3 minutes.

4.  Add the spinach and sprinkle the leaves with the salt and pepper. Sauté, stirring, until the spinach starts to wilt, about 1 minute. *continued*

5. Stir in the Horseradish Cream. Simmer until most of the liquid has evaporated and the cream has thickened enough to bind the hash together. (Don't reduce too much or the cream and butter will separate and you'll have a "broken" sauce; Love Note page 277, Wild Salmon Hash. Don't reduce too little or you'll have a lot of cream on the plate.)

6. Spoon onto plates and serve topped with 2 eggs any style and toast on the side.

## HORSERADISH CREAM

MAKES ABOUT 1¼ CUPS

TURN THIS INTO STONE-GROUND MUSTARD CREAM (WHICH IS GREAT WITH PULLED pork hash) by omitting the horseradish and adding an extra tablespoon of stone-ground mustard.

1 cup heavy whipping cream

1 tablespoon plus 1½ teaspoons prepared horseradish

1 tablespoon plus 1½ teaspoons stone-ground mustard

2 teaspoons Dijon mustard

In a small bowl, whisk together all the ingredients. This can be made several days ahead and kept refrigerated in an airtight container.

## LOVE NOTE

**Corned beef is usually beef brisket** or beef round that has been soaked in seasoned brine. The term *corn* comes from an Old English word that refers to the salt and seasonings used to cure the meat. It's not easy to find corned beef at grocery stores except around St. Patrick's Day, so buy some cooked corned beef from a deli. You'll need about 12 ounces. (I'd buy a pound, make a nice sandwich, and use the rest for the hash.)

# Wild Salmon Hash

BEING IN THE PACIFIC NORTHWEST, WE CAN'T RESIST OFFERING FRESH WILD SALMON even on our breakfast menu. Besides, with Mother's nestled among many of downtown Portland's hotels, we end up serving a lot of out-of-towners who like to sample the region's fare—and we wouldn't want to disappoint! Luckily, you can substitute with any fish you like—cod, red snapper, or halibut—so just choose what's plentiful in your neck of the woods. Leeks are great with fish; they have a wonderful oniony flavor without being overpowering and let the beautiful flavor of the fish come through.

2 to 3 leeks (about ½ pound)

2 tablespoons butter, preferably clarified (Love Note 2, page 145, Nana's Chicken Fried Chicken)

1 pound fresh wild salmon (or other fish), skin and bones removed, cut into 1-inch dice

3 cups diced Roasted Reds (page 215; also Love Note, page 263, Tofu Scramble)

1 teaspoon kosher salt

1½ teaspoons freshly ground black pepper

1 cup heavy cream

¼ cup chopped fresh chives, for garnish (optional)

1. Trim off the root end and dark green leaves from the leeks, leaving just the white and light green parts. Slice lengthwise, then crosswise into ¼-inch-thick half-moons. Place in a bowl filled with cold water and swish around to remove sand and dirt. Lift the leeks out and drain in a colander. You should have about 3 cups.

2. Place a large (12- to 14-inch), nonstick sauté pan over medium-high heat for several minutes. When hot, add the butter, tilt to melt it or coat the pan, and then add the leeks. Sauté for about 3 minutes, or until the leeks soften and start to turn golden around the edges.

3. Add the salmon and sauté until it begins to turn opaque, about 3 minutes.

*continued*

4. Add the potatoes and sauté, stirring occasionally, for 5 to 6 minutes. Season with the salt and pepper.

5. Add the cream and simmer until most of the liquid has evaporated and the cream has thickened enough to bind the hash together. (Don't reduce too much or the cream and butter will separate and you'll have a "broken" sauce; Love Note.)

6. Serve with 2 eggs any style and toast. Garnish with chives, if desired.

## LOVE NOTE

**I simmer cream until it has thickened** enough to use as a sauce, or as in this recipe, a binding agent. Cream does a good job of reducing to a sauce without having to rely on thickeners like flour or roux. The reason cream (and other high-fat dairy products like crème fraîche) works in this way is because it's higher in fat than in protein. You can simmer it until the water evaporates, whereas simmering milk until the water evaporates ends in a curdled mess. Milk is higher in protein than fat, and it's the protein that curdles when exposed to high temperatures (and acidity, which is why you have to be careful when adding lemon juice, vinegar, or wine to sauces made with milk instead of cream).

Even cream has a point of no return, though. Simmering it for too long will cause what proteins it does have to coagulate and separate from the fat, which ruins any emulsion and makes the sauce taste and look oily. This is one of the ways a sauce can "break."

# Mother's Biscuits and Gravy

LIGHT BUTTERMILK BISCUITS TOPPED WITH CREAMY GRAVY LOADED WITH SAUSAGE —this is serious comfort food. Our biscuits have been known to transport 75-year-old men back to their mother's side in their childhood kitchen.

I try biscuits and gravy everywhere I go, and I have yet to find any place with biscuits and gravy as good as these. I believe in them so much that I've been known to tell my guests that if they don't think they're the best they've ever had, I'll buy!

| | |
|---|---|
| 1 tablespoon unsalted butter | 2 cups warm Country Sausage Gravy (page 282) |
| 4 Buttermilk Biscuits (below), split in half horizontally | ¼ cup finely chopped fresh Italian (flat-leaf) parsley |

1. Heat a large (12- to 14-inch) sauté pan or griddle over medium-high heat. Once hot, add the butter and tilt the pan to melt and coat it. Add the biscuits, cut side down, and cook until they're lightly golden and toasted, about 2 minutes. Alternatively, place the biscuits cut side up in a toaster oven and toast until the tops are golden.

2. Remove the biscuits from the pan or oven and place 2 halves on each plate. Ladle ½ cup of gravy on top of each pair. Serve immediately topped with chopped parsley.

## BUTTERMILK BISCUITS

MAKES 18 BISCUITS

THESE BISCUITS ARE JUST ONE OF THE THINGS DEBBIE PUTNAM, THE PASTRY CHEF AT Mother's, has been making for our bread baskets since we opened in 2000. We make them with self-rising flour (flour that already has salt and leavening mixed in), but they can be made with all-purpose flour, too. The dough is very wet and yields moist, fluffy biscuits that are not only delicious topped with Country Sausage Gravy (especially when they're a day old) but also perfect alone, with just a smattering of whipped butter.

This recipe makes a lot of biscuits: You can freeze the leftovers, let them thaw for an hour or so, and rewarm them in a 300°F oven. Or freeze unbaked biscuits and bake them fresh anytime the mood strikes (Love Note 1).

6 cups self-rising flour (Love Note 2)

⅓ cup granulated sugar

2¼ teaspoons kosher salt

¾ cup (1½ sticks) cold unsalted butter, cut into small cubes

2½ cups buttermilk

2⅓ cups heavy cream

1½ cups all-purpose flour, for dredging

4 tablespoons (½ stick) unsalted butter, melted

1. Heat the oven to 450°F. Spray a 13x9x2-inch baking dish with nonstick cooking spray (use a smaller pan if you want to cook some biscuits now and freeze the rest for later).

2. In a large bowl, combine the self-rising flour, sugar, and salt. Using a pastry blender, two knives, or a whisk, cut the cold butter into the dry ingredients until the butter is the size of peas (Love Note 3). Alternatively, you can combine the dry ingredients in the bowl of a stand mixer. Add the butter pieces and mix first on low and then on medium-low speed until the pieces are the size of peas, about 1 minute.

3. Combine the buttermilk and heavy cream in a measuring cup. Pour it into the butter-flour mixture and stir with a wooden spoon until mostly incorporated. Then, using your hands, mix just until incorporated—no more than 3 or 4 quick kneadings. Or briefly mix on low speed with the mixer, turning it on for a couple of seconds and then off to scrape the sides of the bowl. Repeat until just combined. (Don't overmix, and don't worry that the batter is wet, goopy, and nonuniform. It

*continued*

is OK to have some pockets of flour and chunks of butter. That's what will make the biscuits flaky and moist. The most important thing is not to overmix!)

4. Put the all-purpose flour in shallow bowl. Using an ice cream scoop with a $\frac{1}{3}$-cup capacity or a $\frac{1}{3}$-cup dry measuring cup, scoop out a heaping portion of the batter and drop it into the flour. Sprinkle some flour on top, pick up the dough, and cup it in the palm of your hand. Gently jiggle the dough in your palm so that the excess flour falls away, leaving just a light coating (or lightly toss the dough between both hands).

5. Starting in one corner, arrange the biscuits in a row down the long side of the pan so you have a row of six. (You must start the first one very close to the corner and place the next one nearly on top of the first in order for all six biscuits to fit.) After filling the row, place more two biscuits across the short side (you should now have 3 across and 6 down). Continue scooping and arranging the remaining dough in pieces directly next to each other (they should be touching and just slightly squished) in rows until you have used all the dough. (If you used a different-size baking pan or aren't cooking all the biscuits at once, your baking pan may not be filled corner to corner with biscuits. In this case, crumple a piece of foil to fit into the blank spaces to help the biscuits keep their shape during baking.)

6. Bake for 10 minutes, or until the biscuits start to brown, and then reduce the heat to 375°F and bake until the biscuits are light brown all over, being sure to rotate the pan now and then (so the biscuits bake evenly), another 20 to 25 minutes. You'll know they're done when the biscuits start to pull away from each other, they don't have any bounce when poked, and a knife inserted between some of them in the middle of the pan comes out clean.

7. Remove the pan from the oven, brush the tops of the biscuits with the melted butter, and let cool for 10 minutes before cutting into individual biscuits and serving. (You could pull them apart, but I like to cut the biscuits along the obvious separations to make them a little straighter and prettier.)

*continued*

## LOVE NOTES

**1** **To bake frozen biscuits,** place them on the prepared pan and bake at 450°F for 10 minutes, or until lightly browned, and then reduce the heat to 375°F and bake for about 25 minutes more, until they're toasty brown all over.

**2** Debbie prefers **self-rising flour** (she's from the South, after all). If you can't find it, you can make your own

by combining 2 tablespoons baking powder and 2 teaspoons salt for every 4 cups all-purpose flour. Be sure to mix well.

**3** Don't worry if you see **clumps of butter**—that's good! The little bits of butter here and there melt during cooking and yield a flaky, tender biscuit.

## COUNTRY SAUSAGE GRAVY

MAKES 2 QUARTS

FOR THE BEST GRAVY, GET THE BEST BREAKFAST SAUSAGE YOU CAN AFFORD, BUT don't get anything dolled up with other ingredients like apples or sun-dried tomatoes. Simple breakfast sausage is all this gravy needs to be delicious. This recipe makes a lot because the gravy has to cook for a while, so you might as well freeze some to serve on Nana's Chicken Fried Chicken (page 143), Pulled Pork (page 318), or another plateful of biscuits and gravy some other time.

1½ pounds bulk pork breakfast sausage

Butter or bacon fat, if necessary

½ cup all-purpose flour

3 cups whole milk

3 cups heavy cream

1½ teaspoons granulated garlic

1½ teaspoons granulated onion

1½ teaspoons freshly ground black pepper

¾ teaspoon dried thyme

¾ teaspoon cayenne pepper

½ teaspoon kosher salt

1.  Place a medium (6- to 8-quart) Dutch oven over medium-high heat. When hot, add the sausage and sauté, stirring occasionally and breaking the meat into small chunks, until lightly browned, about 5 minutes.

2.  Set a metal sieve or strainer over a heatproof bowl. When the sausage is cooked through, scrape the contents of the pan into the strainer and let the fat drip through. Pour the collected fat into a heatproof measuring cup. If necessary, add either melted butter or bacon fat to equal ⅓ cup (Love Note).

3.  Pour the measured fat back into the Dutch oven. Add the flour and mix well with a wooden spoon over medium heat to make a roux. Cook, stirring frequently, until the mixture resembles fine, wet sand, about 3 to 5 minutes. Whisk the milk into

the roux a little at a time, scraping up the bits of sausage from the bottom of the pot and allowing the roux to absorb the liquid before adding more. This will help prevent lumps.

4.  Slowly whisk in the cream and bring the mixture to a boil, and then lower the heat to a slow simmer. Add the sausage, garlic, onion, black pepper, thyme, and cayenne and continue to cook for about 30 minutes, stirring frequently with a wooden spoon to be sure the bottom does not burn.

5.  Add the salt, stir well, and serve.

## LOVE NOTE

**There are hundreds of brands of sausage,** so it's impossible to know how much fat your sausage will release. Ideally, this gravy is made with just the fat from the sausage, but that isn't always possible, and you need enough fat to make the roux. You can substitute butter or bacon fat . . . it's your call. We usually get enough fat from our sausage, but we sometimes have to use bacon fat, too.

# Mother's Buttermilk Pancakes

I DON'T CARE WHAT ANYONE SAYS, THERE IS A DISTINCT DIFFERENCE BETWEEN pancakes made from scratch and those made from a mix. Treat yourself and your family to these and watch them disappear. You won't need a nap after these…they're so light and just right! To make morning preparations easier, mix up the dry ingredients and wet ingredients the night before. Keep them separate until morning, though, or some of the leavening agents will get activated and the batter will lose some of its rising power.

3 cups all-purpose flour
(Love Note 1)

1½ teaspoons baking soda

3 teaspoons baking powder

¼ cup granulated sugar

½ teaspoon kosher salt

4½ cups buttermilk

3 large eggs

6 tablespoons (¾ stick) unsalted butter, melted

Vegetable oil or clarified butter, for brushing the griddle or pan

Whipped butter, for serving

Maple syrup, for serving

1. Heat the oven to 200°F. In a large mixing bowl, combine the flour, baking soda, baking powder, sugar, and salt. Mix thoroughly with a whisk.

2. In another mixing bowl, whisk together the buttermilk and eggs.

3. Slowly pour the buttermilk mixture into the dry ingredients while gently stirring, and mix just until combined. (Don't overmix or you will activate the gluten in the flour and the pancakes will be chewy, like bread, instead of fluffy.) The mixture will be a little lumpy (and that's OK, but if you have pockets of flour bigger than a dime, smash them against the side of the bowl to break them apart without having to stir the batter more). Pour in the melted butter and gently mix just until incorporated. (Sometimes melted butter solidifies when added to cold ingredients. Adding it now helps disperse it evenly in the batter and smooth out some of the lumps.)

4.  Place a griddle (Love Note 2) or wide (preferably 14-inch) sauté pan over medium heat for several minutes. If using an electric griddle, set the heat to 350°F.

5.  Sprinkle the griddle with a few drops of water; they should bounce around before evaporating. If they sizzle away quickly, the heat is too high. If they just sit there and slowly steam, the heat is too low. When the griddle is properly heated, brush with oil or clarified butter, and then wipe with a paper towel so it's evenly greased. (Big spots of oil or butter will promote uneven browning and your pancakes will have dark and light spots. Don't skip this step even if you have a nonstick griddle.)

6.  Use a 4-ounce ladle (Love Note 3) to pour several 5- or 6-inch pools of batter onto the griddle, an inch or two apart. (Just let batter fall off ladle; don't try to shape it.)

7.  Cook until bubbles begin to pop on the surface of the pancakes, the edges look a little dry, and the underside is golden, about 2 minutes (try not to flip before they're ready, because the more you flip the cakes the less fluffy they will be). Flip them over and continue cooking until the pancakes are cooked through, about 1 minute more. (If the undersides of the pancakes are browning or burning before the tops get a chance to form bubbles and dry out, the heat is too high. If it's taking much longer than 2 or 3 minutes for the bubbles to form, the heat is too low.)

8.  Repeat with the remaining batter. Keep the pancakes warm on a heatproof platter or baking sheet in the oven.

9.  Serve topped with whipped butter and maple syrup.

*continued*

## VARIATION: Buttermilk Waffles

This pancake batter makes excellent waffles in both a Belgian waffle iron and a traditional waffle iron. You can use the batter as is or add 2 more tablespoons of melted butter to thin it out a little and make the waffles crispier. If the batter still seems too thick and doesn't spread out well in the waffle iron, add another ¼ cup of buttermilk. The batter will yield about 22 waffles using a ½-cup measure.

## LOVE NOTES

**1** I like my **pancakes thin and light** so they won't sit in my stomach like a lump. But if you want yours a little thicker, stir in ½ to 1 cup more flour.

**2** **A built-in griddle** is not a common feature in ranges these days. Luckily, there are many different griddles you can buy to put on your stove, from heavy cast iron to lightweight nonstick aluminum. Some sit on just one burner; some are elongated to stretch across two; there are also electric models that plug in, sit on the countertop, and allow you to set a precise temperature.

**3** **Ladles** come in standard sizes, from 1 to 12 ounces, and they help measure as you serve. At Mother's we use a 6-ounce ladle, which holds about ¾ cup of batter. That makes a big, plate-size pancake, too big for serving at home. I like a 4-ounce (½-cup) ladle instead, which makes 6-inch pancakes. To find out how many ounces your ladle is, fill it with water, pour the water into a measuring cup, and read the results. If you don't have a ladle that's the right size, use a dry measuring cup to scoop the batter.

# Almond Poppyseed Pancakes

I LOVE THE FLAVOR OF ALMONDS IN CAKES, COOKIES, AND MUFFINS, AND IT ALSO translates deliciously to pancakes. With almond paste, almond extract, and sliced toasted almonds, these pancakes are very rich in flavor, and the poppyseeds add even more nuttiness and crunch. While they almost border on dessert, they aren't sweet, so don't leave off the maple syrup; it completes the dish and makes these a perfect breakfast treat.

3½ ounces almond paste
(Love Note 1)

2 cups whole milk

1 cup (8 ounces) sour cream

1 tablespoon almond extract

4 large eggs

3 cups all-purpose flour

¼ cup granulated sugar

1 tablespoon baking powder

1½ teaspoons kosher salt

½ cup poppyseeds (Love Note 2)

4 tablespoons (½ stick) unsalted butter, melted

Vegetable oil or clarified butter, for brushing the griddle or pan

1 cup sliced almonds, toasted (Love Note 3)

Whipped butter, for serving

Maple syrup, for serving

1. Heat the oven to 200°F. Place the almond paste in the bowl of an electric mixer fitted with the whisk attachment. Whisk on low speed while adding the milk, a little at a time, to loosen up the paste until it's smooth and not lumpy. Alternatively, you can process the almond paste with a little of the milk in a food processor until smooth (add just enough milk to help the almond paste thin out).

2. Add the sour cream, almond extract, and eggs. Whisk or process until well-blended and smooth.

3. In a large mixing bowl, add the flour, sugar, baking powder, salt, and poppyseeds. Whisk well to thoroughly combine.

*continued*

4. Slowly pour the liquid ingredients into the dry ingredients while gently stirring, and mix just until combined. (Don't overmix or you will activate the gluten in the flour and the pancakes will be chewy, like bread, instead of fluffy.) The mixture will be a little lumpy (and that's OK; if you have pockets of flour bigger than a dime, smash them against the side of the bowl to break them apart without having to stir the batter more). Pour in the melted butter and gently mix just until incorporated. (Sometimes melted butter solidifies when added to cold ingredients. Adding it now helps disperse it evenly in the batter and smooth out some of the lumps.)

5. Place a griddle or wide (preferably 14-inch) sauté pan over medium heat for several minutes. If using an electric griddle, set the heat to 350°F.

6. Sprinkle the griddle with a few drops of water; they should bounce around before evaporating. If they sizzle away quickly, the heat is too high. If they just sit there and slowly steam, the heat is too low. When the griddle is properly heated, brush with oil or clarified butter, and then wipe with a paper towel so it's evenly greased. (Big spots of oil or butter will promote uneven browning and your pancakes will have dark and light spots.)

7. Ladle ½ cup of batter per pancake onto the griddle, an inch or two apart. Sprinkle evenly with 1 tablespoon toasted almonds.

8. Cook until bubbles begin to pop on the surface of the pancakes, the edges look a little dry, and the underside is golden, about 2 minutes. Flip them over and continue cooking until the pancakes are cooked through, about 1 minute more. (If the undersides of the pancakes are browning or burning before the tops get a chance to form bubbles and dry out, the heat is too high. If it's taking much longer than 2 or 3 minutes for the bubbles to form, the heat is too low.)

*continued*

9. Repeat with the remaining batter. Keep the pancakes warm on a heatproof platter or baking sheet in the oven.

10. Serve with whipped butter and maple syrup.

## LOVE NOTES

**1** **Almond paste** is more than just ground almonds—it's ground almonds mixed with sugar and a little oil and maybe corn syrup for moisture. You can buy it in tubes in the baking aisle at most supermarkets. Don't confuse it with marzipan, which has a lot more sugar. You can freeze leftover almond paste in a zip-top bag. Defrost in the refrigerator before using.

**2** Most stores carry **poppyseeds in jars** in the spice aisle. But jarred spices always cost a premium price because of the packaging. If you love making poppyseed pancakes, try to get your seeds in bulk to save money. If your store doesn't carry poppyseeds in bulk, look online. Two reputable retailers include Penzeys Spices (www.penzeys.com) and King Arthur Flour (www.kingarthurflour.com).

**3** The **natural oil in nuts turns rancid** fairly quickly. Always taste your nuts before you use them to make sure they're still fresh. Keep nuts in the freezer for longer storage.

To toast almonds (or any nuts), spread them out on a rimmed baking sheet and place in a preheated 350°F oven for about 10 minutes, or until lightly golden and fragrant. Watch carefully to keep them from burning.

# Gingerbread Pancakes

A LOCAL STARBUCKS[SM] ASKED ME TO CREATE RECIPES FOR THEM TO DISTRIBUTE WITH their holiday coffee beans. I figured the only thing better than gingerbread pancakes with a warm cup of coffee on a cold winter morning would be adding some of that coffee to the batter itself. It really deepens the flavor of the spices. This is perfect for the winter holidays and is especially delicious with Pear-Ginger Compote (page 293).

3 cups all-purpose flour

1 cup firmly packed dark brown sugar (Love Note)

2 teaspoons baking powder

1 teaspoon baking soda

1 teaspoon kosher salt

5 teaspoons ground ginger

2 teaspoons ground nutmeg

1 tablespoon ground cinnamon

1 teaspoon ground cloves

1¾ cups buttermilk

½ cup brewed coffee, cold or at room temperature

4 large eggs

8 tablespoons (1 stick) unsalted butter, melted

2 tablespoons lemon juice (1 lemon)

Vegetable oil or clarified butter, for brushing the griddle or pan

Softened or whipped butter, for serving

Maple syrup, for serving

Pear-Ginger Compote (page 293), for serving (optional)

1. Heat the oven to 200°F. In a large bowl, whisk together the flour, brown sugar, baking powder, baking soda, salt, ginger, nutmeg, cinnamon, and cloves.

2. In another bowl, whisk together the buttermilk, coffee, and eggs.

3. Make a well in the dry ingredients. Slowly pour the buttermilk mixture into the dry ingredients while stirring gently. Mix until just combined. (Do not overmix.

*continued*

The batter is supposed to be lumpy. If you see lumps larger than a dime, just squish them against the side of the bowl. Anything smaller will disappear when the pancakes are cooked.) Stir in the melted butter and lemon juice.

4. Place a griddle or wide (preferably 14-inch) sauté pan over medium heat for several minutes. If using an electric griddle, set the heat to 350°F.

5. Sprinkle the griddle with a few drops of water; they should bounce around before evaporating. If they sizzle away quickly, the heat is too high. If they just sit there and slowly steam, the heat is too low. When the griddle is properly heated, brush with oil or clarified butter.

6. Use a 4-ounce ladle to pour several 6-inch pools of batter onto the griddle, an inch or two apart.

7. Cook until bubbles begin to pop on the surface of the pancakes, the edges look a little dry, and the underside is golden, about 2 minutes. Flip them over and continue cooking until the pancakes are cooked through, about 1 minute more. (These pancakes tend to get a little dark faster than normal because of the extra sugar in the recipe. If the underside of the pancakes are browning or burning before the tops get a chance to form bubbles and dry out, the heat is too high. If it's taking much longer than 2 or 3 minutes for the bubbles to form, the heat is too low. Adjust the temperature accordingly.)

8. Repeat with the remaining batter. Keep the pancakes warm on a heatproof platter or baking sheet in the oven.

9. Serve with softened or whipped butter and maple syrup, and/or Pear-Ginger Compote, if desired.

## LOVE NOTE

**Dark brown sugar has more molasses** than light brown, which gives it
a more intense flavor. Many brown sugars are made from sugar that has
been refined until white, then sprayed with molasses to give it the color
and moisture we expect from brown sugar. Thankfully, there are still some
manufacturers, particularly C&H, who make brown sugar by only partially
refining the sugar so that some of the natural molasses remains saturated
in the crystals. To me the difference is like that between fresh-squeezed
juice and juice from concentrate.

## PEAR-GINGER COMPOTE                    MAKES ABOUT 4 CUPS

THIS VERSATILE COMPOTE IS EXCELLENT ON GINGERBREAD PANCAKES, OATMEAL, OR
even potato pancakes. If you end up with a windfall of pears, make a double batch and
freeze it. With a little imagination, you'll find many more uses for it.

2 pounds firm-ripe Bartlett or
d'Anjou pears, peeled and cut into
½-in. chunks (about 4 cups)

½ cup granulated sugar

½ cup pear nectar, apple juice, or
water

1 tablespoon lemon juice
(½ lemon)

1 tablespoon peeled and grated
fresh ginger

*continued*

1.  Place the pears, sugar, pear nectar or juice, lemon juice, and grated ginger in a medium (4- to 6-quart) saucepan. Stir to combine. Cover the pot and bring to a simmer over medium-high heat.

2.  Remove the lid, reduce the heat to medium-low, and cook, stirring occasionally, until the pears are tender but still hold their shape (you don't want mush), 15 to 20 minutes.

3.  Remove from the heat and serve warm, or let cool and refrigerate or freeze.

# Pumpkin Pancakes

WE ALL GO A LITTLE PUMPKIN CRAZY IN THE FALL: PUMPKIN PIE, PUMPKIN BREAD, pumpkin soup. These pie-spiced pancakes are another delicious way to get a fix. At Mother's Bistro, we use candy corn to make pumpkin faces around Halloween…and not just on the kids' cakes! It makes them that much more festive.

3¾ cups all-purpose flour

5¼ teaspoons baking powder

3 teaspoons ground cinnamon

1¼ teaspoons ground allspice

1¼ teaspoons ground ginger

½ teaspoon kosher salt

⅓ cup packed light brown sugar

1 (15-ounce) can pumpkin, or 2 cups fresh pumpkin purée

6 large eggs

3 cups whole milk

8 tablespoons (1 stick) unsalted butter, melted

Vegetable oil or clarified butter, for brushing the griddle or pan

Whipped butter, for serving

Maple syrup, for serving

1. Heat the oven to 200°F. In a large mixing bowl, whisk together the flour, baking powder, cinnamon, allspice, ginger, salt, and brown sugar. (If the brown sugar is lumpy, run the mixture through a sifter or fine-mesh sieve.)

2. In a medium bowl, whisk together the pumpkin and eggs until combined. Whisk in the milk.

3. Slowly pour the liquid ingredients into the dry ingredients while gently stirring, and mix just until combined. (Don't overmix or you will activate the gluten in the flour and the pancakes will be chewy, like bread, instead of fluffy.) The mixture will be a little lumpy (and that's OK; if you have pockets of flour bigger than a dime, smash them against the side of the bowl to break them apart without having

*continued*

to stir the batter more). Pour in the melted butter and gently mix just until incorporated. (Sometimes melted butter solidifies when added to cold ingredients. Adding it now helps disperse it evenly in the batter and smooth out some lumps.)

4.  Place a griddle or wide (preferably 14-inch) sauté pan over medium heat for several minutes. If using an electric griddle, set the heat to 350°F.

5.  Sprinkle the griddle with a few drops of water; they should bounce around before evaporating. If they sizzle away quickly, the heat is too high. If they just sit there and slowly steam, the heat is too low. When the griddle is properly heated, brush it with oil or clarified butter, and then wipe with a paper towel so it's evenly greased. (Big spots of oil or butter will promote uneven browning and your pancakes will have dark and light spots.)

6.  Ladle ½ cup of batter per pancake onto the griddle, an inch or two apart.

7.  Cook until bubbles begin to pop on the surface of the pancakes, the edges look a little dry, and the underside is golden, about 2 minutes. (Pumpkin pancakes get dark quickly because of the natural sugar in the pumpkin and the additional sugar in the recipe. If the undersides of the pancakes are browning or burning before the tops form bubbles and dry out, the heat is too high. Lower the heat by a few degrees, flip them over, and continue cooking until the pancakes are cooked through, about 2 minutes more.

8.  Repeat with the remaining batter. Keep cooked pancakes warm on a heatproof platter or baking sheet in the oven, and serve with whipped butter and maple syrup.

# Mother's Crunchy French Toast

IF I HAD TO PICK OUR ONE SIGNATURE BREAKFAST DISH, THIS WOULD BE IT. FRENCH toast goes by the name *pain perdu* in France, which translates as "lost bread." It's a recipe created to save stale bread from being "lost" to the garbage by soaking it in eggs and milk to get it moist and tender again and then frying it up. Although you can certainly use whatever stale bread slices you have lingering in the fridge (except something strong-flavored like rye), fresh challah provides a wonderful richness (Love Note 1). A roll in cornflakes adds a wonderful, addictive crunch.

4 large eggs

¾ cup heavy cream

¾ cup half-and-half

½ teaspoon ground cinnamon

2 tablespoons granulated sugar

Pinch ground nutmeg

½ teaspoon pure vanilla extract

4 cups cornflakes

1 loaf egg (challah) bread, sliced into six 1-inch-thick slices (Love Note 1)

9 tablespoons (1 stick plus 1 tablespoon) unsalted butter (divided), preferably clarified (Love Note 2; also Love Note 2, page 145, Nana's Chicken Fried Chicken)

Confectioners' sugar, for serving (optional)

Softened butter, for serving

Maple syrup, for serving

1. If your pan isn't big enough to cook all the French toast at the same time, heat the oven to 200°F. In a large bowl, whisk together the eggs, cream, half-and-half, cinnamon, sugar, nutmeg, and vanilla.

2. Place the cornflakes in another large bowl and crush with your hands until the pieces are small (but not like breadcrumbs) and somewhat uniform in size. Place a rimmed baking sheet nearby to hold the prepared bread.

*continued*

3. Dip a slice of bread into the cream mixture, immersing both sides (saturate it, but do not let it fall apart).

4. Dip the slice into the cornflakes on both sides, pressing to adhere the flakes; set aside on the baking sheet. Repeat with the remaining slices.

5. Place a griddle or wide (preferably 14-inch) sauté pan over medium heat for several minutes. If using an electric griddle, set the heat to 350°F.

6. Sprinkle the griddle with a few drops of water; they should bounce around before evaporating. If they sizzle away quickly, the heat is too high. If they just sit there and slowly steam, the heat is too low. When the griddle is properly heated, add 1 tablespoon of clarified butter for each piece of French toast and tilt to coat the pan.

7. Add the prepared bread in an even layer. Cook until golden on one side, about 4 minutes. Lift each piece with a spatula and put ½ tablespoon butter in its spot. Flip the toast onto the butter to cook the other side, about 4 minutes more. Repeat with the remaining slices of bread. Serve immediately or keep warm in the oven until all the French toast is cooked.

8. Cut each piece of bread in half diagonally to make triangles. Arrange 3 triangles like shingles on serving plates, sprinkle with confectioners' sugar, if desired, and serve with softened butter and maple syrup.

*continued*

## LOVE NOTES

**1** **Challah** (pronounced HALL-uh) is a slightly sweet, eggy Jewish bread that's becoming increasingly common at gourmet grocery stores and bakeries. Many bakeries often carry it only on Fridays, for the Jewish Sabbath. If you can't find it, substitute any soft, sweet bread, such as brioche, Hawaiian bread, or thick slices of Texas toast.

**2** **Clarified butter is important** for this recipe because it allows you to cook the French toast at a high enough heat to get a proper sizzle going, ensuring that the toasts stay crunchy. If the butter isn't clarified, the milk solids will melt and impart moisture, which can impede crunchiness. And when the solids inevitably burn, they'll give a burnt flavor to the food.

# Basic Scones

PROPER SCONES ARE CRUMBLY, SWEET BISCUITS WITH A SLIGHTLY DRY TEXTURE, making them the perfect accompaniment to coffee, tea, or hot chocolate. This recipe can support hundreds of variations—try adding your favorite spices, fresh fruit, dried fruit, citrus zests, or flavorful extracts. The key is to leave the butter in pieces and not to overmix.

**FOR THE SCONES**

2¼ cups all-purpose flour

⅓ cup granulated sugar

1 tablespoon baking powder

11 tablespoons (1 stick plus 3 tablespoons) cold unsalted butter, cut into small pieces (Love Note 1)

Dried fruit like raisins or cherries or ½ cup toasted nuts like hazelnuts, almonds, or pecans (optional)

2 tablespoons orange or lemon zest

¾ cup cold heavy cream

**FOR THE VANILLA ICING (OPTIONAL)**

1 cup confectioners' sugar

¼ teaspoon pure vanilla extract

2 to 3 tablespoons water or heavy cream, or for variation try lemon or orange juice

**TO MAKE THE SCONES**

1. Heat the oven to 425°F. In a large bowl, whisk together the flour, sugar, and baking powder until well combined. Or place in a food processor and pulse to combine.

2. Add the butter pieces and toss to coat in flour. Using a pastry blender, whisk, or two knives working in opposite directions, cut the butter into the dry ingredients until the pieces are about the size of peas. If using a food processor, cut in the butter using about twelve 1-second pulses, and then transfer the mixture to a mixing bowl. (Be careful not to overmix.) If adding mix-ins like nuts, zest, or dried fruits, toss them in now.

*continued*

3. Add the cream and stir just enough to blend (do not overmix or you'll develop the gluten in the flour and the scones will be chewy).

4. Turn the dough out onto a lightly floured surface and press it together to incorporate all the crumbs. Pat it into a 1-inch-thick circle. Cut the dough into 8 triangles, and arrange them 1 inch apart on a parchment-lined baking sheet (Love Note 2). Bake until lightly browned on top, 12 to 15 minutes.

**TO MAKE THE ICING**

1. Mix the confectioners' sugar and vanilla extract in a small bowl. Add the water or heavy cream and mix to achieve a drizzling consistency. (When you lift your spoon out of the icing, it should fall like in a ribbon into the bowl. If not, add more sugar to thicken it or water to thin it.)

2. Remove the scones from the oven and let cool for a few minutes. If using icing, dip the end of a whisk into the icing, and then wave it over the cooled scones. Let the icing set for a few minutes before serving.

## LOVE NOTES

**1.** The pieces of **ice-cold butter** get dispersed and coated in the flour and will eventually create flaky layers, but if the butter is too warm, it will absorb the flour. It's a good idea for other ingredients in recipes like these to be ice cold, too, so that they don't warm the butter when they are combined with it.

**2.** **Unbaked scones freeze beautifully.** Arrange on a baking sheet and freeze until firm, and then pack into a zip-top freezer bag. To bake, place the still-frozen scones on a parchment-lined baking sheet and bake at 375°F for 20 to 25 minutes, until lightly browned on top.

# Best Bloody Marys

MY DAUGHTER, STEPHANIE, WENT TO TULANE UNIVERSITY IN NEW ORLEANS, A CITY where folks sure know how to make a Bloody Mary. When I opened Mother's, she was adamant about which recipe to use—hers! It has a little pepper and a little Tabasco, but what really sends it over the top is the jalapeño-infused vodka. It steeps for only a day, but the flavor it adds to the drink is unbelievable.

**FOR THE BLOODY MARY MIX**

1 (46-ounce) can tomato juice

¼ cup prepared horseradish

3 tablespoons Worcestershire sauce

2 tablespoons lemon juice (1 lemon)

2 tablespoons lime juice (1 lime)

½ teaspoon Tabasco sauce

½ teaspoon Cholula® hot sauce (Love Note 1)

½ teaspoon kosher salt

½ teaspoon freshly ground black pepper

1 teaspoon celery salt

**FOR THE GARNISH SKEWERS**

8 (6-inch) wooden skewers

8 pepperoncini

8 picked onions

8 spears pickled asparagus or pickled green beans

8 (2½-inch) celery pieces

8 pimento-stuffed olives

**FOR SERVING**

12 ounces (1½ cups) Jalapeño Vodka (page 305)

**TO MAKE THE BLOODY MARY MIX**

In a large (at least 2-quart) pitcher or bowl, whisk together the tomato juice, horseradish, Worcestershire sauce, lemon juice, lime juice, Tabasco, Cholula, salt, pepper, and celery salt. Mix thoroughly for a minute or two to disperse the ingredients and dissolve the salt.

*continued*

**TO ASSEMBLE THE GARNISH SKEWERS**

On each skewer, spear 1 pepperoncini (widthwise), 1 pickled onion, 1 asparagus spear or green bean (stick the skewer into one end of the bean then and fold the top end over and skewer it, too), 1 celery piece (pierce through it horizontally; it will be wider than anything else on the skewer), and 1 olive.

**TO SERVE**

1. For each drink, mix 1½ ounces Jalapeño Vodka with ¾ cup Bloody Mary mix. Taste and adjust the seasonings if desired.

2. Pour the mixture into tumblers filled with ice. Garnish each with a skewer (Love Note 2).

## LOVE NOTES

**1** All **hot sauces** are not the same. Tabasco has a sharp and vinegary flavor, while Cholula, a Mexican-style hot sauce, has a thicker, more vegetable-based flavor. I like the flavor it adds here, but if you can't find it, substitute your favorite Mexican-style hot sauce, like Tapatío®.

**2** **Garnishes** are half the fun of Bloody Marys. People have been known to skewer everything from avocados to shrimp. Maybe that's because the spicy, tomato-based drink is so similar to cold tomato soups like gazpacho, which are often garnished with similar accompaniments. These skewers are almost a side dish on their own, and they're easily assembled with jars of tangy pickled vegetables, which you can get at any supermarket (look in the olives aisle).

## JALAPEÑO VODKA

MAKES 750 ML, OR
ABOUT 25.6 OUNCES

THIS MAKES AN EXCELLENT HOLIDAY OR HOSTESS GIFT. MAKE A BIG BATCH AND decant it into several plain or decorative glass bottles (look for these at cookware stores or wine- and beer-making supply stores). Attach a label and the Bloody Marys recipe.

½ jalapeño pepper, split length-wise (don't discard the seeds)

Zest of ½ lemon

Zest of ½ lime

2 small cloves garlic, halved

1 teaspoon coarsely ground black pepper

1 sprig fresh dill (optional)

750 ml bottle inexpensive vodka

1. Place the jalapeño, lemon zest, lime zest, garlic, pepper, and dill sprig into a large pitcher or jar.

2. Pour the vodka over the ingredients in the pitcher. Allow to infuse for 24 hours.

3. Set a cheesecloth-lined sieve over a large bowl (preferably with a spout) and pour the infused vodka through it. Discard the cheesecloth and infusion ingredients. Pour the infused vodka back into its original bottle (or a pretty bottle, if you're giving it as a gift), but be sure to label it with the contents.

# sandwiches

**When you need good food fast—and you don't want to turn to fast food—a sandwich can really hit the spot.** At Mother's I've offered lunch entrées from time to time, but it's the sandwiches that get ordered time and again. You can tuck almost anything between two slices of bread, add a soup or a salad, and have a quick, filling meal.

While a sandwich can be as simple as a slathering of mayo and a couple of slices of cheese, they can also be as inventive as your imagination allows, since they're nothing more than several components layered together. Start by thinking about some of your favorite dishes and then about putting those flavors on a roll. Steak and blue cheese is a match made in heaven, so why not stack thin slices of flank steak and mesclun greens on a sturdy roll and drizzle with a little blue cheese dressing?

### ADDING FLAVOR AND TEXTURE

It might be odd to think of salad dressing as a sandwich spread—or, as I like to say, a schmear—but it can work. A schmear helps take the sandwich to another level, adding moistness and layers of flavor. Almost anything can be a schmear—even hummus and guacamole—but you have to be careful that it doesn't overpower your other sandwich ingredients. Think of flavors that go together—beef with horseradish, chicken with pesto—and let that be your guide. I've developed half a dozen schmears by just whisking mayonnaise with things like chili sauce and roasted garlic.

Accompaniments like lettuce, tomato, onion, and cheese add even more flavors and textures, but don't go overboard. You don't want to put everything but the kitchen sink on a roll. The flavors will overwhelm each other and you won't be able to appreciate what you're eating.

As for the bread, be just as picky about the carrier as you are about the contents. Buy the best-quality bread you can afford, and shop at a bread bakery if you can, where you'll find the best selection, from crispy to soft. Try to choose a bread texture that best matches the contents. Squishy or soft ingredients like grilled portabellas or burgers would ooze out of a crusty roll and make a mess when you take a bite, so choose a soft roll instead.

Keep in mind that hot sandwiches should be served immediately. Many of the sandwiches in this chapter are warm and have cheese, so they're best eaten right away, before the cheese gets cold and hardens. And sandwiches with pretty ingredients or lots of colors—like nicely charred portabella mushrooms or grilled salmon—look especially beautiful when served open-face. When your guests are greeted with such a sandwich on their plate, they won't be able to resist digging in.

# Grilled Ham and Swiss Cheese Sandwich

HAM AND SWISS IS SUCH A DELICIOUS COMBO THAT YOU CAN FIND IT TUCKED INTO everything from croissants to quiche. These ingredients also fill the classic French *croque monsieur,* but rather than label our sandwich with a French name, we just call it what it is . . . a grilled ham and cheese sandwich. But it's not just any sandwich as long as you take time to do it right.

This is first and foremost a ham sandwich, with piles of paper-thin slices of ham and a little cheese, but the technique for grilling it is the same as for a grilled cheese sandwich. And if there's one sandwich that screams Mother Food and should be mastered, it's grilled cheese. It's as kid-friendly as it is adult-friendly, and there are countless variations. But a perfect grilled cheese or ham and cheese sandwich does require some attention. And when making the sandwich for kids, consider the audience. How many kids like crust? Win them over (we do!) by cutting the crust off, and watch the sandwich disappear.

Feel free to change things up and substitute smoked turkey for the ham and Gouda for the Swiss, or substitute Cheddar or Brie. You could even go all Italian with prosciutto, Parmesan, and Fontina.

8 slices rustic, sourdough, rye, or whole-wheat bread (Love Note 1)

4½ tablespoons (just over ½ stick) salted butter, softened (Love Note 2)

½ cup Stone-Ground Mustard Mayonnaise (page 311)

¼ pound Swiss cheese, cut into 8 slices

1 pound baked ham, shaved into paper-thin slices (Love Note 3)

1. Heat the oven to 400°F. Lay the bread slices out on a work surface. Spread one side of each with 1½ tablespoon of butter.

2. Turn over and spread 1 tablespoon of Stone-Ground Mustard Mayonnaise on each slice. Lay 2 slices of cheese on top of 4 slices of bread.

*continued*

3. Heat a griddle, skillet, or large (12- to 14-inch) sauté pan (not nonstick) over medium-high heat. Add the remaining ½ tablespoon butter to the sauté pan and add the ham. Sauté, stirring with tongs, until the ham is warm and golden in spots, 4 to 5 minutes.

4. Remove from the heat and use tongs to evenly divide the ham among the cheese-topped bread pieces. Top each with the remaining slices of bread, butter side up.

5. Return the sauté pan to medium-high heat. Add the sandwiches (if your pan can't fit all the sandwiches at once, cook them in batches) and brown the bread on one side, tucking the contents in and pressing the sandwiches down with a flat spatula once or twice (to help them get brown and to "glue" the sandwiches together via the melting cheese), 2 to 3 minutes. Use a spatula to flip the sandwiches over and brown on the second side, 2 to 3 minutes more. Remove from the pan and place on a baking sheet. Place in the oven and bake until they're crispy and golden on the outside and the cheese has melted on the inside of each sandwich. (You can finish them on the stove if you prefer not to turn on your oven; just continue cooking in the pan, but don't cover or they'll get soggy.)

6. Cut each sandwich in half and serve.

### STONE-GROUND MUSTARD MAYONNAISE

MAKES 1¼ CUPS

1 cup mayonnaise

¼ cup stone-ground mustard

1 tablespoon prepared horseradish

In a small mixing bowl, whisk together the ingredients. Refrigerate until ready to use.

*continued*

# LOVE NOTES

**1** I divide **bread for sandwiches** into two camps: rustic and soft. That's because within each of these camps there's a lot of variation, and what you want to use is a matter of taste. The most important thing to consider is the texture—rustic breads (typically artisan breads like French bread, sourdough, and ciabatta) are chewier. For a sandwich like this, you'll have to slice bread about ¼ inch thick so that the sandwich isn't too hard to bite into. Squishy fillings will likely squish right out of a rustic bread, but sturdy fillings will be right at home.

Soft breads, like hamburger buns, whole-wheat sandwich bread, and rye bread don't stand up as well to sturdy fillings but are perfect for softer ones.

**2** **This is not the time to break out the nonstick cooking spray.** The bread needs to be evenly buttered with real, salted butter for a properly browned and crisp exterior. That's because the milk solids in the butter cook as the sandwich cooks, turning nutty and brown.

**3** **Shaved ham** is simply ham that has been cut as thinly as possible. Often, it's so thin you can almost see through it. Slicing the ham so thinly means the texture becomes ultra-tender and almost luxurious. It's not something you can do yourself with a sharp knife. Just because the deli has presliced meats doesn't mean you can't ask to have something sliced just for you. For this sandwich, ask them to "shave" it or to slice it on the thinnest setting.

# Grilled Portabella Mushroom Sandwich

MEATY IN FLAVOR AND TEXTURE, PORTABELLAS ARE ONE OF THOSE RARE FOODS that make both vegetarians and meat eaters happy. They easily measure 6 inches across and can stand up to the smoke and heat of the grill. Marinating makes the mushrooms extra-special—they almost taste like steak.

While these portabellas are great tucked into a bun, you can also serve them as part of a grilled vegetable platter. You can even slice them and serve on a bed of mesclun greens tossed with Balsamic Vinaigrette (page 30) for a hearty main-dish salad.

**FOR THE MARINATED MUSHROOMS**

¾ cup extra-virgin olive oil

2 tablespoons finely chopped garlic

2 teaspoons balsamic vinegar

1 tablespoon finely chopped fresh Italian (flat-leaf) parsley

4 portabella mushrooms (Love Note)

**FOR THE SANDWICH**

4 sesame seed or poppyseed brioche rolls, Kaiser rolls, or other soft buns (Love Note 1, facing page, Grilled Ham and Swiss Cheese Sandwich), split in half

¼ cup extra-virgin olive oil or 4 tablespoons (½ stick) softened unsalted butter (optional)

½ cup Sun-Dried Tomato Mayonnaise (page 315)

1 cup packed mesclun greens, washed and dried (about 1½ ounces)

1 large tomato, cut into 8 slices

1 teaspoon kosher salt (divided)

¼ teaspoon freshly ground black pepper (divided)

¼ pound smoked provolone cheese, cut into 8 slices

**TO MARINATE THE MUSHROOMS**

1. Whisk together the olive oil, garlic, vinegar, and parsley in a mixing bowl.

*continued*

2. Remove the stems from the portabellas by holding the cap in one hand and using the other to carefully tug on the stem to pop it out (or use a sharp knife and cut it off).

3. Dip each portabella into the marinade (be sure to scoop the marinade up into the gill side and swirl it around a bit, and place in another bowl gill side up. (Dipping them individually ensures each mushroom gets evenly coated.) Pour any remaining marinade over the portabellas and allow them to marinate for at least 10 minutes before grilling.

**TO MAKE THE SANDWICH**

1. Heat the grill to medium-high (you should be able to hold your hand a few inches above the grate for 3 seconds). Position the rack 4 inches from the heat.

2. Arrange the buns cut side up on a baking sheet or platter. If desired, brush with olive oil or softened butter (it will make them toastier and golden brown). Place on the grill, cut side down, until golden and toasted.

3. Transfer the buns back to the baking sheet and set aside. Spread 1 tablespoon of Sun-Dried Tomato Mayonnaise on each half of the toasted buns. Arrange about ¼ cup of the mesclun greens on each top half, followed by 2 tomato slices.

4. Place the marinated portabellas on the grill, gill side up. Season each mushroom with ¼ teaspoon salt and a pinch of pepper (you can just season one side if you like, or divide the amount between both sides). Cook for about 4 minutes or until grill marks appear. (If you're not going to top the portabellas with cheese, grill them with crosshatch marks. See "To Cook and Serve," Step 1, page 157, Grilled Salmon with Sesame Noodles.)

5. Carefully flip the portabellas and grill the other side. (You might get some flare-ups from olive oil that may have pooled inside the cap. If this happens, move the porta-

bellas out of the flames so they don't get overly charred.) After 2 minutes, top each with 2 slices provolone cheese so the cheese melts as the bottoms of the portabellas cook (don't close the grill cover). Grill for another 2 minutes, or longer if necessary for the cheese to melt.

6. When the mushrooms are browned and soft and the cheese has melted, remove from the grill and place on the bottom halves of the sandwiches. Place on serving plates and serve open-face (if for no other reason than it looks pretty), or put the two halves together before serving, if you prefer.

## LOVE NOTE

**Hand-pick portabellas** rather than buy them prepackaged. This way you can avoid mushrooms that are damaged, shriveled, or slimy. To prep portabellas, remove the stems and wipe the caps with a damp paper towel to remove any dirt. You can also lightly dust them off with a dry, soft brush. Do not rinse them or they will absorb water and not grill properly.

## SUN-DRIED TOMATO MAYONNAISE

MAKES 1¼ CUPS

½ cup oil-packed or rehydrated sun-dried tomatoes, drained

2 cloves garlic

½ teaspoon kosher salt

¼ teaspoon freshly ground black pepper

1 cup mayonnaise

Purée the drained sun-dried tomatoes, garlic, salt, and pepper in a food processor until smooth. Transfer to a small bowl and stir in the mayonnaise until well combined. Refrigerate until ready to use.

# Mother's Pulled Pork Sandwich

PULLED PORK IS EASY TO MAKE AND GREAT TO USE IN OTHER DISHES. YOU CAN serve it as a main course smothered in Country Sausage Gravy (page 282; but strain out the sausage so it's nice and smooth and not too meat-heavy), or tuck it into tacos and burritos. You can turn it into a hash for breakfast, or even freeze it for another day.

This pulled pork sandwich is a standout and was created with the assistance of my sous chef at the time, Rick Widmayer. His sweet-and-sour barbecue sauce coupled with the Swiss cheese and caramelized onions do their job perfectly.

2 cups tightly packed Pulled Pork (page 318)

¼ cup pork cooking liquid (Love Note 1), or 1 tablespoon oil or pork fat, for reheating

4 soft hoagie rolls or hamburger buns with sesame seeds (Love Note 2), split in half

½ cup Honey Mustard Barbecue Sauce (page 319)

¼ pound Swiss cheese, cut into 8 slices

½ cup caramelized onions (page 118)

1. Heat the oven to 375°F. Put the pork and cooking liquid in an ovenproof casserole dish with a lid, or put in a baking pan and cover with foil. Place in the oven and cook for 35 to 45 minutes, or until heated through. Alternatively, you can heat the pork on the stove: Place a medium (8- to 10-inch) sauté pan over medium-high heat. Add the vegetable oil or pork fat from cooking the pork shoulder. Add the pork and sauté until warmed through, about 5 minutes. (With this method the pork caramelizes a bit and gets crispy.)

2. Heat the broiler. Place the rolls cut side up on a baking sheet. Place the pan under the broiler and toast the rolls until golden. Remove from the oven. Set the tops of the rolls aside but keep the bottoms on the baking sheet.

3. Using tongs, distribute the hot pork evenly among the bottoms of the rolls on the pan, about ½ cup pork per roll.

4. Top the meat with a drizzle of Honey Mustard Barbecue Sauce, about 2 tablespoons per sandwich. Place 2 cheese slices, shingle-style, over the sauce so the meat is totally covered (make sure the cheese covers the meat, and make sure the meat covers the bread or it will burn when you put the sandwich under the broiler). Place the baking sheet under the broiler (keep careful watch!) until the cheese on top has melted, about 1 minute.

5. Remove from the broiler, and top each sandwich with 2 tablespoons Caramelized Onions.

6. Place the sandwiches on serving plates. Lean the tops against the sandwiches (try not to totally cover them; they're too tasty-looking to hide) and serve.

*continued*

## LOVE NOTES

1. **Save the liquid** left over from cooking the pork shoulder, and use it to moisten the meat while reheating. It's so much more flavorful than water! Just remove any congealed fat before using (but don't discard the fat—you can use it instead of oil if you decide to reheat the pork in a sauté pan).

2. **Soft rolls** are traditional with pulled pork sandwiches because they absorb some of the meat's juices. Also, if the bread is too crusty, everything will ooze out when you take a bite.

## PULLED PORK

MAKES 4 TIGHTLY PACKED CUPS

THIS IS THE PERFECT SLOW-COOKED FOOD FOR A FAST-PACED LIFESTYLE. IF YOU WANT to make the pork while you're out of the house, place it in a slow cooker after browning it, add the remaining ingredients, and cook on high for 4 hours or low for 8 hours.

3 pounds pork shoulder (also known as Boston pork butt), left whole, fat trimmed

2 teaspoons kosher salt

1 teaspoon freshly ground black pepper

2 teaspoons dried marjoram

1 tablespoon vegetable oil

1 cup water

1. Heat the oven to 350°F. Sprinkle the pork evenly with the salt, pepper, and marjoram.

2. Place a 5-quart Dutch oven or deep metal roasting pan over high heat for several minutes. When very hot, add the oil and heat until shimmering. Add the pork and brown for 3 to 4 minutes on each side.

3. Add the water, bring to a boil, and cover. Remove from the heat and place in the oven. Cook for $3\frac{1}{2}$ to 4 hours, or until the pork offers no resistance when pierced with a two-pronged fork. Let cool for about 10 minutes.

4. Use two forks to pull the meat apart, shredding it.

5. Use right away, or refrigerate or freeze it. Reserve some of the cooking liquid and/or the fat for reheating the pork.

**HONEY MUSTARD BARBECUE SAUCE**

¼ cup yellow mustard

1 tablespoon Dijon mustard

½ tablespoon whole-grain
mustard

½ tablespoon cider vinegar

1 tablespoon honey

¼ cup firmly packed light brown
sugar

8 tablespoons (1 stick) salted
butter

1. In a small bowl, whisk together the yellow mustard, Dijon mustard, whole-grain mustard, cider vinegar, honey, and brown sugar until combined.

2. Place a small saucepan over medium heat. Add the butter and warm just until melted.

3. Slowly drizzle in the mustard mixture, whisking constantly until emulsified.

4. Keep the sauce warm but not hot until ready to use. Refrigerate if necessary and reheat just before serving. The sauce keeps refrigerated, in an airtight container, for up to 1 week.

# Mother's Tuna Melt

CREAMY TUNA SALAD FLECKED WITH TANGY, CRUNCHY BITS OF PICKLES, RED ONION, and celery satisfies on so many levels. And our tuna salad is great between two pieces of bread or scooped onto greens. But add some tomatoes and melted Cheddar cheese and you can see why tuna melts have endured on restaurant menus for decades. We like to serve ours open-face on crusty country bread.

4 (6-ounce) cans albacore tuna packed in water or oil, very well drained (Love Note 1)

½ small dill pickle, seeds removed and finely diced (Love Note 2), or 1 pickle spear, finely diced (about ⅓ cup)

⅓ cup finely diced red onion

⅓ cup finely diced celery

1 cup mayonnaise (¾ cup if not using albacore, Love Note 3)

⅛ teaspoon kosher salt

¼ teaspoon freshly ground black pepper

4 large (½-inch-thick) slices rustic country bread

1 large tomato, cut into 8 or more slices

¼ pound medium or sharp Cheddar cheese, cut into 8 slices

1. Heat the broiler. Put the tuna in a mixing bowl and break it up with a fork. Add the diced pickle, onions, celery, mayonnaise, salt, and pepper, and mix well.

2. Arrange the bread on a baking sheet and place under the broiler. Toast until the tops are light golden brown, 1 to 1½ minutes (watch carefully to make sure they don't burn).

3. Turn the bread over, toasted side down, and spread the tuna salad evenly on the untoasted side of each slice. Top each piece with 2 or 3 tomato slices, and then with 2 slices of Cheddar. Place the open-face sandwich under the broiler, heat until the cheese has melted, 2 to 3 minutes, and serve.

*continued*

# LOVE NOTES

**1** Look closely on your supermarket shelf for cans of **high-quality imported tuna,** or even tuna that was caught and canned by local fishermen. Although they might be more expensive than the tuna from big companies like Chicken of the Sea®, they offer big, meaty, solid pieces of albacore packed in oil or water (the oil-packed tends to have the most flavor and a moist, tender texture). Domestic tuna is usually from smaller fish, which are lower in mercury. These fancier varieties are the cans to buy when you're going to prepare the tuna simply, either tossing it into a green salad with vinaigrette or into a simple sauceless pasta.

With the mayonnaise and cheese in this sandwich, though, you can save some money and buy tuna from the big guys. You should still choose "white meat" (aka albacore) packed in water or oil. It's usually in a solid fillet (also called "fancy") and will be much better in quality and flavor than "chunk light meat," which is code for skipjack (a lesser-quality) tuna.

If you buy oil-packed tuna, save the oil and put it in the dish if you can—it has important nutrients, such as omega-3s, extracted from the fish during the canning process.

**2** Some people put **relish in their tuna,** but I use pickles instead. Relish is sweet and has added sugar, which this tuna salad doesn't need.

**3** **Solid albacore tuna is the best-quality canned tuna,** but it can be very dry—it's a solid piece of fish, after all. Chunk tuna absorbs a lot of the liquid it's packed in and is therefore very moist. If you're not using solid albacore, you may need less mayonnaise for the salad. Start with ¾ cup and add more as needed.

# Benny's Chicken Sandwich

BEN ALEXANDER WAS A COOK AT MOTHER'S FOR A FEW YEARS, AND HE WAS A REAL asset. He was very creative, always thinking "outside the box," and never hesitated to tell it like it was. He created this sandwich for his lunch one day, and since my rule is if you don't pay for it, I can have a bite, I tried it. I loved it so much that I put it on the menu and named it after him.

**FOR THE MARINADE**

¼ cup extra-virgin olive oil

2 teaspoons finely chopped garlic (about 2 cloves)

1 teaspoon chili powder

½ teaspoon ground cumin

1 tablespoon fresh lime juice (about ½ lime)

**FOR THE SANDWICH**

4 boneless, skinless chicken breasts (1 to 1¼ pounds)

1 teaspoon kosher salt (divided)

½ teaspoon freshly ground black pepper (divided)

¼ pound medium or sharp Cheddar cheese, cut into 8 slices

4 soft French rolls, split in half

½ cup Spicy Mayonnaise (page 325)

4 leaves romaine, red leaf, or green leaf lettuce, washed and dried

1 large tomato, cut into 8 slices

4 (⅛-inch-thick) slices red onion (about ¼ onion), separated into rings

1 avocado, cut into 6 slices per half (Love Note)

**TO MAKE THE MARINADE**

1. Combine the marinade ingredients in a medium bowl.

2. Add the chicken breasts and turn to coat. Allow to marinate in the refrigerator for at least 2 hours or as long as overnight.

*continued*

1. Heat the grill to medium-high (you should be able to hold your hand a few inches above the grate for 3 seconds). Lightly oil the grate using a paper towel or clean rag doused in vegetable oil. Grasp the towel with tongs so you don't burn yourself while rubbing oil on the surface of the grate. You can spray the grate with nonstick spray instead, but remove the grate first so that you're not spraying the oil at the flames. Place the chicken breasts on the hot, lightly oiled grate and season each with ¼ teaspoon salt and ⅛ teaspoon black pepper (season one side if you like, or divide the amount between both sides). Grill on one side for about 3 minutes. Turn the breasts over and cook for another 2 minutes, or until almost done. Top each breast with 2 slices of cheese and cook for another minute or two to finish cooking the breasts and melt the cheese.

2. While the chicken cooks, place the rolls on the grill, cut side down, for a few minutes to get them warm and toasted.

3. Spread both halves of each roll with 1 tablespoon of Spicy Mayonnaise. Place a lettuce leaf, 2 tomato slices, a few red onion rings, and 3 avocado slices on each top half.

4. When the chicken is cooked and the cheese has melted, place on the prepared roll bottoms. Place on plates and serve them open-face.

**SPICY MAYONNAISE**                                    MAKES ½ CUP

½ cup mayonnaise

2 teaspoons sambal oelek (Love Note 2, page 12, Hummus)

In a small mixing bowl, whisk together the ingredients.

## LOVE NOTE

**To cut an avocado,** cut lengthwise around the pit with a sharp knife. Twist the halves to separate them and expose the pit. Tap the pit with the thicker part of the knife blade until it is partially embedded. Wiggle the knife until the pit loosens and you can pull it out.

To slice the avocado, make cuts in the flesh but don't cut through the skin. Slide a large spoon between the flesh and skin to scoop out the pieces.

desserts

**The best desserts are those packed with flavor without being cloyingly sugary, like the recipes in this chapter.** And if you're intimidated by baking, then these recipes will help you get over your fears. From the cream pies to the cookies, they're guaranteed to work. Even better, they're packed with a career's worth of advice to help you know the *why* as well as the *how*.

While you can play a bit with spices and extracts, types of nuts, or brands of chocolate, it's important to follow recipes to get the technique right. Nowhere is that more important than in baking. It's a science, after all. There are chemical reactions involved—bonds being formed and structures being developed. If you don't understand the science (and you'd have to be a professional to do so), then you really should follow these recipes to the letter. If the recipe calls for six eggs and you only have four, go to the store. If it calls for a springform pan and you don't have one, choose a different recipe (and then go get yourself a springform pan for next time!).

Before you begin, read through the recipe so you will know what's expected, from cooking and cooling times to what size mixing bowl to use. Also, some recipes require special pans and equipment, and you need to make sure you have them on hand before you start. One thing you'll find indispensable is parchment paper. This silicone-treated paper makes your cookie sheets and cake pans nonstick, so your baked goods can be removed without getting damaged in the process. You can find it at most supermarkets or purchase it in bulk from a restaurant supply store. In a pinch, aluminum foil also works.

In the end, there's only one secret to success with these recipes—treat them like formulas, not jumping-off points for experimentation. If you follow the instructions and advice carefully, you'll be rewarded with stellar treats to celebrate any occasion.

## CAKES

Few things in the world of baking are as scientific as making a cake. There are so many reactions and processes going on that just mixing the batter differently can result in a completely different dessert. That's why it's important to follow any cake-making directions to the letter. This is also why you don't have to let cake-making intimidate you. All you have to do is follow the recipe and you'll be fine.

There are a few things to remember when making cakes, cookies, or anything with a tender (rather than flaky) crumb: All your ingredients should be at room temperature unless otherwise noted. Butter must be pliable enough to cream properly with the sugar (so let it sit out for at least 1 hour before using). Eggs and milk need to be at room temperature or they will chill down the butter.

When measuring out flour, spoon it into the cup rather than dip your measuring cup into the flour. Dipping packs the flour a bit, which results in more flour per cup, and this can throw off the quality of the finished product. For an accurate measure, fluff the flour with your spoon to aerate it a little (it has a tendency to settle), spoon it into the cup until heaping, then run the straight edge of a spatula across the top to level it out.

## PUDDINGS

Mothers have been making pudding for ages. After all, it's easy, uses common ingredients likely to be on hand, and is even a bit nutritious. That being said, pudding can also be one of the most elegant ways to end a meal. Decadent boozy tiramisù and creamy panna cotta drizzled in berry coulis are impressively rich desserts.

Most of these recipes rely on cream and eggs, so make sure you choose the freshest possible. Also, follow the directions closely when cooking the puddings on the stove—heat that's too high can curdle eggs, and whisking too vigorously can break down cornstarch. But other than taking a few simple precautions, making pudding is almost child's play.

## COOKIES AND BROWNIES

When it comes to baking, most of us cut our teeth, so to speak, on cookies and brownies. They're easy to make and cook so quickly they're almost instantly gratifying. But there are a few secrets to success when making even these simple sweets.

Creaming butter and sugar together is an integral step for almost any cookie, and the purpose is to incorporate some air into the batter so that the cookies don't bake up flat. What do I mean by "cream"? That just means to whip the butter and sugar together until light and fluffy, or "creamy." It usually takes 2 to 3 minutes with an electric mixer. However, if the butter is too cold or too warm, it won't cream properly, so you need to set the butter out at least 1 hour before baking. When it's the right temperature, it should feel pliable but not greasy. If you don't have an hour to spare, grate the butter on the holes of a large grater. This will increase the surface area so that the butter will warm much more quickly.

Your eggs need to be room temperature, too. If they're too cold, they'll make the butter solidify into curdled-looking clumps. Take the eggs out of the fridge when you set out the butter. If you need to warm the eggs in a hurry, put them in a bowl, cover with hot tap water, and let sit for 5 minutes.

And if you haven't used your baking powder or baking soda in a while, check them for freshness before using. Baking soda should fizz when added to something acidic, like vinegar. Baking powder should fizz when added to hot water.

When it's time to bake, use a heavy-duty baking sheet to keep cookies from burning. If you only have thin, flimsy ones, double them up. To make sure the cookies don't stick to the pan, line the baking sheets with parchment paper—it's better than greasing the baking sheets, which can cause the cookies to spread too much.

To make sure cookies bake evenly, measure the dough accurately—an ice cream scooper works great for this. Also, arrange the cookies at least

2 inches apart so they don't run into each other, and rotate the sheets (from top to bottom and front to back) halfway through the baking time. Also, be sure to let the baking sheets cool between batches.

Don't feel obligated to bake all your cookie dough at once. All of the cookie doughs in this chapter will keep in the refrigerator for a couple of days and can be frozen indefinitely. You can also portion out the dough on cookie sheets, freeze until hard, and store in a zip-top bag in the freezer for fresh-baked cookies anytime, with no need to defrost the dough. For slice-and-bake cookies like shortbread, freeze the whole log and slice off just as many cookies as you want.

### SAUCES

Just a drizzle of something saucy can make a stark-looking dessert seem decadent. There are a few "core" sauces that really go with almost anything, and those are the sauces I've included. They freeze well (just reheat in the microwave at 50 percent power), so there's no excuse not to have some on hand.

When pairing a sauce with a dessert, try to keep the flavors compatible. Also, some people don't love chocolate (crazy, I know!) so don't taint a chocolate-free dessert with a chocolate sauce—unless you know you have an audience of chocolate lovers on your hands.

# Coconut Cream Pie

EVERYONE LOVES THIS PIE—EVEN PEOPLE WHO SAY THEY DON'T LIKE COCONUT.
What sets it apart is the chocolate cookie crust and the coconut rum. If you don't stock
coconut-flavored rum in your home bar, get a bottle—it really takes the flavor here to
another level.

My cream pies aren't mile-high affairs because they're so rich that too much filling
would be overload. The trickiest part about making this, or any other custard-based
pie, is keeping the eggs from curdling. Follow the tips in this recipe and you'll be an
expert in no time!

**FOR THE CHOCOLATE COOKIE CRUST**

6 ounces Nabisco® Famous
Chocolate Wafers (about
30 cookies)

5 tablespoons unsalted butter,
melted

**FOR THE COCONUT FILLING**

1½ cups whole milk

½ cup heavy cream

1 vanilla bean, split in half
lengthwise

6 large egg yolks

½ cup granulated sugar

⅛ teaspoon kosher salt

2 tablespoons cornstarch

1½ cups sweetened, shredded
coconut, toasted, plus more for
garnish (Love Note 1)

4 tablespoons (½ stick) unsalted
butter

2 tablespoons coconut rum, such
as Malibu®

**FOR THE WHIPPED CREAM TOPPING**

1½ cups cold heavy cream

1 teaspoon pure vanilla extract

¼ cup confectioners' sugar

**TO MAKE THE CRUST**

1. Heat the oven to 350°F and place a rack in the middle of the oven. Place the chocolate wafers in the bowl of a food processor fitted with the metal blade and pulse
until ground into evenly sized crumbs. Or place them in zip-top bag and pulverize

*continued*

them with a rolling pin or meat mallet until finely crushed. You should have about 1½ cups of crumbs.

2. Place the crumbs in a medium mixing bowl. Drizzle in the melted butter and mix with a fork until the crumbs are evenly moistened (if using a food processor, drizzle the butter through the feed tube while pulsing).

3. Transfer the buttered crumbs to a 9-inch pie plate, and use your fingertips or the back of a spoon to press the mixture evenly into the pie plate, spreading it up the sides but not over the rim. (I find the back of a spoon works best for pressing the crumbs into place and scraping away the thicker areas where the bottom meets the sides to even out the crumbs.)

4. Bake for 7 to 10 minutes, or until the sides of the crust feel firm to the touch. Transfer to a wire rack to cool completely before filling. (The crust can be made up to 1 day ahead; wrap in plastic and store at room temperature.)

**TO MAKE THE FILLING**

1. Place the milk, cream, and vanilla bean in a medium (4- to 6-quart) saucepan. Heat over medium-high heat, stirring occasionally, until almost about to simmer. (The surface will start to look foamy. This is called "scalding." Do not let it boil.) Remove from the heat and let the vanilla bean steep in the milk for 15 minutes.

2. Place the egg yolks, sugar, salt, and cornstarch in a medium mixing bowl and beat with a whisk until well blended, about 1 minute.

3. Remove the vanilla bean from the milk. Use a knife to scrape out as many seeds as possible and add them back to the milk. Swirl the pod in the milk to remove any remaining seeds. Discard the pod or save for another use (Love Note 2). Add the

*continued*

toasted coconut and place the pot over medium-high heat. Bring to a simmer, and then remove from the heat.

4. Ladle out about ½ cup of the hot milk and whisk it into the egg mixture. (This is called "tempering," which allows the eggs to warm up so they don't get shocked into curdling when you pour them into the hot milk.) Slowly pour the egg mixture into the pot of milk, whisking steadily to keep the eggs from curdling.

5. Place the pot over medium-high heat and bring the mixture to a boil, stirring constantly but not furiously. (You must stir constantly so you don't get scrambled eggs, but don't stir too vigorously either; Love Note 3.) Reduce the heat to low and continue to cook while whisking continuously (make sure to get the sides and edges) until the mixture is very thick, 2 to 3 minutes.

6. Remove from the heat, add the butter and stir until melted, and then stir in the coconut rum.

7. Pour into a shallow pan or bowl and let the filling cool to lukewarm in the refrigerator, covered with plastic wrap (about 15 minutes). Pour into the cooled pie shell. Place a piece of plastic wrap directly on the surface (to keep a skin from forming). Refrigerate the pie for at least 4 hours before serving.

## TO MAKE THE TOPPING

1. Just before serving, make the whipped cream topping: Place the cream and vanilla in the bowl of a stand mixer fitted with the whisk attachment (or, if using a whisk or hand-held mixer, put them in a deep mixing bowl). Beat on medium speed until frothy. Sprinkle in the confectioners' sugar and beat on medium-high speed until stiff peaks form (when the whisk is lifted, the cream will form a point that doesn't droop; Love Note, page 340, Banana Cream Pie).

2. Mound the whipped cream in the center of the chilled pie. Use the back of a large spoon or an offset metal spatula to spread it out to the edge and give it a few decorative swirls. If desired, fill a pastry bag fitted with a star tip with half of the whipped cream and pipe a border around the outside of the pie (pipe a ring of the letter "s," starting a new "s" inside the bottom part of the previous "s" so they interlock). Sprinkle with toasted coconut and serve.

*continued*

## LOVE NOTES

**1** **To toast coconut,** spread it out on a rimmed baking sheet. Bake at 325°F for about 10 minutes, stirring it around occasionally to keep the shreds from burning. The coconut shreds should be mostly golden brown, with a few white ones mixed in.

**2** **Used vanilla beans are great** for lending their flavor to sugar, either confectioners' or granulated. Just rinse and dry the bean, place it in an airtight jar, and cover with sugar. Let sit for at least 1 week or for up to 2 months.

**3** **Cornstarch is an excellent thickener** for cream pies because it has twice the thickening power of flour—and the less thickener you have to add, the more the flavors from your other ingredients will shine through. Cornstarch reaches full gelatinization once it comes to a simmer, but if you boil it too much the starch granules will burst and the filling will thin out. The same is true if you stir the mixture too vigorously. Like all good things, everything in moderation.

# Banana Cream Pie

THE FILLING IN THIS BANANA CREAM PIE HAS PERFECT CONSISTENCY, SO IT STANDS up nicely on the plate. The banana is optional, so you can leave it out for a delicious vanilla cream pie. Follow the chocolate variation (page 340) for a yummy chocolate version (with or without bananas). The filling makes a great pudding, too.

**FOR THE VANILLA WAFER CRUST**

6 ounces vanilla wafers (about 50 cookies)

5 tablespoons unsalted butter, melted

**FOR THE BANANA CREAM FILLING**

1 cup heavy cream

1 cup whole milk

6 large egg yolks

½ cup granulated sugar

¼ cup cornstarch

Pinch kosher salt

2 tablespoons unsalted butter

2 teaspoons pure vanilla extract, or ½ vanilla bean, split in half lengthwise

2 to 4 firm-ripe bananas, thinly sliced (about 2 cups), plus more for garnish

**FOR THE WHIPPED CREAM TOPPING**

1½ cups cold heavy cream

1 teaspoon pure vanilla extract

¼ cup confectioners' sugar

**TO MAKE THE CRUST**

1. Heat the oven to 350°F and place a rack in the middle of the oven. Place the cookies in the bowl of a food processor fitted with the metal blade and pulse until ground into evenly sized crumbs. Or place the cookies in a zip-top bag and pulverize with a rolling pin or meat mallet until finely crushed. You should have about 1½ cups of crumbs.

2. Place the crumbs in a medium mixing bowl. Drizzle in the melted butter and mix with a fork until the crumbs are evenly moistened (if using a food processor, drizzle the butter through the feed tube while pulsing). *continued*

3. Transfer the crumbs to a 9-inch pie plate, and use your fingertips or the back of a spoon to press the mixture evenly into the plate, spreading it up the sides but not over the rim. (The back of a spoon works best for pressing the crumbs into place and scraping away the thicker areas where the bottom meets the sides to even out the crumbs.)

4. Bake for 7 to 10 minutes, or until lightly browned and the sides of the crust feel firm to the touch. Transfer to a wire rack to cool completely before filling. (The crust can be made up to 1 day ahead; wrap in plastic and store at room temperature.)

**TO MAKE THE FILLING**

1. Place the cream and milk in a medium (4- to 6-quart) saucepan, and heat over medium-high heat, stirring occasionally, until just simmering. Remove from the heat. If using a vanilla bean instead of extract, add it now and let it steep in the milk for 15 minutes; remove the pod, then scrape out the seeds with a paring knife and add them back to the milk mixture. Discard the pod or save for another use.

2. Place the egg yolks, sugar, cornstarch, and salt in a medium mixing bowl and beat with a whisk until well blended, about 1 minute.

3. Ladle out about ½ cup of the hot milk and whisk it into the egg mixture. (This is called "tempering," which allows the eggs to warm up so they don't get shocked into curdling when you pour them into the hot milk.) Slowly pour the egg mixture into the pot of milk, whisking steadily to keep the eggs from curdling.

4. Place the pot over medium-high heat and cook the mixture, stirring constantly but not furiously, until it starts to thicken. (Make sure to get into all the nooks and crannies of the pan; Love Note 3, page 336, Coconut Cream Pie.) Reduce the heat to medium and continue to cook, whisking continuously, for 4 to 5 minutes or until very thick. If you're worried the mixture is about to curdle, move the pot off

the stove while continuing to stir. When the mixture starts to pull away from the bottom of the pan, it's ready. (When cool, the mixture will not tighten much more, so make sure it's thick or you will have a runny cream pie.)

5. Remove the pot from heat, add the butter and stir until melted, and stir in the vanilla extract (if not using the vanilla bean).

6. Pour into a shallow pan or bowl and place a piece of plastic wrap directly on the surface (to keep a skin from forming). Allow to cool for 30 minutes in the fridge.

7. When the filling has cooled, stir it well, then spread a third of it into the baked and cooled pie shell and scatter half the bananas over the top. Cover with another third of the filling and the rest of the bananas. Spread the remaining filling over the top (covering the bananas will keep them from turning brown). Place a piece of plastic wrap directly on the surface and refrigerate the pie for at least 4 hours.

**TO MAKE THE TOPPING**

1. Just before serving, make the whipped cream topping: Place the cream and vanilla in the bowl of a stand mixer fitted with the whisk attachment (or, if using a whisk or hand-held mixer, put them in a deep mixing bowl). Beat on medium speed until frothy. Sprinkle in the confectioners' sugar and beat on medium-high until stiff peaks form (when the whisk is lifted, the cream will form a point that doesn't droop; Love Note).

2. Mound the whipped cream in the center of the pie. Use the back of a large spoon or offset metal spatula to spread it out to the edge and give it a few decorative swirls. If desired, fill a pastry bag fitted with a star tip with half the whipped cream. Pipe swirls around the edges (pipe a ring of the letter "s," starting a new "s" inside the bottom part of the previous "s" so they interlock). Immediately before serving, garnish with a few more banana slices.

*continued*

**Cream must be very cold** to whip properly. Many bakers chill their bowls and beaters, too. Make sure to keep careful watch during the process. Cream can go from softly whipped to overwhipped in just seconds. When you see the beater beginning to make tracks in the cream, stop the machine, lift out the beater, and see if it leaves a peak of cream standing in the bowl. If the tip is still droopy, beat for just a few seconds longer.

If you overbeat your cream (it will look clumpy instead of fluffy), you can salvage it as long as it hasn't turned into butter. Scrape the overbeaten cream into another bowl and add a little new cream to the mixing bowl. Whisk until slightly thickened and then fold it into the overbeaten cream.

## VARIATION: Chocolate Banana Cream Pie

For the filling, substitute more whole milk for the cream and add 4 ounces chopped semisweet chocolate along with the butter and vanilla extract in Step 5. For garnish, use a vegetable peeler, zester, or Microplane grater to shave semisweet or dark chocolate onto the whipped cream.

# Mother's Black Bottom Peanut Butter Pie

LOTS OF THINGS COMBINE WITH CHOCOLATE TO CREATE A WINNING COMBINATION—mint, raspberry, coffee, and ginger, to name a few. And while each has its fans and foes, I have yet to meet someone who doesn't love chocolate with peanut butter.

This ultra-rich pie not only has that to-die-for combination in its two-layer filling, but it also boasts a great peanut cookie crust. The peanuts on top aren't just for show—they add a nice crunch and a bit of extra peanut flavor that takes the pie right over the top. There is enough dough to make either a very thick crust or a regular crust and a few cookies for nibbling while the pie sets (Love Note).

**FOR THE PEANUT BUTTER
SHORTBREAD CRUST**

2 sticks (1 cup) unsalted butter, at room temperature

⅔ cup granulated sugar

2 cups all-purpose flour

1 cup smooth peanut butter, preferably Jif®

1 teaspoon pure vanilla extract

**FOR THE FUDGE**

½ cup heavy cream

1 tablespoon corn syrup

4 ounces semisweet chocolate, finely chopped

**FOR THE PEANUT BUTTER FILLING**

½ cup cold heavy cream

1¼ cups (10 ounces) cream cheese, at room temperature

1½ cups smooth peanut butter, preferably Jif

1 tablespoon unsalted butter, at room temperature

1 cup confectioners' sugar

1 tablespoon pure vanilla extract

½ cup whole or coarsely chopped roasted salted peanuts, for garnish

**TO MAKE THE CRUST**

1. Place the butter and sugar in the bowl of an electric mixer fitted with the paddle attachment. Beat at medium-high speed until fluffy and pale in color, about 2 minutes.

*continued*

2. Reduce the speed to low and add the flour, mixing just until incorporated, about 1 minute. Add the peanut butter and vanilla and continue mixing until incorporated.

3. Place the dough (or just most of it if you're going to make shortbread cookies, too) into the pie plate and press it along the bottom and up the sides until evenly distributed and at least ¼ inch thick.

4. Place the pie plate in the refrigerator to chill for at least 1 hour or overnight.

5. Heat the oven to 325°F. Remove the pie plate from the refrigerator and prick the dough all over with a fork. Bake the crust for 30 to 35, minutes or until it looks opaque and set. (It may puff up a little, but that's OK.)

**TO MAKE THE FUDGE**

1. In a small (2- to 3- quart) saucepan, bring the cream and corn syrup just to a boil while stirring now and then. Remove from the heat.

2. Add the chocolate pieces and stir with a wooden spoon until the chocolate has melted and the ingredients are well combined.

3. Reserve ⅛ cup of the chocolate mixture and set aside in a microwavable bowl. Pour the remaining chocolate mixture into the baked pie crust and refrigerate while preparing the peanut butter filling.

**TO MAKE THE FILLING**

1. Place the cream in the bowl of an electric mixer fitted with the whisk attachment. Beat at medium-high speed until stiff peaks form. Scrape the whipped cream into a clean bowl and set aside.

2. Return the mixing bowl to the electric mixer and fit it with the paddle attachment. Place the cream cheese, peanut butter, and butter in the bowl and beat at medium-high speed until fluffy, about 3 minutes. With the mixer running, beat in the confectioners' sugar and vanilla extract. Continue beating for 1 minute more, until all the ingredients are fully incorporated.

3. Remove the bowl from the mixer. Fold the whipped cream into the peanut butter mixture until fully incorporated.

4. Spoon the peanut butter filling on top of the fudge layer in the pie. Use an offset metal spatula to smooth the top. Cover the pie and chill for at least 4 hours, or preferably overnight.

**TO SERVE**

Microwave the reserved fudge for 10 to 20 seconds to soften it, or heat it in a small saucepan over low heat (don't overheat it or it will "break"). Dip a fork into it and drizzle the mixture across the surface of the cold pie. Top with the peanuts, cut into wedges (this is a rich pie, so smaller servings are best), and serve.

## LOVE NOTE

**To make cookies out of leftover crust dough,** shape it into a log, wrap in plastic wrap, and refrigerate for at least 1 hour or freeze for later. Slice the log into ¼-inch-thick rounds and bake on a parchment-lined baking sheet at 350°F for 10 to 12 minutes. You'll probably get about two dozen 2-inch cookies.

# Mother's Apple Crisp

CRISPS HAVE ALL THE FLAVOR OF FRUIT PIES WITHOUT HAVING TO DEAL WITH THE fuss of the crust. When made right, they're downright righteous and something every family member can enjoy.

This recipe makes a lot—it's great for a buffet or large gatherings and keeps and reheats well. And you don't have to stick with one nut in the topping; there are times we've used a combination of almonds, hazelnuts, and walnuts all in the same crisp topping. It's nutilicious! Make a double batch and freeze the extra so you can whip up a crisp at the drop of a hat.

**FOR THE APPLE FILLING**

10 Granny Smith apples or other firm baking apples (about 3½ pounds; Love Note)

1 to 2 tablespoons lemon juice (about 1 lemon)

2 teaspoons ground cinnamon

½ cup granulated sugar

**FOR THE CRISP TOPPING**

1½ cups all-purpose flour

1 cup firmly packed light brown sugar

¼ cup granulated sugar

1 to 2 teaspoons ground cinnamon

1 cup (2 sticks) cold unsalted butter, cut into ½-inch dice

1½ cups chopped pecans or walnuts

Heat the oven to 350°F. Spray the bottom and sides of a 13x9x2-inch baking dish or spray with nonstick cooking spray.

**TO MAKE THE FILLING**

1. Peel the apples, and then cut each of the four sides off the apple as close to the core as possible. (This way you save a step by coring and slicing at the same time.) Slice the quarters into ¼-inch-thick slices.

*continued*

2. Place the apples in a large mixing bowl, and add the lemon juice, cinnamon, and sugar. Toss to coat. Pour the mixture into the prepared dish.

**TO MAKE THE TOPPING**

1. Place the flour, brown sugar, granulated sugar, and cinnamon in a large mixing bowl. Add the butter pieces and toss to coat. Using a pastry blender or large whisk, cut the butter into the dry ingredients until it forms large crumbs. Stir in the nuts. Alternatively, place the dry ingredients in the bowl of an electric mixer fitted with the paddle attachment or a food processor fitted with a metal blade. Mix or pulse to combine, then scatter the butter over the mixture. Mix on low speed or pulse until the mixture forms small clumps (about 3 minutes). Stir in the nuts.

2. Scatter the topping over the fruit, squeezing it with your hands as you go to create larger pieces (they will cook up extra-crispy and provide more texture). Lightly press the topping down into the fruit.

3. Bake on the middle rack in the oven until the topping is brown and the filling is bubbly, 45 to 55 minutes. Remove from the oven and cool on a wire rack for 30 minutes before serving. Serve alone or with vanilla ice cream, whipped cream, or a drizzle of heavy cream.

## LOVE NOTE

**Granny Smiths are my go-to baking apple** because they do a great job of keeping their shape when cooked, and their tartness provides a wonderful complexity and contrast to the dessert. But there are other varieties of apples that hold up well, too, including Cortland, Golden Delicious, Jonagold, Pippin, and Pink Lady. If you like, use a mix of different varieties.

# Devil's Food Cake

THIS CAKE IS MADE WITH PURÉED BEETS, WHICH IS A TRADITIONAL WAY OF MAKING devil's food that dates to wartime rationing. This is the signature chocolate cake at Besaw's Cafe, where I was a chef, but I added it to my repertoire at Mother's because I couldn't resist its texture, flavor, and earthiness. This is the only chocolate cake recipe you'll ever need; and vegetables in your cake can justify dessert!

The chocolate ganache frosting is simply melted chocolate and cream blended together and cooled. This mixture is the basis for truffles, so you can imagine how great it is on cake. It can also be swirled into homemade ice creams for a decadent "truffle swirl."

**FOR THE CHOCOLATE GANACHE FROSTING**

1 cup heavy cream

16 ounces semisweet chocolate, finely chopped

**FOR THE CAKE**

2 cups all-purpose flour

2 teaspoons baking soda

¼ teaspoon kosher salt

3 ounces chopped semisweet chocolate

8 tablespoons (1 stick) unsalted butter, at room temperature

2¼ cups packed (1 pound) light brown sugar

3 large eggs, at room temperature

½ cup buttermilk, at room temperature, divided

1 (15-ounce) can beets (not pickled!), with the juice, puréed until very smooth in a food processor or blender

**TO MAKE THE FROSTING**

1. Place the cream in a medium saucepan and bring to a simmer over medium-high heat.

2. Remove the cream from the heat and whisk in the chocolate. Keep whisking until the chocolate is melted.

3. Let the mixture cool on the counter, stirring occasionally, until spreadable, about 2 hours (the time it should take to make, bake, and cool the cake; Love Note 1).

*continued*

**TO MAKE THE CAKE**

1.  Heat the oven to 350°F. Using butter, oil, or nonstick cooking spray, thoroughly grease the bottom and sides of two 9-inch cake pans and line their bottoms with parchment (Love Note 2).

2.  Sift together the flour, baking soda, and salt. Set aside.

3.  Place a medium saucepan about one-third full of water over medium-high heat and bring to a simmer. Reduce the heat to low to keep the water warm but barely simmering. Place the chopped chocolate in a double boiler or bowl that fits over the saucepan. Set the bowl over the barely simmering water and heat, stirring now and then, until the chocolate is melted (Love Note 3). Set aside and cool to lukewarm.

4.  Place the butter and sugar in the bowl of an electric mixer fitted with the paddle attachment. Beat on high speed, stopping to scrape the sides of the bowl now and then, until light, fluffy, and pale in color, about 5 minutes.

5.  Reduce the speed to medium-high and add the eggs, one at a time, beating until fully incorporated after each addition. Reduce the speed to low and pour in the melted and cooled chocolate. Increase the speed to medium and beat for another minute, until incorporated. Scrape down the sides of the bowl.

6.  With the mixer on low speed, add one-third of the dry ingredients. When incorporated, add ¼ cup buttermilk. Repeat the process, ending with the last third of dry ingredients. When incorporated, add the puréed beets with their juice and mix on low speed until incorporated. Scrape down the sides of the bowl as needed.

7.  Evenly divide the batter between the prepared pans (they should be about three-quarters full).

*continued*

8. Bake for 35 to 40 minutes, or until a toothpick inserted in the center comes out clean (there should be no streaks of batter, just a few crumbs clinging to it) and the cake is pulling away from the sides.

9. Transfer the cakes to wire racks to cool for about 20 minutes. Run an offset spatula or knife around the edge of the pans to release the cake. Place a wire rack over each pan and invert the cake onto it. Allow the cakes to finish cooling before frosting.

**TO FROST THE CAKE**

1. Place one cake (bottom side up) in the center of a serving plate (that way you have a flat surface to frost). Tuck a few strips of parchment paper under the edges of the cake (to keep the plate clean and presentable while frosting). Place one-quarter of the frosting in the center and spread with an offset spatula to cover the surface. If the top of the second cake looks mounded on top, use a serrated knife to cut off the mounded area to make it flat. Place this cake (bottom side up) on the frosted layer (placing it upside down means the smoothest side will be on top, where it matters).

2. Place one-third of the frosting in the center and use an offset spatula to spread it all over the top and sides of the cake. (This is called a "crumb coat." It's a thin layer of frosting that fixes all the crumbs in place so they won't end up where you can see them. Don't worry, it's not meant to look pretty.)

3. Wipe the spatula clean and spoon out the rest of the frosting onto the top of the cake. (If you want to pipe a decorative border, reserve about $2/3$ cup frosting.) Spread all over the top and sides as evenly as possible. Use the spatula or the back of a spoon to smooth it out. If desired, fill a pastry bag with the reserved ganache and pipe a decorative border. (You can simply pipe the letter "s" and then start the next letter "s" in the bottom of the first so that they are interlocking.)

4. Pull the strips of parchment out from under the cake and serve.

# LOVE NOTES

**1** If you need to **cool ganache quickly,** fill a large bowl with ice and place the bowl with the chocolate-cream mixture inside. Once ganache becomes spreadable, use it right away before it hardens and becomes difficult to spread. If you're not ready to use it, move it to a warm place to keep it soft.

If the ganache gets cold and hard, rewarm it in a double boiler until it is the right consistency. Be careful! Ganache is prone to breaking—the fat in the cream and cocoa butter separates from the solids and the mixture ends up looking greasy. If it breaks, cool it, and then pulse in a food processor until re-emulsified.

**2** The easiest way to get **parchment circles** is to purchase them from a cake-decorating supply shop. Another way is to place your cake pan on top of a sheet of parchment, trace around it with a pencil or an X-Acto® knife, fold the circle into fourths and use scissors to cut just inside the line, and unfold.

**3** **Chocolate burns easily,** so chop it into small, evenly sized pieces when melting. Melt it gently in a double boiler or a wide, dry heatproof bowl set over a pot of barely simmering water. You can also melt the chocolate in a microwave at 50 percent power and stir every 15 to 30 seconds until the chocolate is melted (be careful with white and milk chocolates, which burn at lower temperatures than semisweet and bittersweet). If the chocolate overheats, the cocoa butter in the chocolate can separate out (called "seizing"), and you can wind up with a greasy, clumpy mess. There's no way to fix this, so you'll have to throw it all out.

Chocolate can also seize if liquid (like a drop of water) comes into contact with it. Just a small amount of liquid will cause some of the cocoa and sugar particles in the chocolate to clump together. The only way to fix it is to add a lot more liquid—enough to saturate all the particles until it is smooth again, but it's likely you'll still have some seized particles that don't melt away. This is fine for chocolate that will be mixed with liquid ingredients anyway, but not so good when you need pure melted chocolate. So be careful not to let any water from the water bath splash into the chocolate when melting and not to let any steam get into the bowl.

# Mother's Carrot Cake with Cream Cheese Frosting

SERVES 10 TO 12; MAKES ONE
13X9X2-INCH SHEET CAKE OR
ONE 9-INCH LAYER CAKE

THIS WONDERFUL CARROT CAKE IS A WELCOME CHANGE FROM THE USUAL SUSPECTS. Puréed carrots, rather than shredded, make it moist, while shredded coconut and crushed pineapple add subtle tropical flavors.

**FOR THE CAKE**

1 pound carrots, peeled and thinly sliced (about 4 medium carrots)

3 cups walnuts (divided)

2 cups all-purpose flour, plus more for flouring the pans

2 teaspoons baking soda

2 teaspoons ground cinnamon

¼ teaspoon ground nutmeg

1 teaspoon kosher salt

1 cup vegetable oil

2 cups granulated sugar

3 large eggs

2 teaspoons pure vanilla extract

1 cup packed sweetened shredded coconut

1 (20-ounce) can crushed pineapple, drained (about 1 cup pineapple)

**FOR THE CREAM CHEESE FROSTING**

6 tablespoons (¾ stick) unsalted butter, at room temperature

1 pound (two 8-ounce packages) cream cheese, at room temperature

3½ cups confectioners' sugar

1 teaspoon pure vanilla extract

**TO MAKE THE CAKE**

1. Fill a saucepan with a couple inches of water. Set over high heat and bring to a boil. Place the sliced carrots in a steamer basket and set over the saucepan. Cover and steam the carrots until very tender when pierced with a fork, about 20 minutes. (You can also bring a pot of water to a boil, add the carrots, cover, and cook until tender.) Place the carrots in the bowl of a food processor fitted with a metal blade and purée until smooth. You should have 1⅓ cups puréed carrots. Alternatively, you can purée with an immersion blender or with a food mill. (Don't use a blender or you'll need to add liquid.)

*continued*

2. Heat the oven to 350°F and place a rack in the center. Spread the walnuts on a baking sheet and toast until lightly browned, 8 to 10 minutes. Chop the walnuts and set aside.

3. Meanwhile, grease the bottom and sides of a 13x9x2-inch baking dish or two 9-inch cake pans with butter, oil, or nonstick cooking spray. Line the bottom(s) with parchment paper and grease the paper (Love Note 2, page 351, Devil's Food Cake). Sprinkle in a little flour and turn the pans to evenly coat the greased areas. Turn the pans over and tap them against the bottom of the sink to remove the excess (Love Note 1).

4. Sift the flour, baking soda, cinnamon, nutmeg, and salt into a medium bowl.

5. Place the oil and sugar in the bowl of an electric mixer fitted with the paddle attachment. Beat at medium speed until combined. Add the eggs one at a time and beat at medium speed until well incorporated before adding the next. Add the vanilla and carrots and beat for 1 minute more. Reduce the speed to low and add the sifted dry ingredients, mixing just until combined. Stir in the coconut, 1 cup of the walnuts, and the drained pineapple.

6. Pour the batter into the prepared pan(s) and bake in the center of the oven for 35 to 40 minutes, or until a toothpick inserted in the center comes out clean (crumbs can cling to it, but no streaks of batter) and the cake is pulling away from the sides of the pan(s). Remove the pan(s) from the oven and place on a wire rack to cool. After 15 minutes, place a cooling rack(s) over the pan(s) and invert (so the cake falls out of the pan and onto the rack). Peel off the parchment and continue to cool the cake for at least 1 hour before frosting.

**TO MAKE THE FROSTING**
In an electric mixer fitted with the whisk attachment, whisk together the butter and cream cheese on medium-high speed for 1 minute. Gradually whisk in the sugar, 1 cup

at a time. Stop the machine and scrape down the bottom and sides of the bowl. Add the vanilla and whisk at medium-high speed until very smooth and fluffy, about 2 minutes. Stop the machine and scrape down the bowl again, and then mix for 1 minute more. Set aside.

### TO FROST A 13X9X2-INCH CAKE

1. Place a serving platter on top of the cake and invert it again so the cake is sitting on it (Love Note 2). Tuck a few strips of parchment paper under the bottom edges of the cake (this keeps the serving plate clean as you frost). Use an offset spatula to scrape one-third of the frosting onto the top of the cooled cake. Spread the frosting over the top and sides (this is a thin coating called a "crumb coat," which fixes all the loose crumbs in place). Wipe your spatula clean and scrape the remaining frosting onto the top of the cake. Spread evenly over the top and sides.

2. Press the remaining chopped toasted walnuts around the sides and over the top of the cake. Refrigerate if not serving immediately.

### TO FROST A TWO-LAYER CAKE

1. Place a serving plate on top of one cake and invert it again so the cake is sitting on it (Love Note 2). Tuck a few strips of parchment paper under the bottom edges of the cake (this keeps the serving plate clean as you frost). Use an offset spatula to scrape one-third of the frosting onto the top of the cake; spread it evenly over the top. Carefully set the other cake on top, with the flat side facing up, and scrape one-third of the frosting onto the top of it. Spread this frosting over the top and sides of the cake (this thin layer of frosting is a crumb coat, which will adhere the crumbs to the cake so they don't end up on the surface of the final layer of frosting). Clean off your spatula and scrape the remaining frosting onto the top of the cake. Spread evenly over the top and sides.

2. Press the remaining chopped toasted walnuts around the sides and over the top of the cake. Refrigerate until ready to serve.

*continued*

## LOVE NOTES

**1** **Buttering the dish,** lining it with parchment, then buttering and flouring that too might seem like overkill, but properly greasing your baking pans is important. You won't be a happy camper if you can't get the cake out of the pan or if it breaks while coming out. So coat the baking pans evenly in a thin layer of butter, vegetable oil, vegetable shortening, or nonstick cooking spray—even if you're using parchment paper. Using parchment gives you insurance that your cake will come out of the pan. And buttering and flouring the parchment as well as the pan provides an extra barrier to keep the batter from saturating the parchment and negating its nonstick qualities.

Don't be skimpy when sprinkling the pan with flour; add about 2 tablespoons and turn the pan around, letting the flour coat all the greased areas. The flour keeps the butter from melting off the pan and acts as yet another barrier between the batter and the pan. To get rid of the excess, turn it over and, holding it over the sink, tap it a few times while giving it a quarter turn (but don't let the parchment fall out).

**2** **Cakes are fragile** and can easily tear or fall apart when handled. Inverting the cakes onto racks and serving dishes is the best way to maneuver them without damaging them.

# Mama's Cheesecake

ALTHOUGH DENSE RICOTTA CHEESECAKES ARE TYPICAL IN ITALIAN RESTAURANTS, they just don't do it for me. So when I opened Mama Mia Trattoria I decided to serve this cheesecake, which is one of the fluffiest and creamiest you'll find. The amaretto adds just a hint of complexity. Omit it if you must, but substitute another flavoring like lemon juice plus a little lemon zest for that extra something.

**FOR THE GRAHAM CRACKER CRUST**

8 ounces graham crackers (about 14 full-size crackers)

6 tablespoons (¾ stick) unsalted butter, melted

**FOR THE CHEESECAKE FILLING**

1½ pounds (24 ounces) cream cheese, at room temperature

1½ cups granulated sugar

1½ cups (12 ounces) sour cream

3 large eggs, at room temperature

1 cup plus 2 tablespoons heavy cream

½ teaspoon pure vanilla extract

2 tablespoons Disaronno® amaretto liqueur

**TO MAKE THE CRUST**

1. Heat the oven to 325°F, and place a rack in the center. Place the crackers in the bowl of a food processor fitted with the metal blade and process until evenly ground into crumbs. Alternatively, you can place them in zip-top bag and pulverize them with a rolling pin or meat mallet until finely crushed. You should have about 2 cups of crumbs.

2. Place the crumbs in a medium mixing bowl. Drizzle in the melted butter and mix with a fork until the crumbs are evenly moistened. (If using a food processor, drizzle the butter through the feed tube while pulsing.)

*continued*

3. Press the crumb mixture evenly onto the bottom of a 10-inch springform pan. Bake the crust for 10 minutes, or until lightly browned and firm to the touch. Remove from the oven and let cool while you prepare the rest of the ingredients.

**TO MAKE THE FILLING**

1. Place the cream cheese and sugar in the bowl of an electric mixer fitted with the paddle attachment. Beat at medium speed for 8 to 10 minutes, stopping the mixer every now and then and scraping the sides and bottom with a rubber spatula. Beat in the sour cream. Add the eggs, one at a time, beating well after each addition. Stop to scrape down the sides of the bowl. Add the heavy cream, vanilla, and amaretto, and beat until well combined.

2. Stack two large sheets of aluminum foil on the counter and center the springform pan on top. Wrap the foil up the sides of the pan (this is to keep water from the water bath from seeping in during baking).

3. Pour the filling into the pan on top of the baked crust. Set the pan in a roasting pan or baking dish and place on the center rack in the oven. Pour enough hot tap water into the roasting pan to reach 1 inch up the sides of the springform pan.

4. Bake for 1½ hours, or until the cheesecake is slightly brown on top and the center no longer jiggles. Remove from the oven and transfer the springform pan to a wire rack to cool for 1 hour. Chill the cheesecake in the springform pan in the refrigerator overnight before serving. (Don't try to rush this. Cheesecake needs time to firm up in the fridge.)

5. Once the cheesecake is chilled, remove the springform pan ring. To serve, dip a knife in hot water and wipe dry before slicing into the cake (this heats the knife so it makes neater slices). Cut into small wedges (dipping the knife and wiping it clean and dry each time) and serve plain or with Caramel Sauce (page 384), Hot Fudge (Dark Chocolate) Sauce (page 382), or Berry Coulis (page 385), if desired.

# Best Chocolate Pudding

WHEN I WANT TO MAKE DESSERT WITH THE KIDS, I ALWAYS THINK OF CHOCOLATE pudding (besides chocolate chip cookies, of course). It's not too hard to make, it's slightly nutritious given the milk, and kids love to stir it. The cornstarch and cocoa dissolve best when mixed with just enough liquid to saturate the powders and make a paste. Otherwise, they'll form clumps that won't cook out.

3 tablespoons cornstarch

3 tablespoons unsweetened Dutch-processed cocoa powder (Love Note)

Pinch kosher salt

½ cup granulated sugar

4 large egg yolks

1 cup half-and-half

2 cups whole milk

4 ounces bittersweet or semisweet chocolate, finely chopped

1 tablespoon crème de cacao, Godiva® chocolate liqueur, or pure vanilla extract

1 cup whipped cream, for garnish (optional)

1. Place the cornstarch, cocoa powder, salt, and sugar in a small (2- to 3-quart) saucepan and whisk to combine.

2. In a small bowl, whisk the egg yolks, half-and-half, and milk together until combined. Pour a couple of tablespoons of the egg yolk mixture into the dry ingredients in the saucepan, whisking well to make a thick paste (this will help prevent lumps). Slowly whisk in the rest of the egg mixture, a little at a time, making sure it's incorporated before adding more.

3. Set the saucepan over medium-high heat and cook, whisking steadily but not furiously, until thickened and just starting to boil. (You need to stir constantly—make sure to get the sides—to prevent scorching, but don't stir vigorously or you'll break the cornstarch granules and the pudding won't set up.) Lower the heat to medium

*continued*

and continue to cook at a gentle simmer for another 5 minutes, stirring constantly. Remove from the heat and stir in the chopped chocolate until melted.

4. Whisk in the crème de cacao, chocolate liqueur, or vanilla extract. If there are any lumps, strain the pudding through a fine-mesh sieve into a clean bowl.

5. Pour the pudding into 1-cup serving dishes or cups. If you don't like a skin (I do!), place a piece of plastic wrap directly on the surface of each pudding. Chill until cold, about 4 hours. Serve alone or with whipped cream, if desired.

## LOVE NOTE

The difference between **Dutch-processed cocoa and regular** cocoa is that the Dutch style has been treated with alkali to neutralize the natural acidity in the cocoa. The result is a more mellow cocoa flavor and darker color—perfect for a rich pudding like this where you want deep color and rounded flavor. Regular unsweetened cocoa, often labeled "natural cocoa," has a more complex flavor.

Be careful when using cocoa powder in baking recipes. Dutch-processed is pH neutral, so it doesn't work with baking soda—it can't provide the acidity needed for the baking soda to react and create gas bubbles for leavening. Therefore it's normally used with baking powder, which contains its own acidic ingredient. Regular cocoa powder is already acidic, though, so it's best used with baking soda, because using it with baking powder would be overkill. It's not always easy to be sure if a cocoa powder is Dutch-processed or not. Check the fine print on the back label. Droste® is a common brand of Dutch-processed.

# Tiramisù

THERE ARE MANY RECIPES FOR TIRAMISÙ, BUT THIS IS ONE OF THE BEST (EVEN A local paper thought so!). Follow the directions exactly, use the thickest mascarpone you can find, and make sure you keep everything cold and in the refrigerator until mixing together, or it will be runny and won't hold up on the plate.

6 shots of espresso (about ¾ cup; Love Note 1)

⅓ cup brandy

¼ cup Kahlúa® or other coffee liqueur

4 large eggs, separated (Love Notes 2 and 3)

⅔ cup granulated sugar (divided)

1 pound mascarpone

1 cup heavy cream

40 savoiardi ladyfingers (about two 7-ounce boxes; Love Note 4)

Unsweetened cocoa powder and shaved chocolate, for garnish (optional)

1. In a small bowl, combine the espresso, brandy, and Kahlúa. Set aside.

2. In the bowl of an electric mixer fitted with the whisk attachment, combine the egg yolks and ⅓ cup of the sugar. Whisk at high speed until very fluffy, pale yellow, and stiff, at least 7 minutes.

3. Stop the mixer, scrape down the sides of the bowl, and add the mascarpone. Continue whipping until very stiff, another 2 minutes. (If the mixture starts to look curdled, stop mixing. If you continue to beat, you'll end up with butter.) Transfer the mixture to a large bowl and place in the refrigerator while completing the remaining steps.

4. Wipe out the bowl of the electric mixer and add the cream. Whisk at medium speed until frothy. Increase the speed to medium-high and sprinkle in half of the remaining sugar (you don't have to be precise). Continue whipping until the cream

*continued*

holds stiff peaks. Fold the whipped cream into the mascarpone mixture and return the bowl to the refrigerator.

5. Thoroughly wash and dry the electric mixer bowl and whisk attachment and add the egg whites. Beat the egg whites at medium speed until frothy. Increase the speed to high (don't scrape the bowl or you could deflate the whites) and sprinkle in the remaining sugar. Continue beating until the whites hold stiff peaks.

6. Gently fold one-third of the egg whites into the mascarpone mixture (folding in a small amount of the whites at first lightens the mixture and makes it easier to fold in the remaining whites without overmixing, which would deflate the whites). Fold in the remaining whites and return the mixture to refrigerator.

7. One at a time, dip the ladyfingers briefly (make sure they're submerged) into the espresso mixture and place side by side in a 9x13x2-inch baking dish until the bottom of the pan is covered. (Make sure you dip for only a second—you don't want the ladyfingers to be soaked to the center or your tiramisu will end up mushy.) Depending on how you arrange the ladyfingers, you should get 19 to 20 in the dish; you may have to trim a little off the ends of the ones in the corners.

8. Spread half the mascarpone mixture (about 4 cups) over the ladyfingers.

9. Repeat with another layer of dipped ladyfingers, followed by the remaining mascarpone mixture.

10. Cover with plastic wrap and place the dish in the refrigerator to chill overnight before cutting.

11. Cut the tiramisù into thirds lengthwise and crosswise to make 9 portions. Use an offset spatula to lift each portion onto a serving plate, sprinkle with cocoa powder and top with shaved chocolate, if desired (Love Note 5), and serve. *continued*

# LOVE NOTES

**1.** If you don't have an **espresso machine,** I highly recommend stopping at the nearest café to pick up the shots rather than using instant espresso. The flavor is far superior.

**2.** **Separating eggs** requires care and caution. If just a drop of yolk gets in the whites, they won't whip up. That's because the yolk has fat, and just a little fat, oil, or soap (even residue on plastic containers) can keep the whites from whipping.

To ensure the whites stay pristine, crack an egg into a small bowl, scoop out the yolk with your (clean) fingers, and place it in a separate bowl. Then dump the egg white into its own bowl. Repeat with the remaining eggs. This way, if a yolk breaks during cracking, you'll only have to toss out one egg, not the whole batch. By the way, whites whip best when they're at room temperature.

**3.** This dish is made with **uncooked eggs.** Although the risk of salmonella is very low (about 0.005 percent according to the American Egg Board), substitute pasteurized eggs if you'd prefer.

**4.** The **best ladyfingers** for this recipe are very dry and crisp. They're often called savioardi and are imported from Italy. If you can't find these and your supermarket only has soft, cakelike ladyfingers, you will need to let them dry out in the oven first. Moist lady-fingers will soak up too much liquid and the tiramisù will be mushy. To dry them out, arrange them on a baking sheet and place in a 250°F oven for about 20 minutes, until brittle, flipping each one over halfway through.

**5.** To make **chocolate shavings,** you'll need a block of chocolate and a vegetable peeler. Place the chocolate block in the microwave for just a few seconds to soften it a bit. Place it on its side, so a narrow end is facing you, and run the vegetable peeler along the length. The chocolate will curl around the peeler like a wood shaving. Repeat until you have all the shavings you need. If you don't have a block of choco-late, just use the peeler to shave bits of whatever chocolate you have on hand.

# Mama Mia Trattoria's Panna Cotta

*PANNA COTTA* MEANS "COOKED CREAM" IN ITALIAN, AND THAT'S PRETTY MUCH WHAT this is—luscious sweetened cream steeped with a vanilla bean. It's thickened by gelatin rather than eggs, so the pure cream flavor really comes through. This dessert is best in the summer months, when berries are prolific, but you can serve it anytime with Berry Coulis (page 385) made with frozen berries. Panna cotta freezes beautifully. Just defrost it overnight in the fridge.

¼ cup water

2 teaspoons unflavored gelatin (Love Note 1)

2¾ cups heavy cream

½ cup sweetened condensed milk

1 vanilla bean

Fresh berries, chopped fruit, or Berry Coulis (page 385; optional)

1. If planning on unmolding the panna cotta for serving, spray 4 or 6 (6- or 8-ounce) ramekins with a light coating of nonstick cooking spray.

2. Place the water in a medium mixing bowl (Love Note 2) and evenly sprinkle the gelatin on top. Let rest undisturbed while the gelatin absorbs the liquid. (This is called "softening the gelatin." It will help the gelatin dissolve smoothly when whisked with the hot cream. It might seem solid or wrinkly when it absorbs the liquid, but that's OK.)

3. Meanwhile, place the heavy cream and sweetened condensed milk in a medium (4- to 6-quart) saucepan. Split the vanilla bean lengthwise and scrape the seeds into the cream mixture, then toss in the pod.

4. Place the pot over medium-high heat and bring to a simmer, stirring occasionally. Turn off the heat and let the mixture steep for 15 minutes.

*continued*

5. Remove the vanilla pod from the cream and scrape any remaining seeds into the mixture, swirling the pod in the cream to get out as many seeds as possible. (Discard the pod, or rinse and save it for another use; Love Note 2, page 336, Coconut Cream Pie.)

6. Slowly pour the cream into the bowl with the gelatin, whisking constantly, until the gelatin is dissolved. Pour the mixture through a fine-mesh sieve into a pitcher or large liquid measuring cup with a spout (this will catch any bits of vanilla pod and make it easier to pour the mixture into the ramekins). Divide the mixture among the prepared ramekins. Cover the ramekins with plastic wrap (to keep them from drying out or picking up odors from other foods), place in the refrigerator, and chill for at least 4 hours or overnight.

7. To serve: Top the pudding in the ramekins with fruit or a spoonful of coulis, if desired. Or, if you want to remove the panna cotta from the ramekins for a prettier presentation, dip each ramekin in hot water for 30 seconds to loosen it. Run a paring knife around the edge, and invert the ramekin onto a serving plate. Slowly pull the ramekin off. Top with fruit or coulis.

## VARIATION: Lemon Panna Cotta

Soften the gelatin in ½ cup fresh lemon juice instead of ¼ cup water. Use 2½ cups of cream instead of 2¾ cups. Add ½ cup sugar to the cream before simmering. The acid in the lemon juice thickens the cream, so this panna cotta turns out with a lush, dense texture, like cheesecake, without the chewy firmness that results from too much gelatin.

*continued*

# LOVE NOTES

**1** **Why measure the amount of gelatin** instead of just using one packet? Well, a ¼-ounce packet of unflavored gelatin has, on average, about 2½ teaspoons. But the amount in the packet often varies, with some containing less than 2 teaspoons and others almost 1 tablespoon. To be safe, your best bet is to measure the gelatin. If you like the texture more firm (which actually makes it easier to unmold), use up to 1 extra teaspoon of gelatin.

**2** **For efficient mixing,** it's always better to use a mixing bowl that's too big rather than too small. If you chose a bowl just big enough for the gelatin, it would be too small when it came time to whisk in the cream. That's another reason why it's important to read recipes through before starting, so you'll be able to choose the correct size bowls before you begin.

# Bread Pudding

WARM, SQUISHY, AND SWEET, BREAD PUDDING IS THE MOST MOTHERLY OF ALL
desserts because it's delicious *and* practical. It's one of the many genius ways mothers have transformed stale bread into something their families can enjoy. This recipe
is reason enough to stockpile odds and ends of leftover bread (just make sure it's not
strongly flavored, like rye). Keep them in a bag in the freezer until you've accumulat-
ed enough. While I do this at home, in the restaurant I use egg-rich challah bread to
create a very rich, decadent, almost upscale bread pudding. If you don't have leftover
bread or are serving this for company, I urge you to seek out challah or similar eggy
bread, such as Texas toast or brioche.

1 (2-pound) loaf challah bread, or
the equivalent amount of leftover
bread

4 tablespoons (½ stick) unsalted
butter, melted, plus more for
greasing the pan

7 large eggs

3 large egg yolks (Love Note)

1 cup granulated sugar

Pinch kosher salt

2 teaspoons pure vanilla extract

3 cups heavy cream

1 cup whole milk

Caramel Sauce (page 384;
optional)

1.  Heat the oven to 350°F. Grease a 13x9x2-inch baking dish. Cut some of the crust
    off the bread (you don't have to cut it all off), and then cut the bread into large
    (1½-inch) cubes. (You should have 20 cups of bread cubes.)

2.  Arrange the cubes in a single layer on two rimmed baking sheets and brush the
    tops with the melted butter. Bake for 10 to 15 minutes, stirring them once or twice
    to crisp them evenly. Remove from the oven and let cool for at least 10 minutes.
    Turn the oven off.

3.  Meanwhile, in a large mixing bowl, whisk together the eggs, egg yolks, sugar, salt,
    and vanilla. *continued*

4. Place the cream and milk in a medium saucepan and bring just to a boil over medium-high heat. While the milk comes to a boil, evenly arrange the toasted bread cubes in the prepared dish. (It might seem like too much, but the bread will compress once the liquid is added.)

5. Slowly add the hot cream to the egg mixture in a slow, steady stream while whisking. (Start with just a splash. You don't want to add it too fast or the eggs will curdle.)

6. Pour the cream mixture evenly over the bread cubes. Place a sheet of foil over the bread and weigh it down with a couple of small plates or a smaller baking dish on top (you might have to put a couple of cans on top to add more weight so the bread stays submerged). Let sit for at least 1 hour, pressing down now and then. (This will allow the bread to soak up the egg mixture. Refrigerate the pan if you will be letting it sit longer than an hour.)

7. Turn the oven back on to 350°F, and place a rack in the center. Remove the weights from the pudding and bake, covered with foil, for 20 minutes. Remove the foil and

*continued*

*continued*

## LOVE NOTE

**Save the egg whites** from recipes where you use only the yolk. If you don't want to make an egg white omelet, freeze the whites in an airtight container or zip-top bag (label it with how many whites are in it) and use them next time you have a recipe calling for just whites, such as meringue or angel food cake. Defrost the whites in the refrigerator overnight, and then set them on the counter to come to room temperature before whipping. You can also freeze and defrost egg yolks the same way.

bake for another 15 to 20 minutes, or until a knife inserted in the center comes out clean (there should be no uncooked egg coating the knife) and the pudding is puffy on top.

8. Allow the pudding to cool on a wire rack for at least 10 minutes before cutting into squares and serving with Caramel Sauce, if desired.

## VARIATIONS

### White Chocolate Bread Pudding

Decrease the sugar by ¼ cup. After whisking the hot cream into the eggs, whisk in 10 ounces finely chopped white chocolate until melted. Proceed with the recipe and serve warm with White Chocolate Sauce (page 383) or Caramel Sauce (page 384).

### Dark Chocolate Bread Pudding

After whisking the hot cream into the eggs, whisk in 8 ounces finely chopped semisweet or bittersweet chocolate until melted. Proceed with the recipe and serve warm with Hot Fudge (Dark Chocolate) Sauce (page 382) or White Chocolate Sauce (page 383).

### New Orleans Bread Pudding

Heat ⅓ cup bourbon in a small saucepan. Remove from the heat and stir in 1 cup golden raisins. Cover and let the raisins steep for 20 minutes. Strain the bourbon and reserve for Bourbon Crème Anglaise (page 387). Toss the steeped raisins, 1 cup chopped toasted pecans (Love Note, page 380, Lovey's Fudge Brownies), and bread in a large bowl. Pour in the egg and cream mixture and gently toss. Transfer to the prepared baking dish and proceed with the rest of the recipe. Serve with another ½ cup toasted pecans sprinkled on top and a drizzle of Bourbon Crème Anglaise (page 387) or Caramel Sauce (page 384).

# Triple Chocolate Chubbies

THESE ARE THE PERFECT COOKIES FOR THE CHOCOLATE LOVER. IT'S THE MOST chocolatey cookie ever and nice and soft in the middle, kind of like a brownie.

1½ cups pecans or walnuts, or a mix of both (Love Note, page 380, Lovey's Fudge Brownies)

12 ounces semisweet chocolate, finely chopped (Love Note)

4 ounces unsweetened chocolate, finely chopped

¾ cup (1½ sticks) unsalted butter, cut into ½-inch pieces

½ cup all-purpose flour

½ teaspoon baking powder

¼ teaspoon kosher salt

4 large eggs

1 cup packed light brown sugar

½ cup granulated sugar

1½ teaspoons instant espresso powder

2 teaspoons pure vanilla extract

2 cups chocolate chips or chopped chocolate (buy the best chocolate you can afford)

1. Heat the oven to 350°F. Arrange the pecans or walnuts on a rimmed baking sheet and toast for 10 minutes or until lightly browned. Remove from the oven (turn the oven off, too) and coarsely chop.

2. Fill a medium saucepan with several inches of water. Place over medium-high heat, heat until simmering, and then reduce the heat to low so the water just barely simmers. Place the semisweet chocolate, unsweetened chocolate, and butter in a double boiler or heatproof bowl that fits over the saucepan. Set over the barely simmering water and heat, stirring occasionally, just until melted. Remove from the heat and set aside to cool to lukewarm.

3. Meanwhile, in a medium bowl, sift together the flour, baking powder, and salt. (I prefer sifting the dry ingredients together because baking soda has a tendency to clump and a whisk isn't very effective at breaking up the tiny clumps.)

*continued*

4. Place the eggs and sugars in the bowl of an electric mixer fitted with the paddle attachment. Beat at medium-high speed until thick and creamy, about 3 minutes.

5. With the mixer on medium-low speed, slowly pour in the cooled chocolate-butter mixture, beating until combined. Add the espresso powder and vanilla.

6. With the mixer on low speed, add the dry ingredients, mixing just until combined. Then mix in the chocolate chips and nuts. Place the bowl in the refrigerator to chill the dough for at least 1 hour.

7. Heat the oven to 350°F. Position the racks in the upper and lower thirds of the oven. Line two baking sheets with parchment paper.

8. Drop the dough by rounded tablespoon onto the prepared baking sheets, leaving 2 inches between the cookies. Bake for 12 minutes, rotating the baking sheets from top to bottom and front to back halfway through baking. (The cookies will be shiny around the outside but soft in the center.) Let cool on the baking sheet for a minute before moving to a wire rack to cool completely (they'll firm up as they cool).

9. Repeat with the remaining dough, cooling the sheets completely between batches.

### LOVE NOTE

**Not all chocolate is created equal.** The quality of chocolate depends on the quality of the cacao beans used, how they were roasted and handled, and the quality of the other ingredients that were used in making the chocolate. Trusted supermarket brands including Ghirardelli®, Scharffen Berger®, and Lindt®.

# Maple Pecan Sandies

THESE BUTTERY COOKIES MELT IN YOUR MOUTH AND ARE PERFECT WITH A WARM cup of coffee on a brisk fall day.

1½ cups pecans (pieces or halves)

1 cup (2 sticks) unsalted butter, at room temperature

½ cup granulated sugar

¼ teaspoon kosher salt

1 large egg yolk, at room temperature

2 tablespoons maple syrup

1 teaspoon pure vanilla extract

2 cups all-purpose flour

1.  Heat the oven to 350°F. Position the racks in the upper and lower thirds of the oven. Line two baking sheets with parchment paper.

2.  Place the pecans on one of the baking sheets and toast for 10 minutes, or until lightly browned and fragrant (it will take less time if you're using pieces rather than halves). Set aside until cool; turn off the oven.

3.  Place the butter, sugar, and salt in the bowl of an electric mixer fitted with the paddle attachment. Beat on medium speed until light and fluffy, 1 to 2 minutes, stopping to scrape the sides of the bowl now and then.

4.  With the mixer on medium speed, beat in the egg yolk, maple syrup, and vanilla until well combined, about 1 minute. Stop the mixer and scrape down the sides of the bowl.

5.  With the mixer on low speed, slowly sprinkle in the flour, mixing just until incorporated. Mix in the toasted pecans.

*continued*

6.  Divide the dough into three equal portions. Roll each portion into a log. (For bite-size cookies, make the log 1 inch in diameter; for larger cookies, make it 2 inches.) Wrap the logs in plastic and refrigerate for at least 1 hour or up to 3 days. The dough can also be frozen for later use (thaw on the counter for 10 to 15 minutes before slicing).

7.  To bake, heat the oven to 350°F. Cut the logs into ¼-inch-thick slices. Place the cookies 1 inch apart on the prepared pans. Bake until lightly golden around the edges, about 12 minutes, rotating the baking sheets from front to back and top to bottom halfway through baking.

8.  Cool the cookies on the baking sheet for a minute before transferring to a wire rack to cool completely.

9.  Repeat with the remaining dough, cooling the baking sheets completely between batches.

# Shortbread Cookies

I LOVE THE BUTTERY SIMPLICITY OF SHORTBREAD COOKIES. THEY'RE A SNAP TO make, you can change the flavorings by adding different extracts or spices, and the dough can be tucked into the freezer for cookies anytime the mood strikes. Just let the frozen logs sit at room temperature for about 10 minutes, then slice the logs and bake as usual—no need to fully defrost.

| | |
|---|---|
| 1 cup (2 sticks) unsalted butter, at room temperature | ¼ teaspoon kosher salt |
| | 2 cups all-purpose flour |
| ½ cup granulated sugar | 2 teaspoons pure vanilla extract |

1. Place the butter, sugar, and salt in the bowl of an electric mixer fitted with the paddle attachment. Beat at medium speed, stopping the machine to scrape down the sides of the bowl at least once, until the mixture is fluffy, about 3 minutes.

2. Scrape down the sides of the bowl. With the mixer on low speed, add the flour and vanilla and mix briefly (not even 30 seconds), just until incorporated.

3. Lay a large piece of plastic wrap on a work surface. Scrape the dough into the center of the wrap and gather the dough into a ball. Fold one of the long ends of the wrap over onto the dough and use it to help you press and shape the dough into a 12-inch-long log. Wrap the plastic around the log and refrigerate for at least 1 hour, or freeze and bake later.

4. To bake, heat the oven to 350°F. Position the racks in the upper and lower third of the oven. Line two baking sheets with parchment paper.

5. Remove the plastic wrap and cut the log into ¼-inch-thick slices. Place the slices on the prepared pans, 1 inch apart, and bake until they just start to turn golden

*continued*

around the edges, 12 to 14 minutes, rotating the baking sheets from top to bottom and front to back midway through baking.

6. Let the cookies cool on the baking sheet for 2 minutes before transferring to a wire rack to cool completely.

7. Repeat with the remaining cookies, cooling the baking sheets completely between batches.

## VARIATIONS

### Peanut Butter Shortbread

To make the dough, follow the recipe for the crust in Mother's Black Bottom Peanut Butter Pie (page 341), but cut the ingredients in half (to make about thirty 2½-inch cookies), or make the full batch of dough and freeze what you don't use. If desired, mix in ½ cup chocolate chips or finely chopped roasted and salted peanuts or toffee bits. Continue with the shaping, slicing, and baking instructions.

### Chocolate Shortbread

Instead of 2 cups flour, use 1½ cups flour plus ½ cup unsweetened cocoa powder. Omit the vanilla.

### Chocolate Mint Shortbread

Add 2 teaspoons mint extract to the chocolate shortbread dough. Add ½ cup chocolate chips, if desired. (Keep the baked cookies separate from other cookies or they'll all start tasting a little minty.)

# Lovey's Fudge Brownies

NAMED AFTER OUR PASTRY CHEF'S GRANDMOTHER, WE SERVE THESE BROWNIES
piled with a variety of homemade ice creams, drizzled with our own hot fudge and
white chocolate sauces, and topped with whipped cream. These brownies satisfy any
chocolate craving—they're perfect alone or with all the other goodies.

8 tablespoons (1 stick) unsalted
butter, cut into pieces, plus more
for greasing the pan

4 ounces unsweetened chocolate,
finely chopped

1 cup granulated sugar

¼ teaspoon kosher salt

1 teaspoon pure vanilla extract

2 large eggs

½ cup all-purpose flour

½ cup chopped, partially toasted
pecans or walnuts (Love Note;
optional)

1. Heat the oven to 350°F. Grease an 8-inch-square baking pan and line the bottom
   with parchment paper, allowing the paper to hang over the edge of the pan by
   2 inches (these "handles" will help you get the brownies out of the pan). Grease the
   bottom of the paper.

2. Fill a medium saucepan with a few inches of water. Set over medium heat and bring
   to a simmer, and then reduce the heat to low so the water is barely simmering.

3. Place the butter and chopped chocolate in a double boiler or small heatproof bowl
   that fits over the saucepan. Set over the barely simmering water and heat,
   stirring occasionally, just until melted. Remove from the heat and set aside to
   cool slightly.

4. Place the sugar, salt, vanilla, and eggs in the bowl of an electric mixer fitted with
   the paddle attachment. Beat at medium-high speed until combined, about 30 seconds. (Alternatively, you can whisk them together by hand until well combined.)

*continued*

5. With the mixer on low, add the melted chocolate mixture (or add it while whisking by hand); continue mixing until well combined. Add the flour and mix just until incorporated.

6. Stir in the nuts, if using, and pour the batter into the prepared baking pan, spreading evenly with a spatula. Bake for 25 to 30 minutes, or until the edges are puffed, the top is crackled, and a toothpick inserted in the center comes out clean (with a few wet crumbs clinging to it, but no streaks of batter). If the brownies aren't done, continue to bake, checking them every 5 minutes for doneness.

7. Remove the pan from the oven and set on a wire rack. Let the brownies cool completely in the pan. Grasp the ends of the parchment paper and lift the brownies out. Cut into thirds lengthwise and crosswise to make 9 roughly 3-inch squares.

## LOVE NOTE

**To pretoast nuts:** Heat the oven to 350°F. Place the nuts on a baking sheet and toast in the oven for 5 to 10 minutes. Remove from the oven and let cool. Generally, the longer the item will bake, the less time you should toast the nuts to keep them from burning in the finished product. I would toast nuts for 10 minutes for a baked good that will cook for 15 minutes or less, but only 5 minutes for a baked good that will be in the oven for 15 to 40 minutes. Any longer than that and I wouldn't pretoast the nuts at all.

## VARIATION: Cream Cheese Brownies

SWIRL THIS SWEETENED CREAM CHEESE INTO THE BROWNIES, FOR AN
extra-decadent treat. Serve with a tall glass of ice-cold milk.

8 ounces cream cheese, at room
temperature

¼ cup granulated sugar

1 teaspoon pure vanilla extract

1 large egg

1. In an electric mixer fitted with the whisk attachment, whisk together the cream
   cheese and sugar until fluffy, about 2 minutes.

2. Add the vanilla and egg and whisk together until very smooth.

3. Follow the instructions for making the fudge brownies. Pour half the brownie
   batter into the prepared pan, spreading evenly with a spatula. Drop half the cream
   cheese mixture over the batter in large dollops. Pour the remaining brownie batter over the top, spreading evenly, and then drop dollops of the remaining cream
   cheese mixture on top. Run a knife back and forth across the pan to swirl the
   mixtures together.

4. Bake and cool according to the recipe directions.

# Hot Fudge
# (Dark Chocolate) Sauce

THIS RICH, SWEET SAUCE IS PERFECT ON ICE CREAM SUNDAES, BUT IT'S ALSO
wonderful drizzled on any chocolatey dessert. It will keep in the refrigerator for 1 week.

1 cup heavy cream

8 tablespoons (1 stick) unsalted
butter

2/3 cup granulated sugar

2/3 cup packed light brown sugar

Pinch kosher salt

1 cup unsweetened Dutch-
processed cocoa, sifted (Love
Note, page 360, Best Chocolate
Pudding)

1. Place the cream and butter in a medium saucepan over medium heat. Bring to a
   simmer, stirring occasionally.

2. Add the granulated and brown sugars and stir until dissolved.

3. Add the salt and cocoa and whisk well until very smooth. Remove from the heat
   and let cool to lukewarm.

4. If decorating desserts, pour into a squeeze bottle or dip a fork into the sauce and
   wave it back and forth across the dessert to make decorative drizzles. If necessary,
   reheat in the microwave at 50 percent power for 30-second intervals until warm.

# Berry Coulis

USE THIS FLAVORFUL SAUCE TO PERK UP PIES, PANNA COTTA, EVEN PANCAKES.

1 cup fresh or thawed frozen
berries of your choice

¼ cup granulated sugar, or to
taste

1 teaspoon lemon juice (about
¼ lemon), or to taste

1. Place all of the ingredients in a blender or food processor and purée. Taste and add more sugar or lemon juice, depending on the sweetness of the berries (and your personal preference).

2. Strain the mixture through a fine-mesh sieve set over a bowl. Use the coulis right away, or refrigerate in an airtight container for up to 1 week. Or freeze, and then defrost in the refrigerator overnight or in the microwave. Stir before using.

# Crème Anglaise

CRÈME ANGLAISE IS A CUSTARDY SAUCE THAT'S DELICIOUS WITH MANY DESSERTS, particularly bread pudding. You can flavor it many different ways—add different liqueurs like amaretto for a hint of almond, Frangelico® for hazelnut, or Grand Marnier® for orange. About 2 tablespoons liqueur will do it, but don't omit the vanilla bean or extract—it does a great job of rounding out the flavors.

You can also add espresso powder for coffee flavor or grind up some coffee beans and let them steep in the warm cream, but strain and reheat before mixing with the egg yolks. (You can use this same method to steep whole spices and even herbs.) Once chilled, this sauce can be frozen in an ice cream maker and made into ice cream. Just be careful not to overcook the cream or you will have scrambled eggs.

| | |
|---|---|
| 1 cup heavy cream | 5 large egg yolks |
| 1 cup whole milk | ½ cup granulated sugar |
| ½ vanilla bean, split lengthwise, or ¼ teaspoon pure vanilla extract | Pinch kosher salt |

1. Place the cream, milk, and vanilla bean in a saucepan (if you're using vanilla extract you'll whisk it in later). Set over medium-high heat and bring just to a simmer, stirring occasionally. Remove from the heat.

2. Meanwhile, place the egg yolks, sugar, and salt in a medium mixing bowl and beat with a whisk until well blended, about 1 minute.

3. Remove the vanilla bean from the milk. Use a knife to scrape out as much of the seeds as possible and add them to the pot. Swirl the vanilla bean in the sauce to be sure you get out the rest of the seeds (discard the pod or save it for another use; Love Note 2, page 336, Coconut Cream Pie).

4. Ladle out about ½ cup of the hot milk and whisk it into the egg mixture. (This is called "tempering." It allows the eggs to warm up so they don't get shocked into

curdling when you pour them into the hot milk.) Slowly pour the egg mixture back into the pot of milk, whisking steadily to keep the eggs from curdling.

5. Place the pot over medium heat and cook the mixture, stirring constantly so you don't get scrambled eggs, until it is thick enough to coat the back of a spoon, 3 to 5 minutes. (Your finger should leave a distinct trace when you run it along the back of the spoon. Do not let the mixture boil.)

6. Remove from the heat. Strain the sauce through a fine-mesh sieve set over a bowl. Allow to cool slightly. If you didn't use a vanilla bean, stir in the vanilla extract, as well as any other flavorings if desired.

7. Cover with plastic wrap and chill in the refrigerator for at least 2 hours before serving. It will keep in an airtight container in the refrigerator for 3 days.

## VARIATION: Bourbon Crème Anglaise

This is perfect with New Orleans Bread Pudding (page 372), especially since you can use the bourbon left over from soaking the raisins. Stir in 2 tablespoons bourbon after the Crème Anglaise is cool.

# Equivalency Charts

## Liquid/dry measures

| U.S. | METRIC |
|------|--------|
| 1/4 teaspoon | 1.25 milliliters |
| 1/2 teaspoon | 2.5 milliliters |
| 1 teaspoon | 5 milliliters |
| 1 tablespoon (3 teaspoons) | 15 milliliters |
| 1 fluid ounce (2 tablespoons) | 30 milliliters |
| 1/4 cup | 60 milliliters |
| 1/3 cup | 80 milliliters |
| 1/2 cup | 120 milliliters |
| 1 cup | 240 milliliters |
| 1 pint (2 cups) | 480 milliliters |
| 1 quart (4 cups; 32 ounces) | 960 milliliters |
| 1 gallon (4 quarts) | 3.84 liters |
| 1 ounce (by weight) | 28 grams |
| 1 pound | 454 grams |
| 2.2 pounds | 1 kilogram |

## Oven temperatures

| °F | GAS MARK | °C |
|----|----------|-----|
| 250 | 1/2 | 120 |
| 275 | 1 | 140 |
| 300 | 2 | 150 |
| 325 | 3 | 165 |
| 350 | 4 | 180 |
| 375 | 5 | 190 |
| 400 | 6 | 200 |
| 425 | 7 | 220 |
| 450 | 8 | 230 |
| 475 | 9 | 240 |
| 500 | 10 | 260 |
| 550 | Broil | 290 |

# Recipe Index by Chapter

# Index